Lecture Notes in Computer Science   8354

Commenced Publication in 1973
Founding and Former Series Editors:
Gerhard Goos, Juris Hartmanis, and Jan van Leeuwen

Bhaskar Krishnamachari   Amy L. Murphy
Niki Trigoni (Eds.)

Wireless
Sensor Networks

11th European Conference, EWSN 2014
Oxford, UK, February 17-19, 2014
Proceedings

 Springer

Volume Editors

Bhaskar Krishnamachari
University of Southern California, Ming Hsieh Faculty
Department of Electrical Engineering
3740 McClintock Avenue, Los Angeles, CA 90089, USA
E-mail: bkrishna@usc.edu

Amy L. Murphy
Fondazione Bruno Kessler (FBK)
Center for Scientific and Technological Research (IRST)
Via Sommarive 18, 38123 Povo (TN), Italy
E-mail: murphy@fbk.eu

Niki Trigoni
University of Oxford, Department of Computer Science
Wolfson Building, Parks Road, Oxford OX1 3QD, UK
E-mail: niki.trigoni@cs.ox.ac.uk

ISSN 0302-9743   e-ISSN 1611-3349
ISBN 978-3-319-04650-1   e-ISBN 978-3-319-04651-8
DOI 10.1007/978-3-319-04651-8
Springer Cham Heidelberg New York Dordrecht London

Library of Congress Control Number: 2013957971

CR Subject Classification (1998): C.2.0-4, C.3, C.4, E.4, F.2.2, H.2.m

LNCS Sublibrary: SL 5 – Computer Communication Networks
and Telecommunications

Typesetting: Camera-ready by author, data conversion by Scientific Publishing Services, Chennai, India

Printed on acid-free paper

Springer is part of Springer Science+Business Media (www.springer.com)

Preface

This volume contains the proceedings of EWSN 2014, the 11th European Conference on Wireless Sensor Networks. The conference took place in Oxford, UK, during February 17–19, 2014. The aim of the conference was to discuss the latest research results and developments in the field of wireless sensor networks.

EWSN received a total of 50 paper submissions, of which 12 were selected for publication and presentation, yielding an acceptance rate of 24%. Paper submissions were received from 26 countries around the world. EWSN adopted a double-blind review process, where the identities of the paper authors were also withheld from the reviewers. In total, 195 reviews were written, with all papers being evaluated by at least three independent reviewers, and most receiving four reviews. In addition, the 41 members of the Technical Program Committee participated in a week-long online discussion, focusing on the merits of the submissions both individually and in comparison to one another, then making the final decisions. The final program covered a wide range of topics that were grouped into four sessions: Network Protocols, System Issues, Reliability, and Sensing.

The conference program included other elements in addition to the presentation of research papers. The keynote was given by BP America Professor John A. Stankovic from the University of Virginia who spoke about "Technical Solutions Underlying Wireless Health Systems." A poster and research demonstration session attracted numerous submissions, for which separate proceedings are available.

We would like to thank everyone who contributed to EWSN 2014. In particular, we would like to thank the Technical Program Committee for their reviews, and the entire Organizing Committee for their support. Finally, we also would like to thank the local organization team, Dr. Andrew Markham, Dr. Andrew Symington, Mrs. Elizabeth Walsh, and Ms. Andrea Pilot, for their help with the conference planning.

February 2014

Bhaskar Krishnamachari
Amy L. Murphy

Organization

General Chair

Niki Trigoni   University of Oxford, UK

Program Chairs

Bhaskar Krishnamachari   University of Southern California, USA
Amy L. Murphy   Bruno Kessler Foundation, Italy

Local Organization

Andrew Markham   University of Oxford, UK

Demo and Poster Chairs

Alberto Cerpa   University of California, Merced, USA
Marco Zuniga   Delft University of Technology,
                              The Netherlands
Timothy Hnat   University of Memphis, USA

Publicity Chairs

Wendi Heinzelman   University of Rochester, USA
Utz Roedig   Lancaster University, UK
Julie McCann   Imperial College London, UK

Industrial Liaison Chairs

Jie Liu   Microsoft Research, USA
Lama Nachman   Intel Labs, USA
Emiliano Miluzzo   AT&T Labs, USA

Webmaster

Andrew Symington   University of Oxford, UK

Technical Program Committee

Tarek Abdelzaher	University of Illinois at Urbana-Champaign, USA
Mario Alves	Polytechnic Institute of Porto, Portugal
Luca Benini	University of Bologna, Italy
Matteo Ceriotti	RWTH Aachen University, Germany
Alberto Cerpa	University of California, Merced, USA
Karthik Dantu	Harvard University, USA
Eli De Poorter	Ghent University - iMinds, Belgium
Ozlem Durmaz Incel	Galatasaray University, Istanbul, Turkey
Cem Ersoy	Bogazici University, Turkey
Chien-Liang Fok	University of Texas at Austin, USA
Jie Gao	Stony Brook University, USA
Andrea Gasparri	Roma Tre University, Italy
Omprakash Gnawali	University of Houston, USA
Vlado Handziski	Technische Universität Berlin, Germany
Paul Havinga	University of Twente, The Netherlands
Shinichi Honiden	University of Tokyo, Japan
Katia Jaffrès-Runser	University of Toulouse, INPT-ENSEEIHT/IRIT, France
Salil Kanhere	University of New South Wales, Australia
Holger Karl	University of Paderborn, Germany
Brano Kusy	Commonwealth Scientific and Industrial Research Organisation, Australia
Koen Langendoen	Delft University of Technology, The Netherlands
Akos Ledeczi	Vanderbilt University, USA
Andrew Markham	University of Oxford, UK
Pedro Marron	University of Duisburg-Essen, Germany
Tommaso Melodia	State University of New York at Buffalo, USA
Sam Michiels	KU Leuven, Belgium
Emiliano Miluzzo	AT&T Labs, USA
Ingrid Moerman	University of Ghent, Belgium
Luca Mottola	Politecnico di Milano, Italy and SICS Swedish ICT
Animesh Pathak	Institut National de Recherche en Informatique et en Automatique, France
Chiara Petrioli	University of Rome La Sapienza, Italy
Vasanth Rajamani	Oracle, USA
John Regehr	University of Utah, USA
Utz Roedig	Lancaster University, UK
Leo Selavo	University of Latvia, Latvia
Cormac Sreenan	University College Cork, Ireland

Violet Syrotiuk   Arizona State University, USA
Thiemo Voigt   Uppsala University, Sweden and SICS Swedish
                              ICT
Pei Zhang   Carnegie Mellon University, USA
Michele Zorzi   University of Padova, Italy
Marco Zuniga   Delft University of Technology,
                              The Netherlands

Table of Contents

Network Protocols

NarrowCast: A New Link-Layer Primitive for Gossip-Based Sensornet
Protocols 1
    Tomasz Pazurkiewicz, Michal Gregorczyk, and Konrad Iwanicki

κ-FSOM: Fair Link Scheduling Optimization for Energy-Aware Data
Collection in Mobile Sensor Networks 17
    Kai Li, Branislav Kusy, Raja Jurdak, Aleksandar Ignjatovic,
    Salil S. Kanhere, and Sanjay Jha

CodeDrip: Data Dissemination Protocol with Network Coding
for Wireless Sensor Networks 34
    Nildo dos Santos Ribeiro Júnior, Marcos A.M. Vieira,
    Luiz F.M. Vieira, and Omprakash Gnawali

System Issues

Efficient and Flexible Sensornet Checkpointing 50
    Andreas Löscher, Nicolas Tsiftes, Thiemo Voigt, and
    Vlado Handziski

Towards Enabling Uninterrupted Long-Term Operation of Solar Energy
Harvesting Embedded Systems 66
    Bernhard Buchli, Felix Sutton, Jan Beutel, and Lothar Thiele

Implementation and Experimental Validation
of Timing Constraints of BBS 84
    Markus Engel, Dennis Christmann, and Reinhard Gotzhein

Reliability

SOFA: Communication in Extreme Wireless Sensor Networks 100
    Marco Cattani, Marco Zuniga, Matthias Woehrle, and
    Koen Langendoen

All Is Not Lost: Understanding and Exploiting Packet Corruption
in Outdoor Sensor Networks 116
    Frederik Hermans, Hjalmar Wennerström, Liam McNamara,
    Christian Rohner, and Per Gunningberg

Making 'Glossy' Networks Sparkle: Exploiting Concurrent
Transmissions for Energy Efficient, Reliable, Ultra-Low Latency
Communication in Wireless Control Networks 133
    Dingwen Yuan, Michael Riecker, and Matthias Hollick

Sensing

Energy Consumption of Visual Sensor Networks: Impact
of Spatio-Temporal Coverage Based on Single-Hop Topologies 150
    *Alessandro Redondi, Dujdow Buranapanichkit, Matteo Cesana,
    Marco Tagliasacchi, and Yiannis Andreopoulos*

K-Sense: Towards a Kinematic Approach for Measuring Human Energy
Expenditure 166
    *Kazi I. Zaman, Anthony White, Sami R. Yli-Piipari, and
    Timothy W. Hnat*

KinSpace: Passive Obstacle Detection via Kinect 182
    *Christopher Greenwood, Shahriar Nirjon, John Stankovic,
    Hee Jung Yoon, Ho-Kyeong Ra, Sang Son, and Taejoon Park*

Author Index 199

NarrowCast: A New Link-Layer Primitive
for Gossip-Based Sensornet Protocols

Tomasz Pazurkiewicz, Michal Gregorczyk, and Konrad Iwanicki

University of Warsaw, Warsaw, Poland
{tp277655,mg277528}@students.mimuw.edu.pl,
iwanicki@mimuw.edu.pl

Abstract. Although gossiping protocols for wireless sensor networks (sensor-nets) excel at minimizing the number of generated packets, they leave room for improvement when it comes to the end-to-end performance, namely energy efficiency. As a step in remedying this situation, we propose NarrowCast: a new primitive that can be provided by asynchronous duty-cycling link layers as a substitute for broadcasting for gossiping protocols. The principal idea behind the NarrowCast primitive is to allow a sensor node to transmit to a fraction of its neighbors, which enables controlling energy expenditures and reliability. We discuss methods of approximating the primitive in practice and integrating it with gossiping protocols. We also evaluate implementations of the approximations with Trickle, a state-of-the-art gossiping protocol, and X-MAC, a popular link layer based on low-power listening. The results show that—without sacrificing reliability—gossiping using even the simplest approximations of NarrowCast can considerably outperform gossiping based on broadcasting in energy efficiency.

1 Introduction

Gossiping is a compelling communication paradigm with numerous applications in sensornets, such as disseminating queries [1], aggregating information [2], or maintaining complex overlays [3], to name a few examples. The essence of gossiping is that each node has a local state, which it repeatedly broadcasts to its neighbors. Likewise, it integrates the states received from the neighbors with the local state. The global effect of these repeated, local state exchanges is that information is disseminated among the nodes, such that they can learn a query, collectively compute an aggregate, or construct an overlay. Importantly, the dissemination process does not require any routing infrastructure and is robust to network dynamics, which is crucial especially under mobility.

The robustness of gossiping comes at a cost, though. The repeated node state broadcasts, which allow gossip-based protocols to tolerate failures, packet loss, and mobility, also introduce a lot of redundancy in the traffic. The redundancy wastes node resources. At best, transmitting, receiving, and processing redundant information drains node energy and reduces the effective channel throughput. In extreme cases, such as a concentration of mobile nodes in an area, the resulting broadcast storms may even lead to a collapse of the entire dissemination process [4]. Gossiping in sensornets thus requires managing redundancy: on the one hand, redundancy must be sufficient to handle network dynamics; on the other hand, its negative performance effects must be minimal.

B. Krishnamachari, A.L. Murphy, and N. Trigoni (Eds.): EWSN 2014, LNCS 8354, pp. 1–16, 2014.
© Springer International Publishing Switzerland 2014

To date, the problem of redundancy management has been addressed at the network layer: in gossiping protocols themselves. For example, a gossiping protocol can make probabilistic decisions on whether to rebroadcast its state or not [5] or can wait listening for and counting its neighbors' broadcasts, so that its own one can hopefully be suppressed [1]. In general, as we elaborate in the next section, multiple techniques exist that allow gossiping protocols to limit the number of broadcast packets.

However, even though reducing the number of packets generated by a gossiping protocol improves the network-layer dissemination performance, we argue that it still leaves a lot of room for improvement with respect to the end-to-end performance, notably energy efficiency. For instance, when analyzed end to end rather than only from the network layer perspective, probabilistically rebroadcasting a packet wastes the energy of potentially many nodes that have already received and processed the packet. Likewise, counting duplicate neighbors' broadcasts requires energy for receiving and processing them. All in all, we argue that while redundancy management mechanisms at the network layer are necessary, if employed alone, they are inherently limited, as it is the link layer below that controls channel access and radio energy expenditures.

In support of our argument, we propose NarrowCast, a link-layer primitive that is a step toward improving the energy efficiency of gossiping in sensornets. NarrowCast targets the suboptimal combination of broadcast communication and gossiping: on the one hand, the link layer spends time and energy on ensuring that a broadcast reaches all neighbors of the transmitter; on the other hand, some of the neighbors discard the received data as redundant at the network layer, thereby wasting this effort. As a counter-measure, the NarrowCast primitive allows a node to transmit to a *fraction* of its neighbors. In effect, assuming that the resulting energy cost is proportional to the fraction, the gossiping protocol gains control over energy expenditures and robustness.

We evaluate NarrowCast in simulation and on a ~100-node testbed. Being conceptually simple a primitive, NarrowCast is not trivial to implement in the real world, especially when aiming at minimal assumptions and maximal performance. For this reason, we present a few implementations that, under different assumptions, approximate NarrowCast for X-MAC [6], a popular sensornet link-layer protocol. We evaluate these implementations with Trickle [1], a state-of-the-art sensornet gossiping protocol. The results confirm that NarrowCast improves the energy efficiency of gossiping.

The rest of the paper is organized as follows. Section 2 surveys related work. Sections 3 and 4, respectively, introduce and evaluate NarrowCast. Section 5 concludes.

2   Related Work

Arguably, the simplest form of gossiping is flooding, that is, rebroadcasting received data once by each node. Flooding lacks any redundancy management. As a result, it does not ensure that data reach all nodes, and may cause broadcast storms [4].

2.1   Managing Redundancy of Gossiping

For these reasons, virtually all gossiping protocols employ techniques for managing redundancy. A popular technique is to have each node locally suppress its broadcast with a given probability [4,5,7,8]. The probability can be preconfigured globally [4,5,7], but this may be suboptimal in networks with heterogeneous node densities or under mobility. Alternatively, the probability can be adapted by each node based on the perceived neighborhood size [8], which requires additional neighborhood estimation mechanisms. In any case, with an appropriate probability, such proactive techniques of redundancy management considerably limit the traffic without impairing robustness.

In contrast to the proactive probabilistic ones, reactive techniques rely on observing the dissemination process and acting accordingly. For example, before rebroadcasting, each node can count broadcasts from its neighbors [1,4,7,9]. If the number of such broadcasts exceeds a threshold, the node suppresses its own one. Again, the threshold can be fixed [1,4,7] or adapted dynamically [9]. Alternatively, each node can estimate the number of new nodes its broadcast would reach and suppress the broadcast if this number is too low [4,7,9]. The estimation can be based on the nodes' positions [4,7,9] or signal quality [4]. Nodes can also piggyback their neighborhood onto broadcast data [9]. Although estimation-based approaches are potentially more accurate, in practice, counting-based ones perform similarly and are easier to implement.

Whereas the previous techniques focus on limiting traffic, improving the reliability of gossiping typically boils down to broadcasting repeatedly and relying on the traffic-limiting techniques—possibly in combinations—to minimize redundancy. In particular, Trickle [1] uses counting and, in addition, dynamically increases interbroadcast intervals (details in Sect. 3.1). Likewise, GOSSIP3 [5] combines counting with probabilistic suppression. TARP [10], in turn, applies an entire sequence of rebroadcast rules.

All in all, in terms of network-layer packets, such algorithms perform well. Yet, their end-to-end energy efficiency is heavily influenced by the underlying link layer, whose medium access control (MAC) protocol determines the energy expenditures.

2.2 Link-Layer Support for Gossiping

However, sensornet MAC protocols are hardly ever optimized for gossiping. To date, the prevalent traffic pattern in sensornets has been all-to-one data collection, for which unicast communication over a virtual tree dominates. The popularity of this pattern is reflected in some MAC protocols that offer dedicated mechanisms [11]. Gossiping, in turn, assumes no virtual topology and currently relies on MAC support for broadcasting. There are two main approaches to providing such support: synchronizing nodes and probing the wireless channel. None of them is tailored to gossiping, though.

MAC protocols following the first approach [11,12,13,14] aim to ensure that a node mostly sleeps, thereby saving energy, but when it does wake up to broadcast, all its neighbors are awake as well. To this end, the nodes maintain synchronization. This, however, is problematic, especially if they move. In particular, since they mostly sleep, discovering them by a mobile node may take a lot of time [14]. Moreover, the node must decide whether to adopt their wake-up schedule or not, which is again not trivial if the global cost of the decision is to be low [14]. Alternatively, nodes may operate on multiple schedules [12], but this requires more energy and schedule-disposal policies. Finally, mechanisms are necessary for adapting to changing network conditions.

In contrast, MAC protocols following the second approach [6,15,16] do not maintain shared state, but rely on so-called low-power listening. As previously, a node mostly sleeps and wakes up only periodically to check if another node is transmitting. However, the node wake-up schedules need not be synchronized. Instead, during a period guaranteeing that each neighbor will wake up—the low-power listening check interval—a broadcasting node either transmits data repeatedly [16] or transmits an announcement preamble followed by the data only at the period end [6,15] (details in Sect. 3.1). Although this asynchrony facilitates applications of such protocols in mobile sensornets, the prolonged transmissions incur a significant energy overhead [6,15,16].

All in all, as we argued previously, irrespective of the link-layer MAC scheme and despite network-layer redundancy management, the energy efficiency of gossiping based on broadcasting leaves room for improvement. To date, however, little work has been done in this direction. Gaba et al. [17] suggest that cross-layer mechanisms could provide gossiping protocols with feedback from the link layer on channel utilization, so that the protocols' reaction to network dynamics could be optimized. Yet, to the best of our knowledge, no sensornet cross-layer optimizations target gossiping. The interplay between gossiping and the link layer is in turn touched upon by Dunkels et al. [18] who provide a unified set of gossiping abstractions for different MAC schemes. Dunkels et al. [19] also propose an additional announcement layer that concatenates data broadcast by different applications. While not aimed particularly at gossiping, this solution could potentially improve gossiping in multi-application scenarios. In general, however, we are not aware of any solution that targets gossiping and takes the NarrowCast's approach: to abandon link-layer guarantees that a broadcast reaches all neighbors, as many of the neighbors will ignore the received data anyway at a higher layer.

3 NarrowCast Primitive

The principal idea behind NarrowCast is simple: to allow a node to transmit to a fraction of its neighbors. While solutions that utilize the primitive in an optimal manner constitute an avenue for future research (see Sect. 5), this paper aims to demonstrate that NarrowCast can offer performance benefits even for existing state-of-the-art solutions.

3.1 Assumptions and Prerequisites

To this end, as a gossiping algorithm for our discussion, we assume Trickle [1], as it is a compelling solution employed, among others, by popular dissemination protocols, collection protocols, and even Internet of Things standards. To guarantee that data eventually reach all nodes, every node running Trickle broadcasts the data repeatedly every T_{max} time units. Since for the sake of traffic T_{max} is normally large (on the order of minutes), the dissemination latency would be large as well. Therefore, as a counter-measure, whenever a new version of the data is produced at a node or the node receives such a version its neighbor, it shrinks its interbroadcast interval to T_{min}. Since T_{min} is in contrast small (on the order of milliseconds), a broadcast storm may occur whenever all neighbors receiving the new data shrink their intervals and attempt to rebroadcast.

To alleviate broadcast storms, Trickle uses two redundancy management mechanisms (see Fig. 1). First, the interbroadcast interval of a node is doubled up to T_{max} with each broadcast by the node, that is, the duration of the i-th interval after learning a new

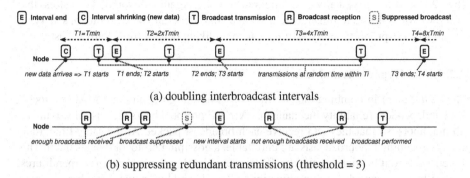

(a) doubling interbroadcast intervals

(b) suppressing redundant transmissions (threshold = 3)

Fig. 1. The redundancy management mechanisms in Trickle

version of data is $T_i = MIN(2^{i-1} \times T_{min}, T_{max})$ [Fig. 1(a)]. This self-regulation mechanism enables recovering from a storm irrespective of the network density. Moreover, instead of transmitting exactly after T_i time units, a node draws a random time from $(0.5 \times T_i, T_i)$, which desynchronizes transmissions. Second, in every interval, each node counts broadcasts received with its version of the data. If their number exceeds a threshold (typically 2–3), the node suppresses its own broadcast in the interval [Fig. 1(b)].

As to the link layer, NarrowCast assumes that the average cost of broadcasting data in terms of energy and channel occupation is proportional to the fraction of neighbors receiving the data. All asynchronous MAC protocols based on low-power listening satisfy this assumption: the more data repetitions or the longer the transmitted part of a preamble, the higher the channel occupation and energy costs, but also the more neighbors awake to receive the data. In particular, our approximations of NarrowCast are built for X-MAC [6], a popular low-power listening MAC, suitable for mobile networks.

In X-MAC, an announcement preamble is a sequence of short frames, a so-called strobed preamble (see Fig. 2). The frames are separated by brief periods in which the transmitting node switches to reception mode. This is useful for unicast packets, as the receiver can acknowledge that it is up, thereby allowing the transmitter to terminate the preamble and send the actual data [Fig. 2(a)]. For broadcast packets, in turn, preambles must be transmitted during an entire low-power listening channel check interval

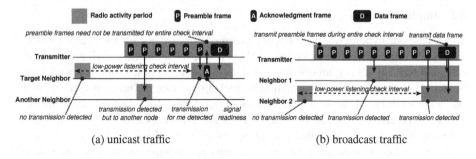

(a) unicast traffic   (b) broadcast traffic

Fig. 2. An example of low-power listening with strobed preambles

[Fig. 2(b)], which is typically preconfigured globally. Again, we would like to stress that while we use X-MAC to illustrate and evaluate our ideas, any MAC protocol satisfying the above cost-proportionality assumption could likely benefit from NarrowCast.

3.2 Main Hypothesis and Idea

Analyzing them in combination, we may observe that gossiping and MAC protocols have independent reliability mechanisms. A MAC protocol bears the cost of waking up all neighbors, so that they can receive each broadcast packet. At the same time, (correctly) assuming that broadcasts are unreliable, a gossiping protocol repeats them. This functionality duplication negatively affects channel utilization and energy expenditures.

To illustrate, consider our combination of Trickle and low-power listening. Suppose that a node broadcasts new data. Its neighbors are awakened by the preceding preamble and receive the data. As a result, they all reset their Trickle intervals to T_{min} and attempt to rebroadcast. Recall that for latency reasons T_{min} is small, on the order of milliseconds. In contrast, to save energy, it is not uncommon for low-power listening preambles to last hundreds of milliseconds. This means that in the initial Trickle intervals multiple nodes want to rebroadcast simultaneously. Hopefully, the MAC protocol ensures that only one succeeds at a time. However, this implies that the others wait, possibly with active radios. Moreover, even though many nodes are already up, the rebroadcasting nodes still have to transmit their preambles, as they may have neighbors that were not in the range of the previous broadcasts, and hence, may yet be sleeping. All in all, the channel congestion and the resulting waiting period may be considerable, which inflates the energy expenditures. The situation is further aggravated when multiple data items are disseminated simultaneously, as is often the case in gossip-based applications.

NarrowCast tries to alleviate these effects by giving control to the network layer over the transmission reliability mechanisms at the link layer, and thereby, over the costs of communication. The idea is to have the link layer provide a communication primitive that allows the network layer (e.g., a gossiping protocol) to transmit, *narrowcast*, to a fraction of neighbors. Under our cost-proportionality assumption on the link layer, such narrowcasts can be proportionally shorter than broadcasts (e.g., have shorter preambles), which reduces channel utilization and energy costs. Moreover, we hypothesize that they need not compromise the reliability of dissemination, as the gossiping protocol will compensate with its own mechanisms (e.g., by repeating transmissions).

3.3 Implementation

To validate our hypotheses, we have implemented NarrowCast for the MiXiM framework [20] of the OMNeT++ simulator [21], a low-level simulation engine for sensor-nets, and for TinyOS 2.1, an operating system for sensor nodes. While NarrowCast is conceptually simple, its implementation is challenging: whereas unicasting a packet to one neighbor or broadcasting it to all is fairly straightforward, it is difficult to ensure that a packet is received by a *given fraction* of neighbors, especially in the absence of shared state. We have thus implemented only approximations of NarrowCast. They all share the idea of shortening packet preambles, but vary in assumptions and implementation effort. For simulation, we have also created a close-to-ideal oracle-based NarrowCast.

Incomplete Preambles (*IP*). The first approximation requires the least implementation effort. Suppose that the global interval in which every node wakes up to check the wireless channel for an ongoing preamble transmission is T_C. A NarrowCast transmission to a given percentage of neighbors, p, is preceded by an incomplete preamble, lasting $p \times T_C$. The motivation behind this idea is that if we assume that neighbor wake-up schedules are uniformly distributed, such an incomplete preamble lasting $p \times T_C$ should on average wake up p percent of neighbors, albeit without any hard guarantees.

Neighbor Cache (*NC*). The second approximation aims to improve the guarantees, assuming that nodes maintain state. More specifically, each node caches its neighbors' wake-up schedules. Before narrowcasting, it consults the cache to compute a preamble fraction that would wake up p percent of its neighbors. The cache is updated by piggybacking transmitters' wake-up schedules on packets. For eviction, the oldest unrefreshed schedules are chosen. While schedule maintenance is not coordinated among nodes, schedules get outdated, which may be problematic especially under mobility.

Colliding Acknowledgments (*CA-* and *CA+*). The third approximation also aims to improve the guarantees, but by means of acknowledgments. Upon waking up and receiving a preamble frame, a node transmits an acknowledgment frame. The frame is transmitted only once for the preamble of a given packet. When a sufficient number of acknowledgments in subsequent slots are observed by the transmitter, depending on the variant, the transmitter terminates the preamble and sends the actual data frame. In the CA- variant, the preamble lasts *at most* $p \times T_C$: it can be terminated earlier, as soon as acknowledgments in k slots are observed. In contrast, in the CA+ variant, the preamble lasts *at least* $p \times T_C$: it is not terminated before this time expires *and* acknowledgments in at least k slots are observed. CA- thus minimizes costs, while CA+ favors reliability.

A major problem with this approximation is that multiple nodes may wake up simultaneously and transmit acknowledgment frames. Dutta et al. showed that if such frames are identical and well timed, their collisions need not be destructive, but only for a few transmitters [22]. Therefore, for scalability, we do not rely on receiving acknowledgment frames, but merely on sensing a high channel state in acknowledgment slots. Nevertheless, this approximation still requires the most implementation effort.

Oracle (*OC*) [only simulations]. Finally, in OMNeT++, we have also implemented an oracle that informs a transmitter when a given percentage of its previously sleeping neighbors have been awaken by preamble frames. Upon such an event, the transmitter terminates the preamble and proceeds with a data frame.

While there are likely many other ways to implement NarrowCast, we believe the previous ones cover enough various techniques to assess the potential of the primitive well.

3.4 Integration with Higher-Layer Protocols

Likewise, there are several ways in which NarrowCast can be utilized by a gossiping protocol like Trickle. Again for brevity, we focus just on two representative ones.

First, instead of broadcasting, the protocol can decide to always narrowcast to a given percentage, p, of neighbors. We denote such a scheme $fix(p)$. For instance, narrowcasting to 50% of neighbors should intuitively reduce energy expenditures, perhaps even twice, without degrading reliability, unless the network is extremely sparse.

Second, a protocol like Trickle, in which the intervals between subsequent transmissions change dynamically, can also dynamically change the percentage of neighbors to which data is narrowcast. In particular, in every Trickle interval, the percentage can be multiplied by a factor $\alpha > 1$, assuming that the initial percentage (in T_1) is p_I. We refer to such a scheme as $dyn(p_I, \alpha)$. The idea behind the scheme is that in the initial intervals data should be propagated fast, perhaps somewhat sacrificing reliability, hence the percentage can be low. Later intervals are in turn longer, and thus, a larger percentage can be utilized to reliably deliver the data to the rest of the nodes, but at a higher cost.

Finally, the NarrowCast-related interfaces provided by a link-layer are simple. The fraction of nodes to which a packet should be narrowcast can be made part of the packet's meta-data, which allows for per-packet manipulations matching the convention of TinyOS. An alternative solution is to designate separate NarrowCast addresses. For example, address ffff is considered a broadcast address in TinyOS. For NarrowCast, in turn, addresses fffx could be assigned, where $2^{x-15} \times 100\%$ denotes the percentage of nodes that should receive a packet destined to this address ($15 > x \geq 0$ or more).

4   Evaluation

We evaluate NarrowCast in OMNeT++/MiXiM and on a testbed. As mentioned previously, in all experiments we used Trickle (with $T_{min} = 256$ ms, $T_{max} = 60$ mins, and suppression threshold = 3) in combination with the aforementioned X-MAC-based implementations of NarrowCast (with different low-power listening check intervals).

The MiXiM framework [20] for OMNeT++ [21] strives to realistically simulate sensornet communication at the signal level. Furthermore, we tried to match the simulated radios to the radios of our sensor nodes, notably in terms of timing, throughput, encoding, and packet reception rate deterioration with distance. We simulated up to 400 nodes in static and mobile networks. In static networks, the nodes were arranged on a torus, and we varied their density. Likewise, for mobility we varied the density by adopting square playgrounds of different sizes, in which the nodes moved with human-scale speeds according to a random-waypoint model (min. speed = 0.3 m/s, max. speed = 1.66 m/s, max. stop time = 1 s). In addition, we let the mobility patterns to warm up for one hour before starting the experiments. Overall, the static networks allow us to systematically study the impact of node density on NarrowCast, whereas the mobile ones enable illustrating the effects of heterogeneity, borders, and connectivity dynamics.

The testbed [23], in turn, spans 10 offices and consists of 102 sensor nodes with CC1101 868MHz radios, 96 of which took part in the experiments. For the employed radio transmission power, the nodes form a network of 7 hops, with a nonuniform density (from 7 to 47 neighbors per node), and more than 15% of asymmetric links. We thus believe that the testbed emulates a medium-scale real-world sensornet well.

Due to space constraints, we focus on experimental results that highlight only the main advantages and drawbacks of NarrowCast, thereby illustrating its potential.

4.1 Attainable Performance

Let us begin with a study of an ideal, oracle-based (OC) implementation of NarrowCast with one new data item gossiped every five minutes, such that the average radio duty cycle remains reasonable for sensornets: at a few percent. We study the dissemination of 60 items (300 minutes) in 400-node torus networks with various densities. Such networks are homogeneous, and hence, for each density, we can configure X-MAC with a global check interval that yields a minimal duty cycle. More specifically, we choose an interval optimal for Trickle based on broadcasting, and use it also for Trickle with narrowcasting. This guarantees that the comparisons are not be biased toward NarrowCast.

Figure 3 compares the simplest oracle-based NarrowCast, *OC-fix*, with broadcasting in terms of duty cycle (a), coverage (b), and latency (c) in relation to network density. Network density is defined as the average of local densities of all nodes. Local density is in turn defined probabilistically for each node: as the sum of packet reception rates from all other nodes (measured before the plotted experiments, independently for each node pair to avoid collisions). As such, this definition captures also extremely poor links.

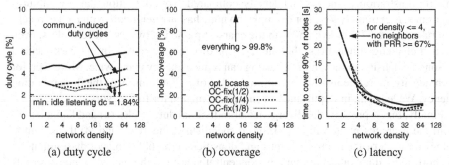

(a) duty cycle   (b) coverage   (c) latency

Fig. 3. Narrowcasting vs. optimally configured broadcasting when gossiping one data item

Duty cycle—the percentage of time a node's radio is active transmitting, receiving, or idly listening—determines the energy consumption of the node. For all densities, gossiping with even the simplest, *fix(p)*, variant of NarrowCast offers a lower duty cycle than optimally configured gossiping based on broadcasting, and the lower p is, the lower the duty cycle [Fig. 3(a)]. In particular, for the lowest plotted values of p, the duty cycle for narrowcasting is lower by up to a factor of 2 from the one for broadcasting.

The reduction is even more noteworthy considering the theoretical minimum of duty cycle (1.84% in the figure), which corresponds to no communication and only periodic low-power listening channel checks. If we subtract from the actual duty cycle the idle listening duty cycle, we obtain what we dubbed a *communication-induced duty cycle*, which describes dissemination efficiency. With this metric, we can observe that, in all but extremely sparse networks, the *fix(p)* variant of narrowcasting disseminates the same amount of information as broadcasting with nearly a factor of $1/p$ less energy. It is not precisely $1/p$, because some costs, such as activating the radio or transmitting actual data, are independent of p. For sparse networks, in turn, the duty cycle grows because *OC-fix* guarantees that p percent of neighbors (rounded up to 1) indeed wake up to receive the data, to which end the transmitted preamble parts may be longer than $p \times T_C$. For a given p, this phenomenon happens at densities around $1/p$, that is, when the expected number of neighbors that wake up on a preamble part lasting $p \times T_C$ drops below 1. Nevertheless, even in the sparsest networks, NarrowCast reduces duty cycle.

At the same time, it does not impair reliability, measured with a standard coverage metric [Fig. 3(b)]: the percentage of nodes that receive each data item. The coverage is hardly ever below 90% (in the plotted experiments, it was above 99.8%), and in general, we have not observed major differences between narrowcasting and broadcasting. This validates our claim that reliability mechanisms in the communication stack are redundant for gossiping, so we can relax some of them without impairing reliability.

By and large, narrowcasting also improves the pace of dissemination, measured, for instance, as the latency to cover 90% of nodes [Fig. 3(c)]. The only exception is the sparsest networks, with densities below $1/p$. In such networks, due to the shorter low-power listening preamble parts and weak links, fewer (out of already few) neighbors of a transmitter have chances to hear the transmitted packet and start contributing to the dissemination process. In effect, not only does the process bootstrap slower, but also the latency penalties accumulate at each hop. Note, however, that we plotted such networks only for illustration, as their actual density, compared to our definition that also captures poor links, is extremely low. For example, no node has any neighbors with packet reception rates above 67% or even 50% in the sparsest plotted networks. Nevertheless, even in such challenged networks, the latency growth is not dramatic. In networks with a reasonable density, in turn, narrowcasting can reduce latency even twice. Moreover, for each density, there seems to be an optimal value of p that minimizes the dissemination latency. We leave an in-depth study of this phenomenon for future work.

Finally, Fig. 4 presents the divergence of individual duty cycles (a) and latencies (b) from the averages plotted in Fig. 3, more specifically, the 10-th and 90-th percentile values for each of the approximations and densities in the 60 rounds of dissemination. In short, individual values are largely concentrated around the means, which suggests that the performance stability of narrowcasting is comparable to that of broadcasting.

All in all, the results confirm our hypotheses. Gossiping with narrowcasting can be more energy efficient than with broadcasting: it disseminates data with a lower channel utilization, and hence, duty cycle and typically latency. At the same time, its reliability is not impaired, being more than sufficient for gossip-based applications.

4.2 Quality of Approximations

However, the previous results concern an ideal, oracle-based implementation of NarrowCast. In contrast, in practice, we can rely only on approximations. Figure 5 thus presents the performance of our approximations (apart from *CA-*, as we explain shortly).

In dense and medium networks, the performance of the simplest approximation, Incomplete Preambles [*IP-fix(p)*, Fig. 5(a)–(c)], is comparable to the oracle-based NarrowCast. In contrast, in sparse networks, the approximation performs poorly in terms of coverage (and hence, the latency to cover 90% of nodes), especially for low values of p. This is because in *IP-fix(p)* packet preambles are always transmitted for a *fixed* fraction, p, of the low-power listening check interval. In effect, while in dense networks or for large p, there is only a remote probability that insufficiently many neighbors wake

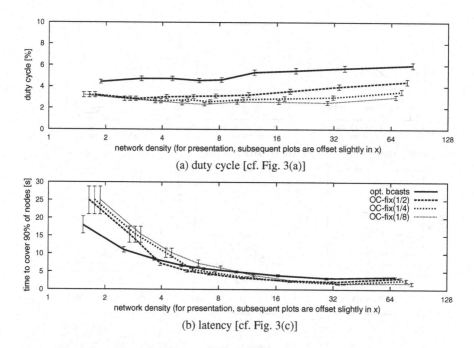

(a) duty cycle [cf. Fig. 3(a)]

(b) latency [cf. Fig. 3(c)]

Fig. 4. Bars illustrating the 10-th and 90-th percentile of the values from Fig. 3

up in this fraction of time to check the channel, in sparse networks and for low values of p, this probability grows, which impairs coverage. Put differently, unlike OC-fix(p), IP-fix(p) is unable to compensate for network sparsity by extending the transmitted preamble parts if necessary, which can be observed by comparing for sparse networks the duty cycles of IP-fix(p) [Fig. 5(a)] and OC-fix(p) [Fig. 3(a)]: for OC-fix(p) they are higher because of the longer preambles. Nevertheless, as we discuss shortly, even for this simple approximation, we can improve the coverage with the dyn(p_I, α) scheme.

The second approximation, Neighbor Cache [NC-fix(p), Fig. 5(d)–(f)], has similar drawbacks as IP-fix(p). Even though a cache of neighbors' wake-up schedules facilitates ensuring that sufficiently many neighbors have a chance to wake up during a preamble transmission, the cache has to be complete. However, this is hard to guarantee in sparse networks and for low values of p, because to add a neighbor to the cache, a node must be lucky to wake up and hear the neighbor transmitting a shortened preamble. The plots illustrate these effects, because in the corresponding experiments the node caches were deliberately purged every third dissemination. While one may argue that the caches could be maintained out of band, for many applications, especially mobile ones, the benefits of NC-fix(p) may still not compensate its drawbacks.

The performance of the final approximation, Colliding Acknowledgments [CA(-/+)-fix(p)], depends on the variant. Transmitting preambles for at most p percent of the low-power listening check interval or until k acknowledgments are observed (the CA- variant, not plotted) inherits the performance problems in sparse networks from IP-fix. In contrast, transmitting preambles for at least p percent of the check interval and until at least k acknowledgments are observed [the CA+ variant, Fig. 5(g)–(i)]

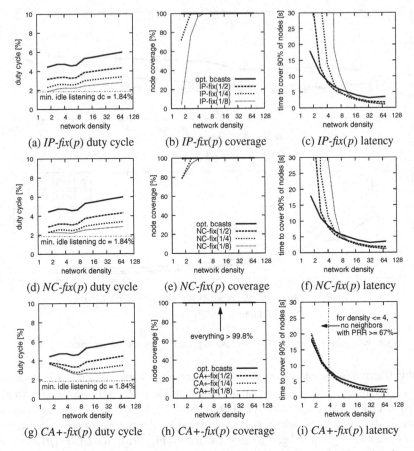

Fig. 5. The performance of the approximations of NarrowCast (for *CA+*, $k = 2$)

performs best of all the approximations in the *fix* configuration. For all plotted network densities, its coverage is above 99.8% and the duty cycle and latency are low. The additional feedback in the form of k acknowledgments addresses the performance issues of the previous approximations in sparse networks, even for k as small as 2. In fact, due to this additional feedback, in the sparsest networks, the duty cycle for *CA+* is slightly higher than for *OC* [Fig. 5(g) vs. Fig. 3(a)] while the latency is lower [Fig. 5(i) vs. Fig. 3(c)]. All in all, *CA+* evidences that NarrowCast can be effectively approximated.

What is more, however, even with a simple, imperfect approximation, such as *IP*, we can maximize reliability by dynamically controlling the fraction of neighbors to which data is narrowcast: by means of the *dyn*(p_I, α) scheme. To illustrate, Fig. 6 presents the performance of *IP-dyn*(p_I, 1.5) for different values of p_I. In other words, after shrinking the Trickle interval, each node starts with a low NarrowCast fraction, p_I, and with each doubling of the Trickle interval, it multiplies this fraction by 1.5, until it reaches 1.

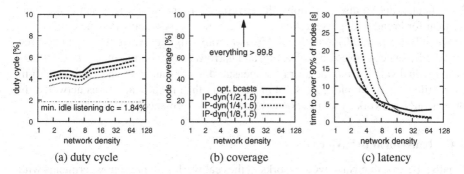

Fig. 6. Improving the reliability of Incomplete Preambles with the $dyn(p_I, \alpha)$ scheme

This scheme provides both a lower duty cycle [Fig. 6(a)] and a high coverage [Fig. 6(b)]. It does not significantly improve the latency in sparse networks [Fig. 6(c)], because in such networks dissemination at a node often progresses only when the node's NarrowCast fraction has grown sufficiently, which takes time. In dense networks, in turn, the latency is lower than for broadcasting. Finally, an additional advantage of *IP-dyn* over *CA+-fix* is simplicity: its TinyOS implementation is just a few lines of code.

In summary, NarrowCast is best approximated with *CA+*. Yet, even simple approximations, such as *IP* can offer a reasonable performance if accompanied with mechanisms for dynamically adjusting the fraction of neighbors to which data is narrowcast.

4.3 Effects of Network Heterogeneity and Dynamics

NarrowCast performs well also under network dynamics. In particular, Fig. 7 shows the performance of *CA+* under mobility on square playgrounds with the same dimensions as the toruses. Since mobility makes determining the optimal low-power listening check interval hard, for each playground, we used the value from the corresponding torus.

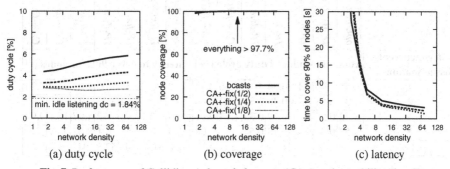

Fig. 7. Performance of Colliding Acknowledgments (*CA+*) under mobility ($k = 2$)

Again, narrowcasting outperforms broadcasting in duty cycle. At the same time, it offers a lower latency and virtually perfect coverage in all but extremely sparse networks. In the sparse networks, in turn, the coverage drops slightly, but so does the coverage for broadcasting. This is because in such networks, nodes get disconnected easily.

In particular, due to disconnections, the coverage for narrowcasting is sometimes better than for broadcasting. Nevertheless, even in the sparsest networks, the coverage is above 90% (in fact, 97.7% in the plots), and more importantly, we have not observed major differences between broadcasting and narrowcasting. Furthermore, the deviation of individual values from the averages, measured, for instance, by the 10-th and 90-th percentile values (not plotted), is not much higher than in the static torus networks. In other words, network dynamics do not impair the performance of NarrowCast.

4.4 Real-World Behavior

Finally, to show that NarrowCast works in the real world, we present experiments with the TinyOS implementations of the different approximations on our testbed. Although we have conducted several experiments with various applications employing Narrow-Cast, for consistency, in this paper we present only experiments with the same application as in the simulations, albeit extended to concurrently disseminate multiple data items. More specifically, d items ($d \in \{1,\ldots,16\}$) are disseminated in the system, and for every such item, each node runs a dedicated instance of Trickle. Periodically, new versions of all items appear simultaneously at random nodes and are started being gossiped. The period is one hour, so that even for $d = 16$, the average duty cycle is low.

Table 1 compares broadcasting and selected approximations of NarrowCast in terms of communication-induced duty cycle and latency to cover 90% of nodes with all items. The coverage is omitted as it was consistently equal to 100%. All depicted values were obtained for the same 96 nodes of the testbed, and the dissemination scenarios were repeated 4 times. The idle listening duty cycles for given values of d were as follows: 0.97% for 1 event, 1.31% for 2 events, 1.64% for 4 events, 3.3% for 8 and 16 events.

Table 1. Testbed results for selected approximations of NarrowCast

# concurrent disseminations (d)	commun.-induced duty cycle [%]							latency to cover 90% of nodes [s]						
	opt. bcast	*IP-fix(1/2)*	*IP-fix(1/4)*	*IP-dyn(1/2,1.5)*	*IP-dyn(1/4,1.5)*	*CA+fix(1/2)*	*CA+fix(1/4)*	*opt. bcast*	*IP-fix(1/2)*	*IP-fix(1/4)*	*IP-dyn(1/2,1.5)*	*IP-dyn(1/4,1.5)*	*CA+fix(1/2)*	*CA+fix(1/4)*
1	0.95	0.39	0.15	0.34	0.2	0.56	0.43	4.39	1.37	2.38	2.05	2.03	3.07	2.23
2	1.37	0.58	0.28	0.48	0.32	0.82	0.64	30.5	3.99	3.82	3.35	2.23	7.9	7.91
4	1.62	0.55	0.31	0.59	0.32	1.13	0.91	42.8	8.22	3.96	7.82	4.97	16.1	9.97
8	1.53	0.81	0.42	0.78	0.54	1.4	1.08	65.3	14.5	6.58	16.1	8.62	33.9	22
16	3.52	1.25	0.67	1.36	0.75	2.6	2.12	121	51.4	34	57.8	31	61.2	60.1

As is typically the case in sensornets, the experimental results differ somewhat from the simulations, despite the fine-tuning of the simulated radios. In particular, the absolute numbers for duty cycle and latency vary due to the differences in the network topologies and wireless communication phenomena not modeled by the simulator. Likewise, colliding acknowledgments perform worse in the real world than in simulation.

This is because whereas in the simulator clear channel assessment is nearly perfect, in our TinyOS implementation, it is configured conservatively. In effect, transmitted acknowledgments are sometimes ignored, which slightly inflates duty cycle and latency. While we were not compelled to address this issue, devising mechanisms optimized for particular radio chips constitutes an interesting problem. There are also a few other minor differences that can be attributed to the testbed topology and experimental settings.

Nevertheless, despite these differences in absolute values, the basic trends from the simulations remain valid. Narrowcasting to a fraction of neighbors instead of broadcasting to all reduces the communication-induced duty cycle by a factor almost inversely proportional to the fraction. By and large, it also reduces the dissemination latency. Finally, it hardly affects the coverage. The testbed experiments thus confirm that the approximations of NarrowCast can in practice improve the performance of gossiping.

5   Conclusions and Future Work

In summary, the results demonstrate that NarrowCast—a link-layer primitive allowing a node to transmit to a fraction of its neighbors—can be effectively implemented in the real world and can indeed improve the end-to-end performance of gossiping protocols. In particular, for Trickle running on top of X-MAC, even the simplest implementations of NarrowCast can reduce the energy consumption and latency by a significant factor, without sacrificing reliability. In general, this reinforces our initial argument that the efficiency of sensornet gossiping protocols leaves room for improvement.

Therefore, since gossiping is a compelling communication paradigm in sensornets, especially under mobility, we believe that our work will inspire novel solutions, designed from the end-to-end perspective. In particular, we are currently working on protocols tailored specifically to NarrowCast. Furthermore, since applications of NarrowCast stretch beyond gossiping, investigating such applications constitutes another research avenue. For instance, we are studying the use of NarrowCast for routing. Finally, we are also working on proving the properties of NarrowCast analytically.

Acknowledgments. This research was supported by the (Polish) National Science Center within the SONATA program under grant no. DEC-2012/05/D/ST6/03582. The authors would also like to thank Albana Gaba for inspiring discussions on cross-layer optimizations.

References

1. Levis, P., Patel, N., Culler, D., Shenker, S.: Trickle: A self-regulating algorithm for code propagation and maintenance in wireless sensor networks. In: Proc. USENIX NSDI 2004, San Francisco, CA, USA, pp. 15–28 (2004)
2. Xiao, L., Boyd, S., Lall, S.: A scheme for robust distributed sensor fusion based on average consensus. In: Proc. IPSN 2005, Los Angeles, CA, USA, pp. 63–70 (2005)
3. Iwanicki, K., van Steen, M.: Multi-hop cluster hierarchy maintenance in wireless sensor networks: A case for gossip-based protocols. In: Roedig, U., Sreenan, C.J. (eds.) EWSN 2009. LNCS, vol. 5432, pp. 102–117. Springer, Heidelberg (2009)

4. Ni, S.Y., Tseng, Y.C., Chen, Y.S., Sheu, J.P.: The broadcast storm problem in a mobile ad hoc network. In: Proc. ACM/IEEE MobiCom 1999, Seattle, WA, USA, pp. 151–162 (1999)
5. Haas, Z.J., Halpern, J.Y., Li, L.: Gossip-based ad hoc routing. IEEE/ACM Trans. Netw. 14(3), 479–491 (2006)
6. Buettner, M., Yee, G.V., Anderson, E., Han, R.: X-MAC: A short preamble MAC protocol for duty-cycled wireless sensor networks. In: Proc. ACM SenSys 2006, Boulder, CO, USA, pp. 307–320 (2006)
7. Williams, B., Camp, T.: Comparison of broadcasting techniques for mobile ad hoc networks. In: Proc. ACM MobiHoc 2002, Lausanne, Switzerland, pp. 194–205 (2002)
8. Gaba, A., Voulgaris, S., Iwanicki, K., van Steen, M.: Revisiting gossip-based ad-hoc routing. In: Proc. IEEE ICCCN 2012, Munich, Germany (2012)
9. Tseng, Y.C., Ni, S.Y., Shih, E.Y.: Adaptive approaches to relieving broadcast storms in a wireless multihop mobile ad hoc network. IEEE Trans. Comput. 52(5), 545–557 (2003)
10. Gburzynski, P., Kaminska, B., Olesinski, W.: A tiny and efficient wireless ad-hoc protocol for low-cost sensor networks. In: Proc. DATE 2007, Nice, France, pp. 1557–1562 (2007)
11. van Hoesel, L., Havinga, P.: A lightweight medium access protocol (LMAC) for wireless sensor networks: Reducing preamble transmissions and transceiver state switches. In: Proc. INSS 2004, Tokio, Japan, pp. 205–208 (2004)
12. van Dam, T., Langendoen, K.: An adaptive energy-efficient MAC protocol for wireless sensor networks. In: Proc. ACM SenSys 2003, Los Angeles, CA, USA, pp. 171–180 (2003)
13. Ye, W., Silva, F., Heidemann, J.: Ultra-low duty cycle MAC with scheduled channel polling. In: Proc. ACM SenSys 2006, Boulder, CO, USA, pp. 321–334 (2006)
14. Dobson, M., Voulgaris, S., van Steen, M.: Merging ultra-low duty cycle networks. In: Proc. IEEE/IFIP DSN 2011, Hong Kong, China, pp. 538–549 (2011)
15. Polastre, J., Hill, J., Culler, D.: Versatile low power media access for wireless sensor networks. In: Proc. ACM SenSys 2004, Baltimore, MD, USA, pp. 95–107 (2004)
16. Sun, Y., Gurewitz, O., Johnson, D.B.: RI-MAC: A receiver-initiated asynchronous duty cycle MAC protocol for dynamic traffic loads in wireless sensor networks. In: Proc. ACM SenSys 2008, Raleigh, NC, USA, pp. 1–14 (2008)
17. Gaba, A., Voulgaris, S., van Steen, M.: Towards congestion-aware all-to-all information dissemination in mobile ad-hoc networks. In: 2010 IEEE GLOBECOM Workshops, Miami, FL, USA, pp. 1690–1695 (2010)
18. Dunkels, A., Österlind, F., He, Z.: An adaptive communication architecture for wireless sensor networks. In: Proc. ACM SenSys 2007, Sydney, Australia, pp. 335–349 (2007)
19. Dunkels, A., Mottola, L., Tsiftes, N., Österlind, F., Eriksson, J., Finne, N.: The announcement layer: Beacon coordination for the sensornet stack. In: Marrón, P.J., Whitehouse, K. (eds.) EWSN 2011. LNCS, vol. 6567, pp. 211–226. Springer, Heidelberg (2011)
20. MiXiM Homepage, http://mixim.sourceforge.net
21. OMNeT++ Homepage, http://www.omnetpp.org
22. Dutta, P., Musaloiu-E., R., Stoica, I., Terzis, A.: Wireless ACK collisions not considered harmful. In: Proc. ACM HotNets-VII, Calgary, Alberta, Canada (2008)
23. Michalowski, M., Horban, P., Strzelecki, K., Migdal, J., Klimek, M., Glazar, P., Iwanicki, K.: A sensornet testbed at the University of Warsaw. Technical Report TR-DS-01/12, University of Warsaw, Warsaw, Poland (2012), http://www.mimuw.edu.pl/%7Eiwanicki

κ-FSOM: Fair Link Scheduling Optimization for Energy-Aware Data Collection in Mobile Sensor Networks

Kai Li[1], Branislav Kusy[2], Raja Jurdak[2], Aleksandar Ignjatovic[1], Salil S. Kanhere[1], and Sanjay Jha[1]

[1] School of Computer Science and Engineering, University of New South Wales, Sydney, Australia
{kail,ignjat,salilk,sanjay}@cse.unsw.edu.au
[2] Autonomous Systems Lab, CSIRO ICT Centre, Brisbane, QLD, Australia
{brano.kusy,raja.jurdak}@csiro.au

Abstract. We consider the problem of data collection from a continental-scale network of mobile sensors, specifically applied to wildlife tracking. Our application constraints favor a highly asymmetric solution, with heavily duty-cycled sensor nodes communicating with a network of powered base stations. Individual nodes move freely in the environment, resulting in low-quality radio links and hot-spot arrival patterns with the available data exceeding the radio link capacity. We propose a novel scheduling algorithm, κ-Fair Scheduling Optimization Model (κ-FSOM), that maximizes the amount of collected data under the constraints of radio link quality and energy, while ensuring a fair access to the radio channel. We show the problem is NP-complete and propose a heuristic to approximate the optimal scheduling solution in polynomial time. We use empirical link quality data to evaluate the κ-FSOM heuristic in a realistic setting and compare its performance to other heuristics. We show that κ-FSOM heuristic achieves high data reception rates, under different fairness and node lifetime constraints.

Keywords: Link scheduling, Optimization, Fairness, Energy, Mobile Sensor Network.

1   Introduction

Recent advances in embedded systems and battery technology have enabled a new class of large-scale mobile sensing applications. Consider a swarm of micro-aerial vehicles fitted with a variety of sensors that can achieve fine-grained three-dimensional sampling of our physical spaces, enabling exciting new applications such as urban surveillance, disaster recovery and environmental monitoring [1–3]. It is now possible to monitor individual movement patterns of wildlife alongside the various aspects of their environment [4–6]. In a typical mobile sensing scenario, sensor nodes mounted on a carrier (e.g., vehicle or animal) collect numerous sensor readings while in transit. The nodes ultimately arrive back at a

B. Krishnamachari, A.L. Murphy, and N. Trigoni (Eds.): EWSN 2014, LNCS 8354, pp. 17–33, 2014.
© Springer International Publishing Switzerland 2014

known rendezvous point (e.g., command center or animal pen), often as a large swarm and remain there for an extended period of time. The data stored on each sensor node is offloaded to a base station (BS) during this time.

A number of considerations make the data collection non-trivial. First, the number of nodes can be quite large (several hundreds) and while the nodes normally arrive back in large groups, their exact arrival sequence is often unknown. Second, the sensor nodes typically have low residual energy levels after being out in the field for an extended period and limited bandwidth due to their weight and size limitations. It is thus critical to collect data from each node before its residual energy is exhausted. Third, the quality of the wireless channel between each node and the BS may vary with time. Having a node transmit during instances when the channel quality is poor is likely to result in packet reception errors, which in turn would require retransmissions and thus increased energy expenditure. Fourth, data should be downloaded from the nodes in a fair way. In particular, the amount of data collected from each node should be greater than a certain application-specific threshold. This is important to maximize the accuracy of data analysis, for example, in the context of mobility modeling and population characteristics for wildlife monitoring.

Conventional scheduling such as the one employed in IEEE 802.15.4 [7] are based on First Come First Served (FCFS), which we refer to as *batch processing*. Batch processing has limited performance in real-world conditions with irregular radio channels and limited bandwidth. Any node with poor link quality occupies the channel due to retransmissions, while the nodes with higher link quality have to wait. Finally, batch processing does not support data collection fairness, potentially downloading a large amount of data from a small subset of nodes.

We consider the scheduling problem in the context of a real-world application for monitoring flying foxes (also known as fruit bats). Flying foxes typically swarm out in search of food at night and flock back to roosting camps during the daytime. A typical roosting camp can consist of hundreds to tens of thousands of animals [8]. Recent work [9] aims to collect fine-grained spatiotemporal data about their movement patterns and environmental surroundings by attaching a sensor collar to these animals. The embedded sensors record the flight and biological data such as GPS, temperature and air pressure while the bats are out and about. The data is offloaded to a BS in the roosting camp when the bats flock back during the daytime. Fig. 1 depicts a typical roosting camp and the sensor collar attached to the animal.

In this paper, we propose κ-fair scheduling optimization model (κ-FSOM) to maximize data harvesting in a large-scale mobile sensor network. κ-FSOM schedules transmissions based on both the link quality and the residual energy of each node. It also guarantees that a certain application-specific amount of data is collected from each node. We first show that this optimization problem is NP-complete. Next, we propose a heuristic algorithm to optimize the scheduling in linear time. The κ-FSOM heuristic prioritizes the nodes for scheduling based on a ratio of the link quality and residual energy. This enables the nodes with the lowest energy reserves and the best chance of achieving successful transmissions

(b) Flying fox with
the sensor collar

(a) Roosting Camp

Fig. 1. Motivating Application: Flying fox monitoring

to transfer their data first. In addition, we develop a state transition model to address the fairness criteria and maximize overall network goodput. While we use the bat monitoring application as a case study, the proposed optimization model and heuristic are application-agnostic and hence applicable to a wide variety of large-scale mobile sensing scenarios with delay tolerance.

The rest of paper is organized as follows: Section 2 presents related work on link scheduling and optimization. We discuss network configuration and MAC protocol in Section 3. Section 4 formulates the scheduling optimization and constraints. In Section 5, we prove that the optimization problem is NP-complete and introduce our heuristic algorithm. In Section 6, we show the performance of the κ-FSOM heuristic and compare it with state-of-the-art. Finally, the paper is concluded in Section 7.

2   Related Work

In this section, we review the literature on link scheduling and optimization in wireless networks. To solve different optimization goals, recent work considers throughput, energy consumption or time delay.

Extensive studies have been conducted on link scheduling in cellular networks. In [10], the link quality is predicted by an application framework which tracks the direction of travel of mobile phone at the BS. They develop energy-aware scheduling algorithms for different application workloads such as syncing or streaming. Some scheduling optimizations which consider multicast [11], quality-of-service assurance [12] and fair relaying with multiple antennas [13] are proposed to achieve optimal delay, capacity gain or network utility.

The majority of related work has focused on addressing the scheduling problem in the context of multi-hop networks [14–16]. However, the notion of fairness in multi-hop networks focuses on fair allocation of time slots among the links in each super frame, which is different from the fairness in data collection of MSN.

A link scheduling for maximum throughput-utility in single-hop networks with the constraint of network delay is presented in [17]. It establishes a delay-based policy for utility optimization. The policy provides deterministic worst-case delay bounds with total throughput-utility guarantee. The author in [18] proposes an opportunistic scheduling algorithm that guarantees a bounded worst case delay in single-hop wireless networks. However, those scheduling algorithms are not applicable in MSNs, because they do not consider the constraints of energy and fairness of collection. In [19], a sensing scheduling among sensor nodes is presented to maximize the overall Quality of Monitoring utility subject to the energy usage. The scheduling algorithm maximizes the overall utility which is to evaluate quality of sensor readings based on the greedy algorithm. For body sensor networks, Sidharth, *et al.* focus on polling-based communication protocols, and address the problem of optimizing the polling schedule to achieve minimal energy consumption and latency [20]. They formulate the problem as a geometric program and solve it by convex optimization.

To the best of our knowledge, there is no research focusing on link scheduling optimization for fair data collection in large-scale single-hop MSNs. The recent work in the literature is not applicable because they do not optimize the scheduling with the requirements of both energy consumption and data reception fairness. The key difference of our work over previous scheduling optimization is that for a single-hop MSN which includes a large number of nodes, data collection is maximized in a fair way before they run out of energy. We formulate the transmission scheduling optimization model in Section 4.

3   Network Configuration and MAC Protocol

In this section, we describe our network setup in the context of the bat monitoring application and propose extensions to IEEE 802.15.4 MAC protocol to improve its performance under our specific constraints.

3.1   Network Configuration

Our sensor nodes [9] are based on a custom-designed light-weight sensing platform. The node embeds a GPS receiver, a three-axis accelerometer, air pressure sensors, a microphone and a flash memory for delay-tolerant data collection. The node is powered by a battery and includes a solar panel for harvesting energy. The bats are nocturnal feeders and can travel long distances (20 km in one night on average) in search for food. Typically the bats return to the roosting camps during the day in large numbers and remain there before heading out again at night. Individual animals can be away for several weeks before returning back to the camp. Thus the total data payload on each node can vary up to a few MB.

We also deploy a number of powered BSs located at animal congregation areas. BSs download data from sensors over a single-hop radio link, using Texas

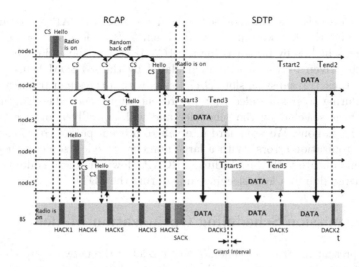

Fig. 2. The timing relationship. $Tstart_i$ and $Tend_i$ stand for the starting and ending time of node i's data transmission respectively.

Instruments CC1101 radios over 915 MHz frequency band. BSs then upload collected data to a central database over 3G.

3.2 MAC Protocol

We propose some modifications to IEEE 802.15.4 super frame structure to address the constraints of our application since 802.15.4 MAC protocol is not feasible for scheduling optimization of MSNs. First, at the beginning of super frame, the BS does not have any information (PRR, energy, data size, etc) about the nodes. Second, the node competes the channel in CAP only when it receives the beacon. If the node misses the beacon due to the poor link quality, it consumes much energy on idle listening. Even worse, the node which misses the beacon has no chance to compete for the channel no matter how small the energy or how good the link quality is. We utilize a 2-stage communication model, with random channel access period (RCAP) followed by scheduled data transmission period (SDTP) (see Fig. 2). The two periods interchange periodically and are synchronized by the BS. Sensor nodes do not keep track of the schedule while away from the BS, they only participate when in the range of the BS.

The purpose of the RCAP is to collect information about sensor nodes, including their current link quality, the amount of available data, and their energy resources. This data fits in a single *Hello* packet and the nodes compete for the channel in a random-access fashion. Nodes check the radio channel for other transmissions by using carrier sensing (CS) to avoid packet collisions and the reception of *Hello* packets is acknowledged by the BS, so the nodes can turn off their radios until the end of the RCAP. However, if *Hello* packets collision happen, the senders have to back off a random time to sense the channel again.

BS calculates the transmission schedule at the end of RCAP by running the κ-FSOM heuristic that we illustrate in Section 5. BS informs all sensor nodes the optimal schedule by broadcasting a *SACK* packet at the end of the RCAP.

SDTP is driven by the schedule calculated by the κ-FSOM heuristic. The nodes find their transmission slot (*DATA* slot) within the super frame and only transmit during their scheduled time to prevent interference. The length of the DATA slots is selected by the scheduler and will typically allow for multiple packet transmissions. We use guard intervals to prevent packet collisions due to time-synchronization errors. With a large number of nodes, some of them may fail to communicate with the BS during RCAP. However, these nodes consume limited energy due to a long sleeping time during the SDTP.

4   Transmission Scheduling Optimization Model

Next, we present an abstract generalizable model of the network, which is used for the optimization model presented in the Section 4.2. We assume that there are N nodes that directly communicate with the BS using single-hop communication. The nodes typically arrive in large groups but their exact arrival sequence is unknown. The residual energy of a node i, when it arrives at the camp is denoted by E_i^0. In order to prevent a node from completely depleting its battery, we assume that a node powers down if the residual energy goes below a certain threshold E_{td}. In this paper, a node in such a state is referred to as a *dead node*. The wireless channel between each node and the BS is typically influenced by a variety of environmental factors and the motion of the node. The channel variability in turn influences the Packet Reception Rate (PRR) of the node. We estimate the PRR as a function of empirically collected RSSI traces from a real testbed as outlined in Section 6.

On the basis of Section 3, the BS aggregates the nodes and channel information in the RCAP in order to schedule the transmissions. In this section, we explain the basic notations and propose the scheduling optimization model under the constraints of reception fairness and node's remaining energy. We formulate the scheduling optimization as an Integer Linear Programming (ILP) problem.

4.1   Problem Formulation

According to the super frame as shown in Fig. 2, we divide the SDTP to a number of slots S, where, $S = \sum_{i=1}^{N} \Delta T_i$. Time slot j ($j \in [1, S]$) is allocated by the BS to only one node's transmission for the purpose of avoiding collisions. Therefore, the allocated time ΔT_i of the node i contains multiple time slots in one super frame. κ-FSOM calculates optimal solutions for multiple super frames so that the schedule is optimized globally. F is defined as the total number of super frames needed for all the nodes to finish their data transmissions. The sequence number of super frame is denoted as f ($f \in [1, F]$). We assume the residual energy when node i arrives at the camp is $E_i^0 (i \in [1, N])$. The PRR is indicated by q_i^f, where $q_i^f \in [0, 1]$. Additionally, q_i^f may change from one super frame to the next due to the time-varying channel.

We assume q_i^f does not change during the super frame since the flying foxes are not highly mobile in the camp. The data payload stored on each node is represented by λ_i and the fairness coefficient is κ where $\kappa \in (0, 100\%]$. Thus, the data reception fairness ensures that the number of data packets the BS collects from each node is not less than $\kappa \cdot \lambda_i$. We define the boolean variable x_{ij}^f as a transmission indicator for node $i \in [1, N]$ associated with the slot $j \in [1, S]$ in the super frame $f \in [1, F]$. $x_{ij}^f = 1$ means node i has jth slot reserved for transmission in super frame f.

The number of data packets received by the BS in a super frame is defined as γ_f, where

$$\gamma_f = \sum_{i=1}^{N} \sum_{j=1}^{S} x_{ij}^f \cdot q_i^f, (f \in [1, F]) \tag{1}$$

Similarly, for all super frames, the data received by the BS from any node i is defined as α_i, where

$$\alpha_i = \sum_{f=1}^{F} \sum_{j=1}^{S} x_{ij}^f \cdot q_i^f, (i \in [1, N]) \tag{2}$$

The energy consumption of nodes arises from the transmissions in RCAP and SDTP as shown in Fig. 2. In this paper, we let $e_{tx-hello}$, $e_{rx-hack}$ and $e_{rx-sack}$ be the energy consumption of transmitting one *Hello* packet, receiving one *HACK* and one *SACK* of the nodes, respectively. The e_{tx} represents energy consumption of transmitting one data packet. Due to the tiny energy consumption of carrier sensing compared to transmitting and receiving packets [21], we neglect the same in our model. The energy consumption of node i in the RCAP is $\breve{E}_A$, where

$$\breve{E}_A = e_{tx-hello} + e_{rx-hack} + e_{rx-sack} \tag{3}$$

We next define $\breve{E}_{Di}$ as the energy that node i consumes on data transmission in all super frames, where

$$\breve{E}_{Di} = \sum_{f=1}^{F} \sum_{j=1}^{S} x_{ij}^f \cdot e_{tx}, (i \in [1, N]) \tag{4}$$

4.2 Optimization Model

Based on the notations in the problem formulation, we formulate the κ-FSOM for finding the optimal schedules as follows. Objective function of the optimization model is to maximize γ_f of all super frames. Constraint (5) specifies the minimum remaining energy to be above E_{td}. A node stops accessing the channel after all its data has been transmitted or constraint (5) is violated. Consequently, it does not waste energy in RCAP in subsequent super frames. For this purpose, φ_i^f is defined as an indicator of RCAP in a super frame for the node. If the node i does not compete for the channel in the RCAP of super frame f, φ_i^f is equal to 0. $\sum_{f=1}^{F}(\breve{E}_A \cdot \varphi_i^f)$ indicates the energy consumption of the node in the RCAP of all super frames.

Constraint (6) guarantees that the BS receives sufficient data packets to meet the fairness requirement. Constraint (7) limits the value of α_i by the total payload λ_i. Constraints (8) and (9) specify that at any data transmission time slot only one node communicates with the BS to prevent transmission collisions.

The only unknown is the total number of super frames during which a node is required to transmit. In other words, φ_i^f is not known. To determine φ_i^f, we define a variable v_{ij}^f for node i at any slot j of super frame f. Accordingly, constraint (10) presents whether node i has stopped the data transmission or not. $\sum_{g=1}^f \sum_{w=1}^j x_{iw}^g q_i^g$ is the total received packets until the current slot j of super frame f. If the amount of data packets received from node i matches the size of payloads λ_i, v_{ij}^f is equal to 0. Constraints (11) and (12) ensure the future slots j' and super frames g have $v_{ij}^f = 0$ if λ_i packets have been received from node i. Constraint (13) guarantees all φ_i^f of the future super frames is 0 if $v_{ij}^f = 0$. As a result, the remaining energy of node i which is restricted by the RCAP indicator φ_i^f stops decreasing in constraint (5). Constraint (14) ensures that the node i stops data transmission if $\varphi_i^f = 0$.

$$maximize \quad \sum_{f=1}^F \gamma_f$$

$$subject\ to:\ E_i^0 - \sum_{f=1}^F (\breve{E}_A \cdot \varphi_i^f) - \breve{E}_{Di} \geq E_{td}, \quad (i \in [1, N]) \tag{5}$$

$$\alpha_i \geq \kappa \cdot \lambda_i, \quad (i \in [1, N], \kappa \in (0, 1]) \tag{6}$$

$$\alpha_i \leq \lambda_i, \quad (i \in [1, N]) \tag{7}$$

$$x_{ij}^f \leq 1, \quad (i \in [1, N], j \in [1, S], f \in [1, F]) \tag{8}$$

$$\sum_{i=1}^N x_{ij}^f \leq 1, \quad (j \in [1, S], f \in [1, F]) \tag{9}$$

$$\lambda_i - \sum_{g=1}^f \sum_{w=1}^j x_{iw}^g \cdot q_i^g \geq v_{ij}^f, \quad (i \in [1, N], j \in [1, S], f \in [1, F]) \tag{10}$$

$$v_{ij}^f \geq v_{ij'}^f, \quad (j' \geq j, j \in [1, S]) \tag{11}$$

$$v_{ij}^f \geq v_{ij'}^g, \quad (g \geq f, j' \geq j, j \in [1, S], f \in [1, F]) \tag{12}$$

$$\sum_{a=1}^{F-f} \varphi_i^{f+a} \leq v_{ij}^f, \quad (i \in [1, N], j \in [1, S]) \tag{13}$$

$$x_{ij}^f \leq \varphi_i^f, \quad (i \in [1, N], j \in [1, S], f \in [1, F]) \tag{14}$$

5 κ-FSOM Heuristic Algorithm

In this section, we first show that κ-FSOM is NP-complete. Next, a heuristic algorithm is proposed to approximate the optimal solution.

Algorithm 1. κ-FSOM Heuristic Algorithm

1: nodes are in AD state and compete the channel
2: The BS calculates η_i^f for the node i, $\forall f \in [1, F]$
3: The BS sorts the nodes by η_i^f, then $\eta_i^f \geq \eta_{i'}^f, (i \neq i', i' \in [1, N])$
4: The BS schedules the node i to transmit
5: **if** $\alpha_i \geq (\kappa \cdot \lambda_i)$ **then**
6:    The node i goes to NA state
7:    The BS schedules the next one to transmit
8: **else**
9:    The node i remains in AD state
10: **end if**
11: **if** every node has $\alpha_i \geq (\kappa \cdot \lambda_i)$ $\forall i \in [1, N]$ **then**
12:    All the nodes transfer to AD state
13:    The BS calculates η_i^f for each node
14:    The BS sorts the nodes by η_i^f, then $\eta_i^f \geq \eta_{i'}^f, (i \neq i', i' \in [1, N])$
15:    **if** $E_i \geq E_{td}$ **then**
16:       The BS schedules the node i to transmit
17:    **else**
18:       The node i changes state to the ND
19:       The BS schedules the next one to transmit
20:    **end if**
21:    **if** $\alpha_i < \lambda_i$ **then**
22:       The node i remains in AD state
23:    **else**
24:       The node i changes state to the ND
25:    **end if**
26: **end if**

Maximizing the collected data presented in κ-FSOM is a typical 0-1 Multiple Knapsack Problem (MKP) [22]. We reduce an instance of a MKP to our scheduling optimization problem by assigning ΔT_i to each knapsack. Therefore, the capacity of the knapsack is equal to ΔT_i. The items to be put in knapsacks are data packets whose size is prorated by q_i^f. The parameters of the energy and fairness conditions (constraint (5) and (6)) are chosen so that they are satisfied by any placement of items. In this way, optimal placement of items in knapsacks is reduced to such an instance of our scheduling problem. Since the problem is obviously an NP problem, this shows that our scheduling problem presented in the Section 4 is NP-complete.

We propose a heuristic algorithm to approximate the optimal solution of κ-FSOM. Due to the prominent effect of E_i^f and q_i^f on the scheduling, a ratio of the link quality and remaining energy of the node i is denoted as η_i^f, where

$$\eta_i^f = \frac{q_i^f}{E_i^f}, \forall i \in [1, N], \forall f \in [1, F] \tag{15}$$

Accordingly, E_i^f is obtained by

$$E_i^f = E_i^0 - \sum_{f'=1}^{f}(\breve{E}_A \cdot \varphi_i^{f'}) - \sum_{f'=1}^{f}\sum_{j=1}^{S} x_{ij}^{f'} \cdot e_{tx} \tag{16}$$

The motivation of calculating η_i^f is to prioritize the nodes based on both the link quality and remaining energy. The κ-FSOM heuristic gives a high transmission priority to the node with larger η_i^f. This method achieves large data reception because for the nodes with the same q_i^f, the node with the smallest E_i^f gets higher transmitting priority. Similarly, for the nodes with the same E_i^f, one with higher q_i^f has higher priority.

In our heuristic, the node works in three states, Access & Data transmission (AD), NonAccess (NA) and NonData (ND). In AD state, the node competes for the channel in RCAP and transmits data in SDTP as shown in Fig. 2. In NA state, the node neither accesses the channel nor transmits data but only receives the $SACK$ packets for the purpose of saving energy in the super frame. More importantly, none of the nodes which are in the NA state transmit data given that no time slots are allocated to them. This helps more nodes achieve fairness. In ND state, the node does not turn on the radio and remains in sleep mode.

The κ-FSOM heuristic develops two steps to maximize the data reception with η_i^f. It is implemented as shown in Algorithm 1.

Initially, all nodes are in AD state and the BS schedules the node i ($i \in [1, N]$) which has maximum η_i^f to transmit data. The BS records the number of data packets from the node. Once the node i meets the fairness of data reception (constraint (6)), it transfers to the NA state. The benefit of NA state is to reduce the channel competition since the number of nodes competing for the channel is decreased. Certainly, after the first step, all the nodes have at least $\kappa \cdot \lambda_i$ data packets being transmitted successfully and the fair reception of data is achieved. At the second step, all the nodes change the state from NA to AD. Then, the BS schedules the node with largest η_i^f to transmit first. To maximize data reception, node i remains in AD state until either constraint (5) or (7) no longer holds. Moreover, if the constraint of (5) or (7) is not fulfilled by the node i, it transitions to ND state. By using this approach, the number of data packets collected by the BS is maximized, meanwhile, the energy and fairness requirements are both achieved. Transition graph is shown in Fig. 3.

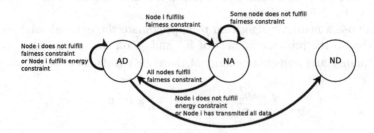

Fig. 3. The state transition of node i

Table 1. Simulation Parameters

Maximum number of bats	N	300
Working temperature	T_A	25 °C
Working frequency	$Freq$	915 MHz
Supply voltage	V_{cc}	3 V
Transmitting current	I_{tx}	35 mA
Receiving current	I_{rx}	15 mA
Remaining energy threshold	E_{td}	1.67 mJ
Bit Rate	R_b	19.2k bps

6   Simulation and Performance Evaluation

Given optimal schedules from κ-FSOM by AMPL, the performance of our heuristic algorithm is compared to the optimal schedules. We study the performance of the κ-FSOM heuristic in the static and dynamic scenarios in MATLAB. Finally, we evaluate the impact of the fairness coefficient κ on network performance.

6.1   Simulation Configuration

The data collection network in the simulation contains one BS and N nodes ($N \in [10, 300]$) which are randomly distributed within the open camp. The node communicates with the BS using CC1101 radio [23].

A data packet which contains time, GPS and biological information has 32 bytes. The length of one *Hello* packet is 10 bytes. Equally, *HACK* and *SACK* have the same length as *Hello*. Therefore, we have

$$e_{tx-hello} = V_{cc} \cdot I_{tx} \cdot \frac{10 \times 8}{R_b} = 0.03mJ \tag{17}$$

$$e_{rx-hack} = e_{rx-sack} = V_{cc} \cdot I_{rx} \cdot \frac{10 \times 8}{R_b} = 0.01mJ \tag{18}$$

$$e_{tx} = V_{cc} \cdot I_{tx} \cdot \frac{32 \times 8}{R_b} = 0.1mJ \tag{19}$$

According to the energy initialization of sensor nodes in simulations [24], E_i^0 in this work is given by a normal distribution with the mean value of 50 Joule, an energy budget that supports the node for several days. However, in our simulations, the value of E_i^0 is given purposely so that some dead nodes which run out of energy can be observed among different scheduling algorithms. The RSSI trace recorded by the sensor collars on the flying foxes [9] is imported to our simulator, which provides an environment to conduct repeatable simulations based on empirical data. Fig. 4 depicts a 780 seconds segment which includes 3120 RSSI samples (The sampling rate of sensor collar is 4 samples per second). In this paper, we convert the RSSI to PRR for the q_i^f by the experimental results of PRR-RSSI relationship [25].

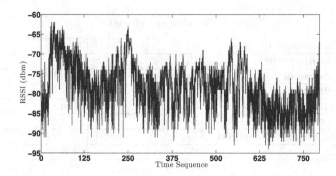

Fig. 4. RSSI trace of the node by the sensor collar on the flying fox

We evaluate three performance metrics: number of data packets received by the BS (data reception), the number of fair nodes and dead nodes. Specifically, the *fair nodes* denote the number of nodes such that node i fulfills $\alpha_i \geq \kappa \cdot \lambda_i$ (the fairness constraint (6)). We compare the performance of our heuristic with κ-FSOM optimal solution at first. Each node carries 80 KB data which is the payload generated by the sensor collar on flying fox in one day. Then, we simulate the κ-FSOM heuristic in the static and dynamic scenarios. In the static scenario, we assume all the nodes are in the camp from the start of experiment to the end. In the dynamic case, the nodes arrive back at the camp at different times. Since the number of nodes communicating with the BS in a short time is small, we increase the data payload to 300 KB in order to explore the limits of the scheduling algorithms. For this reason, a node occupies the channel longer while more nodes enter the camp in the dynamic scenario.

To evaluate the performance of the κ-FSOM heuristic in the static and dynamic scenarios, two Greedy scheduling algorithms and FCFS algorithm are constructed in the numerical investigations. Because two basic elements used in κ-FSOM are the remaining energy represented by E_i^f and link quality q_i^f of node, the Greedy scheduling algorithms are formulated by them. The first Greedy algorithm is called Low Energy Greedy (LEG), namely, the transmission schedule is based solely on the E_i^f of node. Lower E_i^f implies higher priority of transmission at super frame f. High PRR Greedy (HPG) is the second algorithm where the node with higher q_i^f has higher priority. We compare them with the κ-FSOM heuristic algorithm with $\kappa = 10\%$, 50% and 90%.

6.2   Simulation Results

Comparing to optimal schedules To compare to the optimal schedule shown in κ-FSOM, we assess the performance of our heuristic when it operates in ten small-scale networks where the number of nodes is increased from 1 to 10. This initial comparison makes us aware of the performance difference between κ-FSOM and our heuristic. The node i carries 80 KB data, so $\lambda_i = 2500$. In fact,

Table 2. Comparison between the optimal solutions and the κ-FSOM heuristic

Nodes	AMPL (Cplex)			κ-FSOM		
	Packets	Fair nodes	Runtime	Packets	Fair nodes	Runtime
1	2499	1	1 s	2481	1	0.03 s
2	4999	2	4 s	4969	2	0.1 s
3	7499	3	17 s	7469	3	0.04 s
4	9998	4	50 s	9922	4	0.04 s
5	12498	5	1 m 5 s	12477	5	0.04 s
6	14998	6	5 m 15 s	14340	6	0.04 s
7	17498	7	58 m 47 s	17288	7	0.05 s
8	19997	8	5 h 49 m	19792	8	0.05 s
9	22498	9	17 h 25 m	21779	9	0.06 s
10	24997	10	30 h 5 m	24555	10	0.07 s

the comparison is not affected by different κ values, thus we choose κ=50% for both the optimal schedules of κ-FSOM and the κ-FSOM heuristic. The optimal schedules achieve a maximum number of received data packets with the fairness and remaining energy constraints. They are constructed using AMPL and a state of the art ILP solver, Cplex 12.5, in a 2.7 GHz Intel core processor with 8 GB of memory.

Table 2 summarizes running time, the number of collected data packets and fair nodes. It is also found that there is no dead node in all tests. On data reception, the κ-FSOM heuristic and optimal solution have the maximum difference which is 719 when N = 9. On average, the number of packets in our heuristic is less than the AMPL output by around 1.8%. Our heuristic guarantees exactly the same number of fair nodes as optimal schedules. Moreover, our heuristic is much more efficient than κ-FSOM on runtime.

Static Scenario. Fig. 5a and 5c show the performance of the aforementioned four scheduling algorithms on the data reception and fairness. When there are only 10 nodes in the network, they have pretty similar performance. However, FCFS, LEG and HPG collect 92.2%, 90.8% and 83.5% less data packets than our heuristic when N = 300. The number of fair nodes of our heuristic is more than the ones of FCFS, LEG and HPG for 174, 170, 147 nodes when κ = 50% and N = 300. The reason is that LEG scheduling fails when the low energy nodes have poor link quality. The nodes with high PRR are not scheduled, however, they still consume energy on channel competitions in RCAP. For HPG scheduling, the nodes with high PRR occupy the SDTP for multiple super frames until they finish the transmissions. This leads to a large number of dead nodes. However, those nodes could have potentially gained higher data reception. In contrast, our heuristic makes the schedule based on η_i^f which considers both remaining energy and link quality. Moreover, it also achieves the fairness of data collection.

We find the data reception and fair nodes of FCFS, LEG and HPG do not vary significantly from N = 100 to 300. The reason is indicated by dead nodes which are shown in Fig. 5e. It shows FCFS, LEG and HPG have much more dead nodes than the κ-FSOM heuristic starting from N = 50. According to the

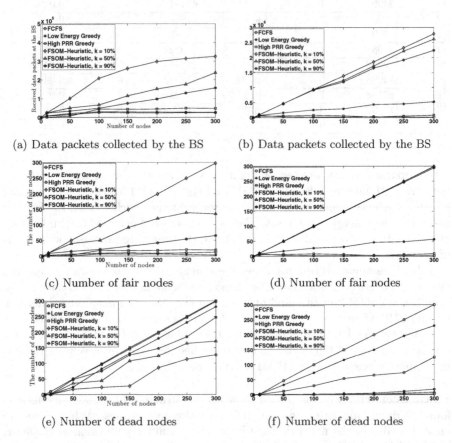

(a) Data packets collected by the BS   (b) Data packets collected by the BS

(c) Number of fair nodes   (d) Number of fair nodes

(e) Number of dead nodes   (f) Number of dead nodes

Fig. 5. (a), (c) and (e) are for static scenario; (b), (d) and (f) are for dynamic scenario

κ-FSOM heuristic, we know that κ is a crucial variable which affects the states transition of node i. The performance of our heuristic varies with different κ value. As shown, they are similar for $\kappa = 10\%$, 50% and 90% when N is 10. From N = 50 to N = 300, $\kappa = 10\%$ performs better than 50% and 90%. The reason is that any node which is scheduled to transmit occupies more super frames when κ is increased due to the fairness constraint (6). It makes the other nodes compete the channel in RCAP repeatedly and cost energy.

Dynamic Scenario. In this set of experiments, we test the scheduling algorithms when nodes fly back as a swarm. Since the arrival pattern of flying foxes in real world is not known, we assume the inter-arrival time of nodes is exponentially distributed which is typically used to model situations involving the random time between arrivals to a service facility [26]. One node has a data payload of 300 KB. From Fig. 5b we find that the κ-FSOM heuristic has up to 37.1 times as many collected data packets as FCFS and HPG. It outperforms LEG by 5 times as well. The reason is explained by Fig. 5d and 5f. The FCFS, LEG and HPG have less fair nodes and more dead nodes than our heuristic, which means the newly arrived nodes fail to transmit since the transmitting node have not finished the transmission. It causes their energy to be depleted very soon. Moreover, in Fig. 5d, we observe the difference of fairness which is achieved by different κ is smaller than the one in static scenario. That is because the BS schedules a small number of nodes in one super frame in dynamic scenario. The first step of κ-FSOM heuristic is completed faster, hence more nodes achieve fairness in dynamic scenario. Likewise, the number of dead nodes in our heuristic has small difference in Fig. 5f. Due to the increase of λ_i in this scenario, there are 16 dead nodes with the $\kappa = 90\%$ in our heuristic at the maximum.

6.3   Effect of Fairness Coefficient κ

Based on the preceding simulations, it is observed that different κ affects the performance of our heuristic. Essentially, the κ decides the fairness level in κ-FSOM. In this experiment, we analyze the impact of κ in the static scenario with 300 nodes. Specifically, the κ is varied from 10% to 100%. The performance of data reception, fair nodes and dead nodes are shown in Fig. 6.

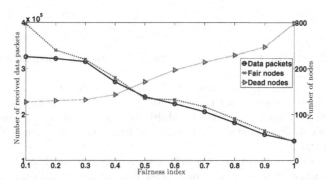

Fig. 6. The effect of κ on the performance of κ-FSOM scheduling

As shown in Fig. 6, data reception rate decreases and the number of dead nodes increases with the increasing κ. This is because the transmission duration of one node is extended when κ is increased. Other nodes deplete their energy due to RCAP if the channel is occupied by someone with high η_i^f for a long time. Their data is not collected by the BS before the nodes exhaust the energy. We also find that the scheduling with smaller κ achieves larger number of fair nodes. However, since the BS gives higher priority to the larger η_i^f node after all nodes satisfy fairness constraint, it does not guarantee most of data can be collected from each node. Therefore, κ changed from 40% to 50% keeps a balance between the data reception from each node and total number of dead nodes.

7   Conclusion

In this paper, we have proposed and evaluated κ-FSOM which is a fair link scheduling optimization model with the objective of maximizing the data reception in the energy-aware data collection of MSN. The super frame structure is developed for the BS to collect data from the nodes. We have proved that the scheduling optimization of κ-FSOM is an NP-complete problem. Therefore, the κ-FSOM heuristic algorithm is proposed to approximate the optimal solutions in polynomial time. Our heuristic schedules the transmissions of data senders based on η_i^f and three working states in two steps. With the application of flying foxes monitoring, we have shown the numerical performance of the κ-FSOM heuristic based on the RSSI traced by the sensor collar. We have compared our heuristic with the optimal schedules of κ-FSOM and presented extensive simulations incorporating both static and dynamic scenarios. Specifically, the κ-FSOM heuristic provides a near-optimal scheduling to the data collection in MSNs.

Acknowledgment. This work was supported by the Australian Research Council Discovery Grant DP110104344 and the Batmon Project in CSIRO's Sensor and Sensor Networks Transformation Capability Platform. The authors thank Dr. Andreas Reinhardt, Dr. Lavy Libman and Dr. Wen Hu for their constructive comments.

References

1. Wood, R., Nagpal, R., Wei, G.Y.: Flight of the robobees. Scientific American 308, 60–65 (2013)
2. Dantu, K., Kate, B., Waterman, J., Bailis, P., Welsh, M.: Programming micro-aerial vehicle swarms with karma. In: ACM SenSys, pp. 121–134 (2011)
3. Sinha, A., Tsourdos, A., White, B.: Multi uav coordination for tracking the dispersion of a contaminant cloud in an urban region. European Journal of Control 15, 441–448 (2009)
4. Israel, M.: A uav-based roe deer fawn detection system. In: Eisenbeiss, H., Kunz, M., Ingensand, H. (eds.) Proceedings of the International Conference on Unmanned Aerial Vehicle in Geomatics (UAV-g), vol. 38, pp. 1–5 (2011)
5. Dyo, V., Ellwood, S.A., Macdonald, D.W., Markham, A., Mascolo, C., Pásztor, B., Scellato, S., Trigoni, N., Wohlers, R., Yousef, K.: Evolution and sustainability of a wildlife monitoring sensor network. In: ACM SenSys, pp. 127–140 (2010)
6. Corke, P., Wark, T., Jurdak, R., Hu, W., Valencia, P., Moore, D.: Environmental wireless sensor networks. Proceedings of the IEEE 98, 1903–1917 (2010)
7. Group, I.W., et al.: Standard for part 15.4: Wireless medium access control (mac) and physical layer (phy) specifications for low rate wireless personal area networks (lr-wpans). ANSI/IEEE 802 15, 4 (2003)
8. Shilton, L.A., Latch, P.J., Mckeown, A., Pert, P., Westcott, D.A.: Landscape-scale redistribution of a highly mobile threatened species, pteropus conspicillatus (chiroptera, pteropodidae), in response to tropical cyclone larry. Austral Ecology 33(4), 549–561 (2008)

9. Jurdak, R., Sommer, P., Kusy, B., Kottege, N., Crossman, C., Mckeown, A., Westcott, D.: Camazotz: multimodal activity-based gps sampling. In: ACM IPSN, pp. 67–78 (2013)

10. Schulman, A., Navda, V., Ramjee, R., Spring, N., Deshpande, P., Grunewald, C., Jain, K., Padmanabhan, V.N.: Bartendr: a practical approach to energy-aware cellular data scheduling. In: Proceedings of the Sixteenth Annual International Conference on Mobile Computing and Networking, pp. 85–96. ACM (2010)

11. Low, T.P., Pun, M.O., Hong, Y.W., Kuo, C.C.: Optimized opportunistic multicast scheduling (oms) over wireless cellular networks. IEEE Transactions on Wireless Communications 9(2), 791–801 (2010)

12. Wu, D., Negi, R.: Downlink scheduling in a cellular network for quality-of-service assurance. IEEE Transactions on Vehicular Technology 53(5), 1547–1557 (2004)

13. Lin, Y., Yu, W.: Fair scheduling and resource allocation for wireless cellular network with shared relays. IEEE Journal on Selected Areas in Communications 30(8), 1530–1540 (2012)

14. Zhou, Y., Li, X.Y., Liu, M., Li, Z., Tang, S., Mao, X., Huang, Q.: Distributed link scheduling for throughput maximization under physical interference model. In: IEEE INFOCOM, pp. 2691–2695 (2012)

15. Leconte, M., Ni, J., Srikant, R.: Improved bounds on the throughput efficiency of greedy maximal scheduling in wireless networks. IEEE/ACM Transactions on Networking 19(3), 709–720 (2011)

16. Papadaki, K., Friderikos, V.: Approximate dynamic programming for link scheduling in wireless mesh networks. International Journal of Computers and Operations Research 35(12), 3848–3859 (2008)

17. Neely, M.J.: Delay-based network utility maximization. In: IEEE INFOCOM, pp. 1–9 (2010)

18. Neely: Opportunistic scheduling with worst case delay guarantees in single and multi-hop networks. In: IEEE INFOCOM, pp. 1728–1736 (2011)

19. Tang, S., Yang, L.: Morello: A quality-of-monitoring oriented sensing scheduling protocol in sensor networks. In: IEEE INFOCOM, pp. 2676–2680 (2012)

20. Nabar, S., Walling, J., Poovendran, R.: Minimizing energy consumption in body sensor networks via convex optimization. In: International Conference on Body Sensor Networks (BSN), pp. 62–67 (2010)

21. Ergen, S.C.: Zigbee/ieee 802.15. 4 summary, UC Berkeley, September 10 (2004)

22. Martello, S., Toth, P.: Knapsack problems: algorithms and computer implementations. John Wiley and Sons, Inc. (1990)

23. TexasInstruments: Cc430f613: Msp430 soc with rf core (2013)

24. Yupho, D., Kabara, J.: The effect of physical topology on wireless sensor network lifetime. Journal of Networks 2(5), 14–23 (2007)

25. Srinivasa, K., Levis, P.: Rssi is under appreciated. The Third Workshop on Embedded Networked Sensors, EmNets (2006)

26. Willkomm, D., Machiraju, S., Bolot, J., Wolisz, A.: Primary user behavior in cellular networks and implications for dynamic spectrum access. IEEE Communications Magazine 47(3), 88–95 (2009)

CodeDrip: Data Dissemination Protocol with Network Coding for Wireless Sensor Networks

Nildo dos Santos Ribeiro Júnior[1], Marcos A.M. Vieira[1],
Luiz F.M. Vieira[1], and Omprakash Gnawali[2]

[1] Universidade Federal de Minas Gerais, Brazil
{nildo,mmvieira,lfvieira}@dcc.ufmg.br
[2] University of Houston, USA
gnawali@cs.uh.edu

Abstract. In this paper, we present CodeDrip, a data dissemination protocol for Wireless Sensor Networks. Dissemination is typically used to query nodes, send commands, and reconfigure the network. CodeDrip utilizes Network Coding to improve energy efficiency, reliability, and speed of dissemination. Network coding allows recovery of lost packets by combining the received packets thereby making dissemination robust to packet losses. While previous work in combining network coding and dissemination focused on bulk data dissemination, we optimize the design of CodeDrip for dissemination of small values. We perform extensive evaluation of CodeDrip on simulations and a large-scale testbed and compare against the implementations of Drip, DIP and DHV protocols. Results show that CodeDrip is faster, smaller and sends fewer messages than Drip, DHV and DIP protocols.

1 Introduction

Wireless Sensor Networks (WSNs) consist of a large number of nodes with sensing, computation, and wireless communication capability. These sensor networks are typically deployed to collect data from the environment or other physical spaces. Many sensor networks have been deployed in outdoor environment such as forests and streets and in indoor setting such as buildings and factories. Wireless communication and energy efficiency are key requirements of these networks, especially in applications where we retrofit existing infrastructure with smart sensing and actuation capabilities.

Many WSN applications require the capability to send messages from a central server or controller node to all the nodes in the network. This type of communication pattern is called *dissemination*. Dissemination is typically used to query, send commands, reconfigure and reprogram the network. A data dissemination protocol for sensor networks needs to overcome several challenges. First, the energy in each sensor node is limited by the battery or energy harvesting capacity, thus it is important to save energy to increase the sensor node's operational lifetime. Second, sensor nodes typically do not have powerful CPUs, so they might not be capable of executing complex communication protocols. Finally,

B. Krishnamachari, A.L. Murphy, and N. Trigoni (Eds.): EWSN 2014, LNCS 8354, pp. 34–49, 2014.

wireless communication is susceptible to transmission errors and packet loss. A dissemination protocol should not only be reliable and energy efficient, but also fast.

In this paper, we present CodeDrip, a data dissemination protocol for Wireless Sensor Networks. CodeDrip uses Network Coding to improve energy efficiency, reliability, and speed of dissemination. Instead of simply retransmitting received data packets, sensor nodes combine various packets into one, and retransmit the combined packet to its neighbors. Therefore, packet loss is mitigated since lost packets might be recovered through the decoding of others combined packets. By avoiding retransmission, the dissemination process might finish faster.

Existing data dissemination protocols for Wireless Sensor Networks present a tradeoff: save energy at the expense of dissemination speed. These protocols use transmission of summaries or version numbers and attempt to selectively transmit the missing data to avoid redundant transmission. While this strategy saves energy, it could incur large delays. Through extensive experiments, we find that CodeDrip provides faster data dissemination while transmitting fewer messages than most previous approaches.

Network Coding is not a new idea in wireless communication. However, previous work such as COPE [11], can not be applied to WSNs because these algorithms require large memory overhead. Network coding schemes such as Rateless Deluge [8] and AdapCode [9] have been previously proposed in wireless sensor networks and are shown to have low memory and computational overhead. However, these WSN dissemination protocols are designed for bulk data dissemination and require $O(n^3)$ instructions for decoding with the Gaussian elimination. There has been no previous study of effectiveness of network coding in dissemination of *small values*. Previously, it was thought that there would be limited opportunity to combine packets in dissemination of small values, hence the focus on bulk data dissemination. We identify the opportunity to make dissemination of small values efficient with network coding and fill this gap in sensor network protocol design space.

Our main contributions are as follows. First, we present the design and implementation of CodeDrip. Second, we study the performance of CodeDrip through extensive simulation and testbed experiments on the KanseiGenie testbed [20]. Third, we compare CodeDrip to the data dissemination of small values with Drip, DIP [18] and DHV [5] and quantify the Network Coding gain and show that Network Coding is useful even for dissemination of small values.

Our work is organized as follows. In the next section, we present work related to CodeDrip. In Section 3, we give an overview of network coding. CodeDrip is explained in Section 4. We present the simulation results in Section 5 and the testbed experiments in Section 6. We conclude in Section 7.

2   Related Work

There is a large body of work in dissemination protocols for WSN. Figure 1 summarizes the major classes of dissemination protocols. In this section, we describe

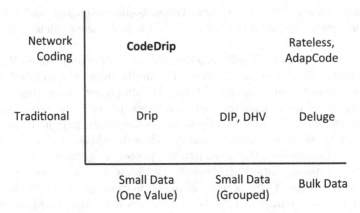

Fig. 1. Selected classes of dissemination protocols in sensor network. CodeDrip uses network coding to make dissemination of small data efficient and fast.

how some of the dissemination protocols fit in the design space of dissemination protocols and application of network coding in dissemination.

2.1   Dissemination of Small Values

Trickle [16] is used as a building block for a number of dissemination protocols that propagate code or small values in WSN. Trickle has two key features that allows it to be efficient: the timer control algorithm and duplicate suppression. Trickle timer doubles its interval every time it fires. Thus, over the long run, the interval converges to a very large maximum value. The timer can be reset to a small value when a new message needs to be sent. Trickle uses version numbers to detect and suppress duplicate transmissions. A node periodically broadcasts its version but stays silent and increases the interval if it hears several messages from its neighbors containing the same version number. When a node receives a new version number, the node resets the timer and transmits the message. CodeDrip uses Trickle timer in its design.

Drip [21] is the simplest data dissemination protocol that uses Trickle timer. Each time an application transmits a message with Drip, a new version number is used. The new version number causes the protocol to reset the Trickle timer and thereby transmissions in the network to disseminate the new value. Redundant transmissions are detected using version numbers and suppressed. When the application does not inject new messages, the timer interval increases which causes the control overhead to level off. When a new message is injected, the new version number causes the timer to reset and the nodes disseminate the message. Figure 2 shows how Drip works when it is used to disseminate three values. Dissemination of each message is paced by its own Trickle timer.

DIssemination Protocol (DIP) [18] is a data discovery and dissemination protocol. DIP continuously measures network conditions and estimates whether each data item requires an update. In DIP, a node periodically broadcasts a summary

Fig. 2. Drip example. There are three values to be disseminated. Each value is independently associated with a Trickle timer. Each packet has a value (rectangles on the left side). Each dot represents when the timer fires and a message is sent.

message, containing hashes of its keys and versions. A hash-tree based algorithm detects if there is an update. DIP scales logarithmically with the total number of items. DHV [5] is a code consistency maintenance protocol. DHV's key contribution is its technique to efficiently determine when to perform code updates. DHV detects and identifies which code item need updates at the bit level. DHV uses the Trickle timer to control transmission rate and duplicate suppression.

DIP and DHV are examples of dissemination protocols that operate at the level of a group of messages (for example, to compute summaries). On the other hand, Drip operates at the granularity of a single message. In DIP and DHV, all nodes must agree on a fixed set of data item identifiers before dissemination. DIP and DHV can scale to a large number of data item updates, however perform worse than Drip on small number of data items or updates [7].

2.2 Bulk and Middle-sized Data Dissemination

A different set of dissemination protocols have been proposed for middle or large-sized objects. Maté [14] and Tenet [19] optimize the design of their dissemination protocols for middle-sized objects. Maté virtual machine disseminates code capsules to install small virtual programs. Tenet disseminates tasks, enabling users to decide what to run in the sensor network during run-time.

Deluge [10] is a data dissemination protocol for code updates. It focuses on disseminating bulk data. Several optimizations in storage, buffering, and transmission enable it to efficiently disseminate objects (such as sensor node code) that do not fit in the limited RAM of sensor nodes. Deluge also uses Trickle timer to time its control packets.

2.3 Network Coding and Dissemination

Early work in network coding showed that, in general, in-network encoding of packets could achieve an optimal capacity that cannot be realized via any feasible routing-only scheme [2]. It was shown that network coding can achieve multicast capacity while routing-only scheme may not. Follow on work showed that it is sufficient for the encoding function to be linear [17]. In wireless environments, network coding has been demonstrated to offer several benefits, such as improved energy efficiency [6](by reducing the number of distinct transmissions), higher throughput and robustness (by allowing nodes to receive potentially multiple copies of a single packet).

A number of network-coding protocols have been proposed in wireless communication, for example COPE [11] and CodeTorrent [13]. COPE [11] demonstrated that the use of network coding can improve the overall wireless network throughput. CodeTorrent [13] performs content distribution in VANETs using network coding. Unfortunately, a direct application of these protocols from mesh networks to WSN is challenging primarily due to memory constraints on sensor nodes that limit the cache size for overheard packets.

Researchers have proposed network coding protocols with low memory and computational overhead. Keller et al. [12] experimentally investigate the delay of flooding based multicast protocols for a sniper detection application using network coding. DutyCode [4] combines the idea of Network Coding and duty-cycle in the MAC layer.

Rateless Deluge [8] is an implementation of Deluge with Network coding. AdapCode [9] is another reliable data dissemination protocol for code update with Network Coding. Both protocols take advantage of Network Coding to improve reliability and send fewer messages than Deluge. These protocols are optimized for bulk data dissemination and have high memory overhead and running time of $O(n^3)$ due to their use of Gaussian elimination. CodeDrip is optimized for dissemination of small values and uses XOR operator for encoding and hence has low computational overhead.

A data dissemination protocol in WSNs with network coding is also presented in [23], but their focus is different from ours. They assume a TDMA-like MAC and focus on a packet-scheduling, determining which packets to combine and transmit given the radio on-off schedule. They prove that the problem is NP-hard and provide a LP formulation. In contrast to their system, CodeDrip runs on CSMA MAC. We also provide a rigorous testbed-based evaluation of dissemination of small values using network coding.

3   Network Coding

Network Coding [3] is a technique that combines packets in the network thereby increasing the throughput, decreasing energy consumption, and reducing the number of messages that are transmitted [22].

In wireless networks, traditionally, dropped packets are recovered using retransmissions. By combining packets using network coding, it is possible to recover the transmitted information without needing to retransmit all the lost packets to all the nodes. We explain how Network Coding works with a simple example.

Consider the topology in Figure 3. The sink node, at the center of the figure, wishes to disseminate two packets, denoted P_1 and P_2. Sensor nodes 1 and 2 are in the communication range of the sink node and might receive the packets. The sink node transmits packet P_1 but only sensor node 1 receives it. Later, the sink node transmits packet P_2, but at this time, only sensor node 2 properly receives packet P_2. Thus, each sensor node receives a different packet.

 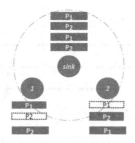 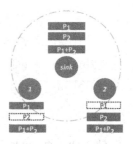

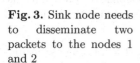

Fig. 3. Sink node needs to disseminate two packets to the nodes 1 and 2

Fig. 4. With traditional retransmission, we need a total of 4 transmissions

Fig. 5. With retransmission with Network Coding, we need only 3 transmissions

With the traditional approach, lost packets are recovered using retransmissions. In our example, the sink node retransmits packets P_1 and P_2. If these retransmissions are successful, sensor node 1 will receive the missing packet P_2 and sensor node 2 will receive the missing packet P_1. Thus, even if these first retransmissions are successful, we need a total of 4 transmissions for both the nodes to successfully receive the message. We show this scenario in Figure 4.

Network Coding allows packets to be combined using a logic operator. We can combine packets using, for instance, the XOR (exclusive or $\oplus$) operator. A new packet is created by performing a bit-wise XOR of each each bit in the packets P_1 and P_2. The new packet is of the same size as the packets P_1 and P_2.

In a network coding system, the sink node, instead of retransmitting packets P_1 and P_2, retransmits a new packet which is $P_1 \oplus P_2$. Sensor node 1, after receiving this packet, is capable of decoding packet P_2 by applying the XOR operator between the packet P_1, which it has already received, over the new packet. Thus, sensor node 1 decodes P_2 since $P_2 = P_1 \oplus (P_1 \oplus P_2)$. In the same way, sensor node 2 is capable of decoding P_1 when it receives the new packet and applies the XOR operator with packet P_2, which it has already received. Thus, sensor node 2 decodes P_1 since $P_2 = P_1 \oplus (P_1 \oplus P_2)$. Thus, we are able to recover both the packets with only three total transmissions, as shown in Figure 5.

This example illustrates the benefit of using Network Coding in the single hop topology example. The number of messages was reduced from 4 to 3. For a larger topology with many more hops, the gains are much larger.

4   Algorithm

CodeDrip uses Network Coding to improve the efficiency of dissemination in Wireless Sensor Networks. In a sensor network deployment, we often need to disseminate different information (e.g., configuration, commands) to the network. With network coding, we can combine different packets and make dissemination more resilient to failure. We can recover lost packets if the sensor node had received a combined message and an original message.

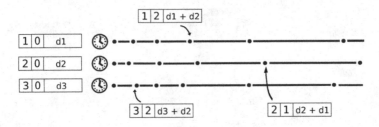

Fig. 6. CodeDrip example. There are three values to be disseminated. Each value has an associated Trickle timer. Each packet transmission might combine the packets.

Like Drip, CodeDrip uses the Trickle timer to time the message transmissions with the goal that the data will eventually arrive at all the nodes in the network. Unlike Drip, CodeDrip sometimes combines messages and transmits the combined messages. CodeDrip does not use topology information to inform its decision about which messages to combine, thus has no control overhead for topology discovery. Later we will describe when CodeDrip decides to transmit combined messages.

To combine messages, different network coding protocols use different operators. CodeDrip uses the $\oplus$ operator, which is a Galois field of 2, instead of a more complex finite field. This choice allows Drip to run efficiently on resource constraint nodes. On most CPUs, the XOR operator is just one hardware instruction.

We modify the packet format for Drip to accommodate the control fields required by network coding. The decoding process needs to know which messages were combined to create the given payload. We add to the message header a field indicating what messages where combined. Each data to be disseminated has a 1 byte identifier. For more than 256 items, we could extend this identifier. Each message, besides its payload, has a set of these identifiers. This set of identifiers is the CodeDrip overhead necessary for the coding and decoding processes. The unmodified Drip message has only one identifier and its payload is the data to be disseminated. A combined message has two or more identifiers corresponding to the packets that were combined. The payload consist of the result of applying the XOR operator among the data that are identified by the list of identifiers.

Figure 6 shows how CodeDrip works. There are three values to be disseminated. Each value has an associated Trickle timer. When the Trickle timer fires (represented by a dot), a message is sent. Figure 6 also illustrates the message content, where packets are combined before transmission.

Each sensor node has two buffers, one for the original messages and one for the combined messages, which are initially empty. After receiving a message, the sensor node verifies if the message is original or combined. If the message is original, the sensor node stores it in the original message buffer and will transmit this message when the Trickle timer fires. Drip also requires an original message buffer to store the data item and its version number.

If the sensor node receives a combined message, the sensor node checks if it can decode the new message from the original messages which it had already received. If it is not possible, the message will be stored in the combined buffer until new messages make it possible to decode the message. In practice, for example, consider the case where only two messages can be combined, the node will only store a combined message in the buffer if it does not have any of its combined packets.

There are two probabilistic decision policies in CodeDrip. The first policy decides what to do when a sensor node receives a message it has already received. Receiving the same message many times indicates that its neighbors already have the message. Thus, it is reasonable that the sensor nodes does not need to send the message right away, since this message is not missing in the neighborhood. A sensor node might decide to suppress the message, in other words, delay sending the message. This process is called suppression and is also present in Drip. The suppression probability determines if the protocol should suppress the message.

The second policy decides if CodeDrip should send the original message or a combined message. This decision is made before sending the message, in other words, when the Trickle timer fires. Each original message is associated with a timer. When this timer fires, the sensor node decides to either send the original message, or to combine with other messages and to send the combination. The other messages to be combined are selected randomly. The combination can happen independently at every node and not just the node that initially generated the packet. The combination probability affects the protocol performance and is evaluated in Section 6.

Since CodeDrip has the potential to decode more than one message with just one transmission, CodeDrip suppresses sending unnecessary messages faster than Drip. For example, CodeDrip can receive the combination of two redundant messages and delay the sender timer of these two messages in a single step while Drip would need to receive both messages.

5   Simulation Experiments

We first perform a set of simulation experiments to study the performance of CodeDrip and how its performance compares to other dissemination protocols. Although simulation experiments use modeled wireless propagation characteristics, which might be very different from what we find in realistic wireless networks, the results are nevertheless helpful in understanding the basic high-level properties of the protocols.

5.1   Evaluation Methodology

We generated WSN topologies by placing the sensor nodes in random locations in the network and constructing a communication graph where the edge weights represent packet loss rate on that link. We made sure that all the topologies are connected. We simulate each scenario ten times and we report the median of

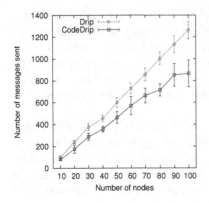

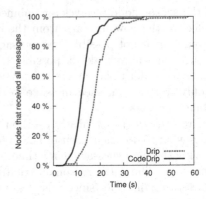

Fig. 7. Number of messages sent for Drip and CodeDrip for different network sizes

Fig. 8. Number of sensor nodes (in percentage) that already received all messages over time. Topology has 100 sensor nodes and 50% packet loss rate.

the metrics. In each simulation, the network disseminated three different data items. We use the simulator called TOSSIM [15] for our experiments. TOSSIM is designed to simulate TinyOS applications. We use these metrics in our study:

- Efficiency: We use the number of messages as a measure of efficiency of the protocol. With energy efficient and duty-cycling MAC, fewer number of transmissions typically leads to less energy expenditure.
- Reliability: We use the fraction of nodes that receive the disseminated message as a measure of reliability.
- Speed: We use the time it takes for all the nodes to receive the disseminated message as a measure of speed. We call it dissemination time or latency.

5.2   Performance Analysis

In the first set of simulations, we compare the number of transmitted messages for CodeDrip and Drip. Figure 7 shows the performance of Drip and CodeDrip for different number of sensor nodes. Roofnet project [1] collected link-level measurements from a realistic mesh network and shown that most communication pairs (sender/receiver) have intermediate (50%) delivery probabilities. Thus, we fix the packet loss rate to 50%. This setting allows us to study CodeDrip's performance in a realistic network. We found that, in larger networks, the overhead for CodeDrip relative to Drip improves as shown in Figure 7. In all our simulation experiments, CodeDrip sends fewer total messages than Drip.

In the second set of simulations, we compare the dissemination latency of CodeDrip and Drip. Figure 8 shows the cumulative fraction of sensor nodes that already received all the disseminated messages according to the dissemination process time in topologies with 100 sensor nodes. Observe that Drip suffers from

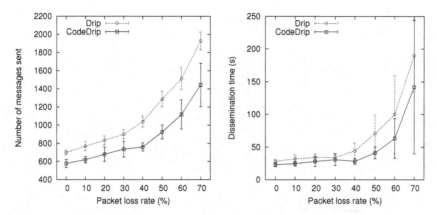

Fig. 9. Number of messages sent and Dissemination time for Drip and CodeDrip for differnet packet loss rates in topologies with 100 sensor nodes

packet loss in the initial stage since there are few nodes transmitting and many packets are lost. In CodeDrip, even when there are few nodes transmitting in the beginning, the data propagates through larger part of the network. We can also observe that dissemination latency is shorter for CodeDrip. While some nodes do not receive the last message with Drip, increasing the dissemination time, with CodeDrip the combined messages increases the probability of receiving the last message, decreasing the dissemination latency.

In the third set of simulations, we study how the link quality affects CodeDrip and Drip protocols. Figure 9 illustrates the performance of Drip and CodeDrip as we vary the link quality in the network with a 100 sensor node topology. We observe that CodeDrip is less affected by the packet loss rate than Drip since CodeDrip needs fewer messages to finish the process. CodeDrip also has smaller dissemination latency compared to Drip. When the packet loss rate is higher than 50%, the measurements have higher variation, which is expected because different decisions are made in dissemination depending on whether the packets are succssfully received.

These results indicate that the dissemination process sends fewer messages when coupled with Network Coding technique. The gains are improved when the packet loss rate are higher.

6   Testbed Experiments

In this section, we describe testbed experiments used to validate the performance results for CodeDrip in a more relistic wireless environment.

6.1   Evaluation Methodology

Testbed experiments involve implementing and running the protocol code on physical motes and collecting instrumentation data to understand the performance.

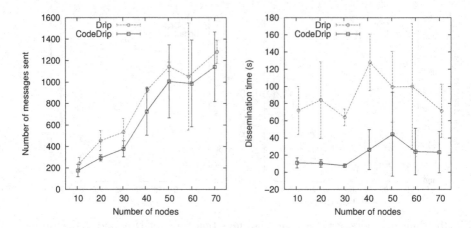

Fig. 10. Number of messages sent and dissemination time for CodeDrip and Drip as we increase the number of physical sensor nodes used in the testbed experiments

We used the public KanseiGenie Wireless Sensor Network Testbed [20] to run our experiments with real sensor motes. This testbed provides access to TelosBs. The motes on the testbed have a 3dB attenuator attached to their antennas. At the lowest power level of transmission, the reliable range is 3 feet. Thus, this testbed allows us to evaluate protocols in a realistic wireless environment with a mix of reliable and unreliable links. We run the protocol code for CodeDrip, Drip, DIP, and DHV on this testbed and collect performance information.

To collect data related to the performance of the protocol, we instrumented the code of the protocols to send a message to the serial port of the TelosB motes. The messages contain the id of the mote, the number of packets the mote sent since the beginning of the dissemination and the number of messages the mote have already received. The system adds a timestamp when a message is sent. These messages are then sent and stored in a central server from which we can download them for performance analysis.

6.2   Performance Analysis

In the first set of testbed experiments, our goal is to compare CodeDrip performance with Drip for different network sizes. Figure 10 shows the number of messages sent and the dissemination time for Drip and CodeDrip. We disseminated 10 values from the sink node. We tested topologies from 10 to 70 sensor nodes. We changed the size of the network by programming the protocol code on select nodes and programming "Blink" program on rest of the nodes. Each point on the graph represents an average of results from 3 experiments and the error bar is the standard deviation. Figure 10 shows that CodeDrip sends fewer messages than Drip and CodeDrip is faster than Drip.

In the second set of experiments, we study the impact of suppression and combination probability on different performance metrics. The probability of

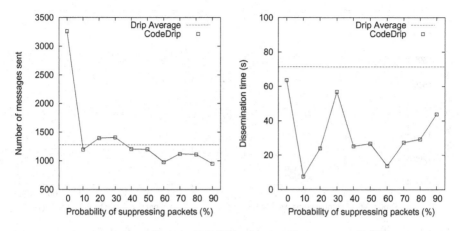

Fig. 11. Number of messages sent and dissemination time for CodeDrip and Drip for different probability of suppression in the testbed experiments

suppressing a received message or combining multiple packets into a single packet before transmission affects the performance of CodeDrip protocol. These results can give us guidelines on how to configure these two parameters in a real-world deployment.

Figure 11 depicts the number of sent messages and the dissemination time by the probability of suppression. The experiments contain topologies with 70 physical sensor nodes. For comparison against Drip, we add a horizontal line that indicates the Drip's average of sent messages and also Drip's average dissemination time. We can observe that for small probability of suppression, CodeDrip sends more messages than Drip. However, the average dissemination time for CodeDrip is always smaller than Drip. For better performance, the probability of suppression should be set between 40% and 80%. In general, increasing the probability of suppression decreases the number of messages but, on the other hand, increases the dissemination time.

Figure 12 shows the results from experiments that analyze the impact of the probability of combination parameter on dissemination performance. The probability of combination determines if the node should combine the messages when the node transmits a message. The results suggest a trend where the number of sent messages increases with the larger probability of combination. We presume that by combining many times, we do not get an original message that could be useful to decode all previous messages. CodeDrip is better than Drip for values below 30%. Again, the average dissemination time for CodeDrip is always smaller than Drip. For better performance, the probability of combination should be set between 10% and 30%.

Thus, we investigated how the probability of suppression and combination affects CodeDrip performance. For the next set of experiments, we set the probability of combination to 30% and probability of suppression to 50%.

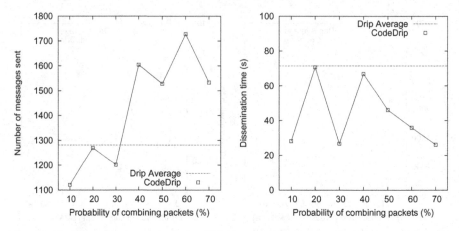

Fig. 12. Number of messages sent and dissemination time for CodeDrip and Drip for different probability of combining packets in the testbed experiments

DIP and DHV are newer dissemination protocols that improve upon Drip for certain types of dissemination. Drip treats every data item as a separate entity for dissemination and DIP and DHV treat them as a group. We now evaluate CodeDrip against both DHV and DIP.

One of the benefits of applying Network Coding is that it reduces the dissemination time. Figure 13 shows the evolution of dissemination with CodeDrip, Drip, DIP, and DHV protocols over time in a topology with 70 physical sensor nodes. The x-axis represents time since the dissemination process started. The y-axis indicates the percentage of nodes that received all 10 disseminated messages. For at least 90% of nodes to receive all messages, CodeDrip takes only 6 seconds, while Drip needs 15 seconds, DIP spends 43 seconds and DHV is not able to get 90% in over 100 seconds.

Figure 14 shows the number of messages sent over time for CodeDrip, Drip, DIP, and DHV protocols in a topology with 70 physical sensor nodes. We observe that the CodeDrip and Drip show a faster growth in the number of sent messages at the beginning of the dissemination process, while DIP and DHV grow more slowly. This is a consequence of how the protocols are implemented. CodeDrip and Drip use different Tricke timer for each value that is being disseminated in the network. DIP and DHV use only one Tricke timer for all values. Although DIP sends fewer messages, not all nodes receive the dissemination content as shown in Figure 13. Thus, CodeDrip transmits fewer packets than DHV and Drip. Although CodeDrip transmits more packets than DIP, CodeDrip does the job of completely disseminating the values, which was not the case for DIP.

Finally, we compare memory overhead of the four dissemination protocols. Table 1 compares the RAM, ROM, and code size usage (in bytes) from CodeDrip, Drip, DIP and DHV. CodeDrip uses more RAM than Drip because of buffers. But, this overhead is marginal since it still consumes less memory than DIP and DHV. CodeDrip consumes fewer ROM memory than Drip, DHV and DIP.

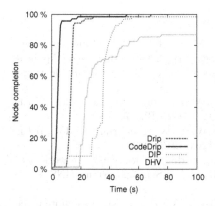

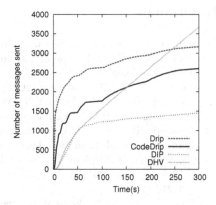

Fig. 13. Percentage of nodes that received all the 10 disseminated values over time for CodeDrip, Drip, DIP, and DHV protocols in the testbed experiments with 70 motes

Fig. 14. Number of messages sent over time for CodeDrip, Drip, DIP, and DHV protocols in the testbed experiments with 70 motes

Table 1. RAM, ROM and Code size usage from CodeDrip, Drip, DIP, and DHV

Metric	CodeDrip	Drip	DIP	DHV
RAM (bytes)	900	845	959	928
ROM (bytes)	17980	21274	22130	21478
Code size (bytes)	42655	50123	49493	49003

7   Conclusions

In this work, we presented CodeDrip, a data dissemination protocol for Wireless Sensor Network. The main idea behind this protocol is to apply Network Coding in the dissemination process, decreasing the number of transmitted messages and consequently saving energy consumption. CodeDrip requires additional space in the packet to store message ids and buffers to store combined messages. These overheads can be controlled by specifying the maximum number of messages that can be decoded and the maximum buffer size. We evaluated the performance of CodeDrip with simulation and testbed experiments. Our results showed that CodeDrip is faster than Drip, DIP and DHV protocols to disseminate information. CodeDrip also requires less ROM memory than Drip, DHV and DIP. Furthermore, CodeDrip transmits fewer packets than DHV and Drip. Although CodeDrip transmits more packets than DIP, CodeDrip's dissemination reliability is higher than DIP's. Thus, CodeDrip is faster, smaller and sends fewer messages than Drip, DHV and DIP protocols.

For future work, we plan to analyze the impact of different topology types and link qualities on the performance of CodeDrip. Another interesting work is to develop new policies to combine messages using more complex operators.

References

1. Aguayo, D., Bicket, J., Biswas, S., Judd, G., Morris, R.: Link-level measurements from an 802.11b mesh network. In: Proceedings of the 2004 Conference on Applications, Technologies, Architectures, and Protocols for Computer Communications, pp. 121–132. ACM, New York (2004)
2. Ahlswede, R., Cai, N., Li, S.-Y.R., Yeung, R.W.: Network information flow. IEEE Transactions on Information Theory 46(4), 1204–1216 (2000)
3. Ahlswede, R., Cai, N., Li, S.Y.R., Yeung, R.W.: Network information flow. IEEE Transactions on Information Theory 46(4), 1204–1216 (2000)
4. Chandanala, R., Stoleru, R.: Network coding in duty-cycled sensor networks. In: 2010 Seventh International Conference on Networked Sensing Systems (INSS), pp. 203–210 (2010)
5. Dang, T., Bulusu, N., Feng, W.-c., Park, S.: DHV: A code consistency maintenance protocol for multi-hop wireless sensor networks. In: Roedig, U., Sreenan, C.J. (eds.) EWSN 2009. LNCS, vol. 5432, pp. 327–342. Springer, Heidelberg (2009)
6. Deb, S.: Network coding for wireless applications: a brief tutorial. In: International Workshop on Wireless Ad-hoc Networks (IWWAN) (May 2005)
7. Gnawali, O., Guibas, L., Levis, P.: A case for evaluating sensor network protocols concurrently. In: Proceedings of the Fifth ACM International Workshop on Wireless Network Testbeds, Experimental Evaluation and Characterizationn, WiN-TECH 2010, pp. 47–54. ACM, New York (2010)
8. Hagedorn, A., Starobinski, D., Trachtenberg, A.: Rateless deluge: Over-the-air programming of wireless sensor networks using random linear codes. In: Proceedings of the 7th International Conference on Information Processing in Sensor Networks, IPSN 2008, pp. 457–466. IEEE Computer Society, Washington, DC (2008)
9. Hou, I.-H., Tsai, Y.-E., Abdelzaher, T.F., Gupta, I.: Adapcode: Adaptive network coding for code updates in wireless sensor networks. In: The 27th Conference on Computer Communications. INFOCOM 2008., pp. 1517–1525. IEEE (2008)
10. Hui, J.W., Culler, D.: The dynamic behavior of a data dissemination protocol for network programming at scale. In: Proceedings of the 2nd International, pp. 81–94. ACM Press (2004)
11. Katti, S., Rahul, H., Hu, W., Katabi, D., Medard, M., Crowcroft, J.: XORs in the Air: Practical Wireless Network Coding. IEEE/ACM Transactions on Networking 16(3), 497–510 (2008)
12. Keller, L., Karaagac, A., Fragouli, C., Argyraki, K.: Evaluation of network coding techniques for a sniper detection application. In: 2011 International Symposium on Modeling and Optimization in Mobile, Ad Hoc and Wireless Networks (WiOpt), pp. 327–333 (2011)
13. Lee, U., Park, J.-S., Yeh, J., Pau, G., Gerla, M.: Code torrent: content distribution using network coding in vanet. In: MobiShare 2006: Proceedings of the 1st International Workshop on Decentralized Resource Sharing in Mobile Computing and Networking, pp. 1–5. ACM, New York (2006)
14. Levis, P., Gay, D., Culler, D.: Active sensor networks. In: Proceedings of the 2nd Conference on Symposium on Networked Systems Design & Implementation, NSDI 2005, vol. 2, pp. 343–356. USENIX Association, Berkeley (2005)
15. Levis, P., Lee, N., Welsh, M., Culler, D.: Tossim: accurate and scalable simulation of entire tinyos applications. In: Proceedings of the 1st International Conference on Embedded Networked Sensor Systems, SenSys 2003, pp. 126–137. ACM, New York (2003)

16. Levis, P., Patel, N., Culler, D., Shenker, S.: Trickle: A self-regulating algorithm for code propagation and maintenance in wireless sensor networks. In: Proceedings of the First USENIX/ACM Symposium on Networked Systems Design and Implementation (NSDI), pp. 15–28 (2004)
17. Li, S.-Y.R., Yeung, R.W., Cai, N.: Linear network coding. IEEE Transactions on Information Theory 49(2), 371–381 (2003)
18. Lin, K., Levis, P.: Data discovery and dissemination with dip. In: Proceedings of the 7th International Conference on Information Processing in Sensor Networks, IPSN 2008, pp. 433–444. IEEE Computer Society, Washington, DC (2008)
19. Paek, J., Greenstein, B., Gnawali, O., Jang, K.-Y., Joki, A., Vieira, M., Hicks, J., Estrin, D., Govindan, R., Kohler, E.: The tenet architecture for tiered sensor networks. ACM Trans. Sen. Netw. 6(4), 34:1–34:44 (2010)
20. Sridharan, M., Zeng, W., Leal, W., Ju, X., Ramnath, R., Zhang, H., Arora, A.: From kansei to kanseiGenie: Architecture of federated, programmable wireless sensor fabrics. In: Magedanz, T., Gavras, A., Thanh, N.H., Chase, J.S. (eds.) Trident-Com 2010. LNICST, vol. 46, pp. 155–165. Springer, Heidelberg (2011)
21. Tolle, G., Culler, D.: Design of an application-cooperative management system for wireless sensor networks. In: Second European Workshop on Wireless Sensor Networks (EWSN), Istanbul, Turkey, January 31-February 2, pp. 121–132 (2005)
22. Vieira, L.F.M., Misra, A., Gerla, M.: Performance of network-coding in multi-rate wireless environments for multicast applications. In: IEEE Military Communications Conference, MILCOM 2007, pp. 1–6. IEEE (2007)
23. Wang, X., Wang, J., Xu, Y.: Data dissemination in wireless sensor networks with network coding. EURASIP Journal on Wireless Communications and Networking 2010(1), 465915 (2010)

Efficient and Flexible Sensornet Checkpointing

Andreas Löscher[1], Nicolas Tsiftes[2], Thiemo Voigt[1,2], and Vlado Handziski[3]

[1] Uppsala University, Sweden
andreas.loscher@it.uu.se
[2] SICS, Sweden
{nvt,thiemo}@sics.se
[3] Technische Universität Berlin, Germany
handziski@tkn.tu-berlin.de

Abstract. Developing sensornet software is difficult partly because of the limited visibility of the system state of deployed nodes. Sensornet checkpointing is a method that allows developers to save and restore full system state of nodes. We present four extensions to sensornet checkpointing—compression, binary diffs, selective checkpointing, and checkpoint inspection—that reduce the time required for checkpointing operations considerably, and improve the granularity at which system state can be examined and manipulated down to the variable level. We show through an experimental evaluation that the checkpoint sizes can be reduced by 70%-93%, and the time can be reduced by at least 50% because of these improvements. The reduced time and increased granularity benefits multiple checkpointing use cases, including automated testing, network visualization, and software debugging.

1 Introduction

Sensornet applications can be rigorously tested in simulation, but the conditions in a deployed network are not easy to model and simulate accurately. Hence, even if the network appears to work well in simulation, it might encounter problems in a real setting as experience has shown [11].

The limited visibility of the internal system state makes it difficult to analyze where the error stems from. Moreover, the actual infrastructure (e.g., a multi-hop wireless network) needed for transmitting error reports or debugging commands may break down once the fault has occurred. When errors have distributed effects over a partial or whole network, the difficulty of debugging increases because the faulty node has to be located before it can be inspected. Systematic testing of node firmware in realistic settings requires visibility into the state of each node to ensure that a certain scenario has been tested. This is challenging to attain without an additional hardware infrastructure, such as in Flocklab [12].

Sensornet checkpointing is a software-based approach to mitigate these issues faced by researchers and software developers [14]. By using sensornet checkpointing, it is possible to save and restore the full run-time state of a sensor node. The run-time state of a node consists of a snapshot of the volatile memory and the current state of the hardware such as timers and LEDs. This improves the

B. Krishnamachari, A.L. Murphy, and N. Trigoni (Eds.): EWSN 2014, LNCS 8354, pp. 50–65, 2014.

visibility into the system tremendously, and provides us with a foundation for making use of testing and debugging techniques formerly not available in the sensor networking domain.

Motivation. The applications of sensornet checkpointing include automated testing, network visualization, and debugging. These applications are affected in different ways by the size required to store and transmit a single checkpoint file.

In the case of automated testing, the number of testing scenarios that can be covered within a bounded time is limited by the time required to transmit checkpoint files between testbed nodes and a workstation. In the case of network visualization, the frequency at which one can update the visualized image of the network is inherently limited by the latency of the checkpointing operation. In the case of debugging, the size of the checkpoint should be limited so as to have a minimal influence on the state of the local node and the network when transferring the checkpoint back to the PC.

Currently, checkpoint files comprise the full system state. Because of the relatively large size of checkpoint files, the time required to transfer them between testbed nodes and a PC is high. In our initial tests in the TWIST testbed, the checkpointing operation took on average 16 s, which limits the efficacy of the aforementioned applications.

Contributions and Roadmap. In order to make sensor network checkpointing more efficient for these applications, we make the following three contributions:

- As the first contribution, we decrease the size of the checkpoint files using two mechanisms described in Section 3. First, we describe a memory-efficient implementation of the Lempel-Ziv algorithm [21] to shrink the checkpointing files. We investigate and adapt the parameterization for the special requirements of checkpointing on resource-constrained devices. Second, we introduce a binary diff algorithm to compress consecutive checkpoints.
- Our second contribution are two novel mechanisms for partial checkpointing. These mechanisms are based on the insight that many debugging applications do not need to work with the full system state. Towards this end, we introduce in Section 4 a new checkpointing format that is self-contained and allows us to store partial system states, thereby enabling what we call *selective checkpointing*. This functional addition to the original checkpointing method not only improves the efficiency in cases where only sub-states are stored but also enables new applications of checkpointing formerly not available. Furthermore, this functionality makes it possible to store and rollback the states of multiple applications independently. We describe a general tool to analyze checkpoint files in the new format.
- Our last contribution is the evaluation of the proposed mechanisms in Section 5. We present a detailed analysis of the compression algorithm in terms of memory consumption and achieved compression ratios demonstrating that we can reduce the checkpoint files to $7\% - 30\%$ of the original size. We also show the capabilities of selective checkpointing in a case study of fault injection, where we reduce the time for a rollback operation by 98%.

After the evaluation, we present related work in Section 6, and conclude our work in Section 7.

2   Background

Sensornet checkpointing makes it easy to save and restore the full run-time state on real sensor nodes. A checkpoint contains the full volatile memory and the state of modifiable hardware registers, such as the ones used for timers and actuators. A small service runs on each node to manage saving and restoration of checkpoints. During either of these operations, the checkpoint service freezes the normal operation of the node by turning off interrupts and taking control of the processor. When checkpointing, the service writes the node state into a file in the flash memory [18]. When restoring the state, the service reads the previously saved system state from the file and substitutes it for the current contents of the memory and the hardware registers.

Checkpoint files can be transferred either through a testbed back-channel, or—in the case of a deployed network—through radio communication. The state of a node can be rolled back using a checkpoint file generated earlier, thereby making it appear as if the network is jumping back in time to an earlier state. The rollback feature makes it possible to replay the network execution from a known state. The state can then be inspected offline with standard debugging tools, but it must be rolled back on a simulated node first. This provides a high visibility into the state of any individual node.

There are many applications for sensor network checkpointing including automated testing [3], visualization of the network where checkpointing enables non-intrusive collection of node-specific information such as routing tables, memory usage and radio connections [14], simulation model validation and debugging by moving the state of all nodes from the testbed to a simulator where it is easier to find the root cause when an error is detected in the testbed [14]. Using rollbacks one can, for example, suspend a testbed run after the initial network set-up has been performed in order to investigate how the network is affected by environmental conditions [2].

3   Accelerated Checkpointing

In our initial experiments with the checkpointing implementation of Österlind et al. [14] we observed that a checkpointing operation on the TWIST testbed takes approximately 16 s on average. The latency of checkpointing depends on the time to store the state on the flash and the time to transfer this file from the flash to the local machine over USB or a testbed backchannel. All those steps are accelerated by reducing the checkpoint sizes.

Through inspection of various kind of memory images induced by running different system firmwares on TMote Sky nodes, we find that a considerable part of the RAM is unused, and therefore filled with zeros. This opens up the possibility to compress the state files considerably.

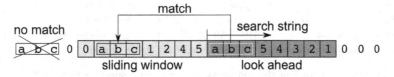

Fig. 1. Sliding window and look-ahead buffer during compression. The string search tries to match the longest string inside the sliding window buffer. The matching string can expand into the look-ahead buffer, but it must start in the sliding window.

To this end, we design LLZ, a memory-optimized lossless compression algorithm based on the Lempel-Ziv algorithm. Furthermore, we use binary diffs of consecutive checkpoints that we apply our compression algorithm on. Both of these mechanisms are designed to have memory footprints commensurate with the requirements of mote-class devices.

3.1   Compression

Compressing checkpoints is a straightforward way to reduce the size of the checkpoints. Compression algorithms are well researched on regular platforms as well as on resource-constrained devices [16]. We conducted initial experiments with run-length encoding compression, but observed a decreasing performance for more complicated checkpoint files. Therefore we choose a compression algorithm based on Lempel-Ziv compression. We select the LZFX compression format [4]. Its reference implementation is designed to be fast and the implementation is small. Both of those properties are important for WSN nodes where computation time and memory overhead matters. The reference implementation of LZFX still uses up memory of around 1 MByte during its compression operations, however. We develop *Low memory Lempel-Ziv (LLZ)*, a memory-optimized compression algorithm using the compression format of LZFX.

Format. We use the LZFX compression format as shown in Figure 2. Data encoded in the compression format replaces redundant data by referring to earlier occurrences in the data stream. Those replacements are called back references. Non-redundant data is encoded uncompressed as literal data.

Every data element is annotated by a codeword, describing the type and the length of the data. In case of uncompressed data, this codeword is followed by the literal data. In case of a back reference to redundant data, the codeword is followed by at least another one, which encodes the address of the reference.

The first three bits specify the type of the data element. If they are zero, the codeword specifies uncompressed data. The next 5 bits define the length $L-1$ of the following uncompressed data. If the first three bits are between 0 and 7, the codeword defines a short back reference. The first three bits are then interpreted as the length of $L-2$ of a back reference. This makes it possible to encode data elements up to 8 bytes long. Longer sequences are encoded with the first three bits set. The following codeword specifies the length of the back reference.

Format	Type	Description
000LLLLL < $L + 1$ bytes>	uncompressed data	<L> = length - 1
LLLooooo ooooooo	BR with length< 9	<o> = addr-1; <L> = length-2
111ooooo LLLLLLLL ooooooooo	BR with length>= 9	<o> = addr-1; <L> = length-2

Fig. 2. The binary format of the compressed data stream specifies three different data elements. The first three bits indicate if uncompressed data or a back reference (BR) is encoded. Back references to redundant data are divided into short back references, with a maximal length of 8, and long back references. Long back references require an additional codeword to store the length of the encoded data.

In both back reference cases, the address $o - 1$ is stored in the last 5 bits of the first codeword and an additional codeword.

Algorithm. LLZ is a memory-optimized variant of the Lempel-Ziv compression algorithm. To produce the compressed data stream, we maintain a sliding window buffer and a look-ahead buffer, as depicted in Figure 1. The sliding window buffer is a fixed size buffer of the last M bytes of the processed uncompressed data. This buffer is the area in which we search for redundant data elements. The look-ahead buffer is a fixed size buffer of the next N bytes of data, we want to compress. It represents the data we want to find inside of the sliding window.

LLZ looks for the longest string match of the look-ahead inside the sliding window. If we find such a match, we can create a back reference pointing to the redundant data. If we are unable to find a fitting match, we encode the data uncompressed. We then forward both buffers by the amount of encoded bytes and repeat this procedure until all data is encoded. We encode longer sequences of uncompressed data with the least amount of codewords possible. Matches that are shorter than three characters are encoded uncompressed as the first three bits would otherwise indicate a literal run.

The efficiency of LLZ depends on the size of the sliding window (parameter M) and the size of the look-ahead buffer (parameter N), as well as the algorithm used for the longest string search. If M is large, the probability of finding good matches increases allowing us to create better back references. If the size N is large, we are able to encode longer data elements. This can lead to better back references as well as better uncompressed encoded data since the codewords to encode these are sparser.

Memory Optimizations. When we implement LLZ on a sensor node we have to take the limited memory into account. To achieve good compression ratios, we want to choose the parameters M and N large. This would yield a higher probability for back references and we would be also able to encode longer data elements. The reference implementation of LZFX compresses blocks of 1MB size which are kept in memory during the compression process. On sensor nodes we are forced to find values that are big enough to yield good compression ratios, but also small enough to fit on sensor nodes.

Performance. Another performance criteria for LLZ is the method used to find a matching string in the sliding window buffer. To speed up the search process, secondary data structures are needed. In the reference implementation, LZFX uses a hash table of $2^{16} = 65536$ bytes for this purpose, but alternative implementations exist [1]. The slowest, but most memory efficient method is to use no additional data structures and search directly in the sliding window buffer. We adjust this algorithm to skip parts of the sliding window that are known to not contain further matches. We do not use an additional buffer to store the current uncompressed data, since we use the sliding window buffer for this. If we choose $N > M$, we extend the sliding window buffer to the size of the look-ahead buffer. The total buffer size is therefore $max(M, N) + N$. The worst case complexity of this longest string search algorithm is $\Theta(M \times N)$.

3.2 Binary Diffs

Checkpointing repeatedly creates multiple full checkpoints even if only small parts of the memory change. We observed, that many memory locations change only slowly or remain almost static after the initialization, while others change rapidly. The size of the following checkpoints can be reduced by only storing the differences to a former checkpoint. Existing tools like bsdiff[15] and XDelta[13] have high memory requirements during the diff operation.

We implemented a memory-efficient binary diff algorithm that reduces the information entropy of the checkpoint files, and thereby ensures that they can be compressed to a greater degree. LLZ works best with repeated data like long strings of the same character, since those sequences can be encoded efficiently. This can be exploited if only small parts of a file change. We apply byte-wise XOR to the two input files and store the result in a diff file. Every byte that is equal in both files is set to zero in the diff file. Every file of those three ones can be retrieved by applying the XOR operation to the two other files.

4   Selective Checkpointing

For many debugging applications storing the full system state is wasteful. Being able to only use full checkpoints also limits the applicability of checkpointing. It is not possible to save the state of parts of the system, like applications, independently. Selective checkpointing provides the functionality to specify which memory sections should be included in the checkpoint. We develop a new file format for checkpoints that supports a general description of checkpoint files. We use this selective checkpointing to develop a checkpoint inspection tool that allows us to analyze and manipulate checkpoints offline.

Selective checkpointing has many advantages over a full state exchange. Partial states are usually much smaller than full states, containing only a few bytes rather than a couple of kilobytes. This results in a much higher performance of the checkpointing and rollback operations as we show in the case study of a fault injection in Section 5.3.

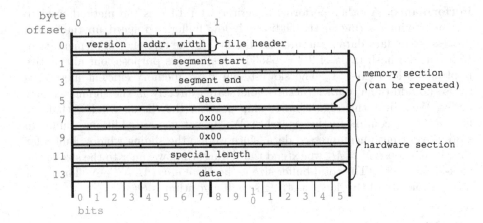

Fig. 3. The new checkpoint file format. It can contain arbitrary many memory sections and can be used for word sizes between 8 and 128 bit.

Another major advantage of selective checkpointing is that partial states do not influence the whole system. This might seem contradictory to the initial goal of checkpointing, saving the complete run-time state of a node and replaying it later. In practice this means that the state of multiple applications running on one node cannot be saved independently since rolling back a checkpoint includes restoring the state of all applications and the operating system. We enable this functionality with selective checkpointing.

A third advantage is that we are not forced to restore the same date during a rollback operation that was formerly saved during a checkpointing operation. The selective checkpointing format is self-contained, meaning that it contains enough information about the stored memory locations to be rolled back. This enables asynchronous checkpointing applications, where one part of the system is manipulated while another one is observed using checkpointing.

By selecting only parts of the full state for a checkpoint, it is possible to create a state that is not consistent. This can happen if the the state of the application depends on data structures in the operating system that are not part of the checkpoint. Although we do not have a mechanism to resolve these dependencies yet, we believe that by carefully selecting the memory sections or employing additional code to resolve such situations, inconsistent checkpoints can be handled. Currently, this has to be done manually though.

4.1   Format

The checkpointing format, as shown in Figure 3, consists of a file header and a header for each memory section that is included in the file. It is also possible to specify a section for hardware information or other special payload, not represented in the volatile memory. The file header consists of 1 byte split into a version field and an address width (AW) field. The version field specifies the format version of the file, and can be used to identify incompatible checkpoint files if the format changes in the future. The address length field specifies the number of bytes an address uses on the target platform. This is important because the address width can differ between architectures. The TI MSP430 devices use 16 bit to 20 bit for addressing, whereas the ARM Cortex M3 platform uses 32 bit. The header for each section consists of a section start (SS) field and a section length (SL) field. Both fields consist of AW bytes to cover the entire memory range. Each section header is followed by SL bytes of payload. A special section is started with an empty SS and SL field, followed by a special section length (SSL) field. The SSL field takes like the SS and SL field AW bytes. The special section header is followed by SSL bytes of payload. With this information, the rollback section can restore the state or partial state correctly. Hardware information can be stored in the special section header. The data stored there is not specified by the format and can be used for any purpose.

This checkpoint format allows for memory efficient handling of the input. We can process one checkpoint file with constant memory overhead, since only the file header and the current section header need to be stored in memory.

4.2   Checkpoint Inspection

We use the selective checkpointing extension to create a *checkpoint inspection* tool, which provides the functionality to analyze and manipulate checkpoints without replaying them on a node or inside a simulator. We argue that a checkpointing framework should include the possibility to create arbitrary new checkpoints and to analyze existing ones, rather than only providing the means for saving and restoring a sensor node's state or a part of a state. We are convinced that this tool enables new applications of checkpointing in the areas of testing and debugging.

There are two types of variables that are interesting for a software tester. The first type is the local variables, which are stored on the stack. They are created when a function is entered and they are destroyed when this function is left. The other type is global variables, which are accessible from every function at any time. In our checkpointing implementation, it is not possible to capture the local variables. This is a trait inherent in Contiki's architecture that is based on Protothreads [8]: all running threads share one stack, which gets reset when a thread yields. It is thus unnecessary to include local variables in the checkpoint. Because of this limitation, Contiki applications need to use global variables that are preserved during task switching, to store their state. Since global variables are stored in the checkpoint as a part of the global state of the operating system, we can access most of the interesting variables.

To get the information needed to analyze a checkpoint offline, our checkpoint inspection tool processes the ELF-encoded firmware of the sensor node. The ELF format provides detailed information about the location, size, and name of every symbol. Unfortunately the ELF format does not provide information about the structures of the symbols, but this information can be retrieved from the source code. The memory sections that are contained in the checkpoint are the BSS and

DATA sections of the firmware. The BSS section contains all global variables that do not have any initialization. The location and size of those variables is, however, static. The DATA section stores all global variables, which are initialized in any kind of way. To have information about all variables, we have to combine both descriptions. This gives us the address of the variables in RAM. The mapping between the RAM address and the position in the checkpointing file is not linear. We can, however, create an address translation using the information provided with the new checkpointing format.

5   Evaluation

We evaluate our improved checkpointing functionality through micro-benchmarks and experiments in the TWIST testbed, using two sensor network applications. The first application collects data over a wireless sensor network and sends it periodically to a sink. Data collection is probably the most common application of wireless sensor networks [10]. This application uses the Rime stack [7] for communication. The second application we use for the evaluation is a small webserver that uses the uIP stack [6] for communication. The communication stack represents a significant part of a typical WSN firmware. By using different communication stacks, we can examine whether their memory usage differs in any considerable manner, and thereby affects the compression results.

   To evaluate the performance of our LLZ compression algorithm, we measure the compression ratios in relation to the selected sliding window size and look-ahead buffer size. In this paper, we define the compression ratio as the size of the compressed file as fraction of the original file size: $ratio = \frac{size_{compressed}}{size_{original}}$. The sliding window size and the look-ahead buffer size range from 8 byte to 512 byte. We calculate the data points that represent the best memory usage to achieve a compression ratio of at least 30%. During early tests, we found that such a compression ratio is easily achievable for most firmwares, and yields a notable performance boost. We also calculate the best compression ratios that are achievable with a memory usage of 128 bytes, and measure how LLZ behaves with increasing memory usage. Lastly, we measure the time needed to create the checkpoints, compress them, and transfer them to the TWIST testbed, and compare the results with those of the original checkpointing method. We transferred the files via SSH from 89 nodes using the TWIST testbed. All timing measurements were repeated multiple times and the listed times are the average times over all runs.

5.1   Compression

Scenario. We compress a complete checkpoint for both applications, including the whole RAM except the regions of the file system and the checkpointing application and compare the results against run-length encoding. We compare also the compression behavior of a RPL implementation in Contiki with a RPL implementation in TinyOS to analyze the influence of different operating system

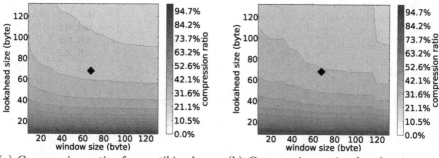

(a) Compression ratios for contiki-rpl application

(b) Compression ratios for the tinyos-rpl application

Fig. 4. The compression ratios of a full checkpoint on TMote Sky are plotted dependent on `look-ahead` and `window` size. The black square shows the best compression ratio for a memory usage below ≤ 128 bytes (left: 11%, right: 10%).

architectures on our approach. We record the time required to create a checkpoint and downloading it to the local machine using a node directly connected to our test machine and the TWIST testbed. We test the times without compression and with compression of the data stream during checkpointing operation.

Results. The compression ratios for both applications, web server and data collection, are shown in Figure 4. A checkpoint of the data collection application can be compressed with a compression ratio of 30% using 48 bytes of buffer memory, i.e., the sliding window and look-ahead buffer. We can achieve a compression ratio of 23% by using 128 bytes of buffer memory. We need 40 bytes to achieve a compression ratio of 30% for a checkpoint of the web server application. With 128 bytes of buffer memory, we can reach a compression ratio of 19%. The best compression ratio we measured was 15% by using 512 of memory for the buffers. The results show that an increased size of the look-ahead buffer size leads to a rapid improvement of the compression ratios for small buffer sizes. The impact of the sliding window buffer size is lower for small buffer sizes. For larger buffer sizes, the effects on the compression ratio in relation to buffer sizes are comparable between sliding window and look-ahead buffer.

The fast improvement of the compression ratios for increasing look-ahead buffer sizes can be explained by the more efficient encoding of consecutive zeros in the checkpointing files. Unused memory segments in the RAM are initialized with zeros. One back reference codeword can encode at most as many bytes as fit in the look-ahead buffer. The improvements of the compression ratios with higher memory usage are as expected. The choice of the operating system has little influence on the compression performance of LLZ.

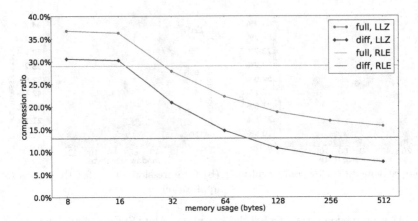

Fig. 5. A comparison of the compression ratios of LLZ and RLE when applied on full or partial checkpoints. LLZ outperforms RLE if sufficient memory for the buffers is used or if the checkpoints are complicated.

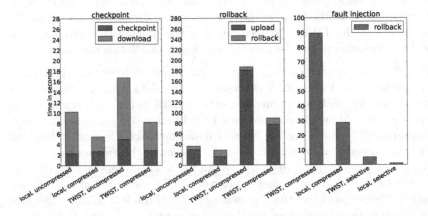

Fig. 6. The accumulated times for checkpointing and rollback are plotted in the left and middle figures using local nodes connected with a USB serial adapter and the TWIST testbed. The times for performing a fault injection are plotted in the right figure. We are able to improve the times for all operations considerably.

The compression results in comparison with the results for run-length encoding (RLE) are given in Figure 5. LLZ performs slightly worse than RLE when there is a very small amount of RAM available for LLZ to use for its search buffer. It outperforms RLE if larger buffers are chosen or with more complex checkpoints, which is the common case.

Figure 6 shows the recorded times for the checkpointing and rollback operations. We observe a notable reduction for all operations using local nodes as well

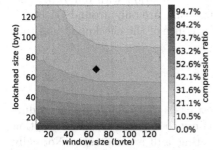

(a) Compression ratios for the data collection application

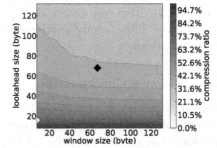

(b) Compression ratios for the web server application

Fig. 7. Compression ratios of a diff between two checkpoints on TMote Sky. The best compression ratios for a memory usage $\leq$ 128 bytes are 12% for the data collect application and 11% for the web server application. The lowest memory usages for a compression ratio $\leq$ 30% is 32 bytes for both applications.

as using the TWIST testbed. By compressing the checkpoint files, we reduce not only the transfer time but also the time for the generation of the checkpoint file. Since we compress the state before writing it to a file in flash memory, the file size becomes smaller, which reduces the time spent on flash writing. The total time of the checkpointing operation is reduced by 4.5 seconds (46.5%) on local nodes, and by 8.4 seconds (50.5%) using the TWIST testbed. The rollback times are reduced by 7.6 seconds (20.8%) on local nodes, and by 97.3 seconds (52.0%) on the TWIST testbed.

5.2   Binary Diffs

Scenario. We evaluate the performance of binary diffs using two checkpoints for both application, which are taken 30 minutes apart from each other. We observe that this time frame is long enough to encounter state changes. We then create a binary diff of both files and compress it afterwards. The diff of both source files should yield better compression ratios than the source files under the same memory restrictions.

Results. We plot the compression ratios for both applications in Figure 7. The best compression ratio using 128 bytes of total buffer memory is 12% for the data collection application and 11% for the web server application. The lowest memory usage to achieve a compression ratio of 30% is 32 bytes for both applications. The best compression ratio we obtained was 7% by using 512 bytes of memory for the search buffers. The dependency of the compression ratios on the buffer sizes is similar to what can be observed when compressing the source files. We could, however, observe an even higher impact of the look-ahead buffer size for low buffer sizes.

Our experiments show that binary diffs in combination with our LLZ compression algorithm can lead to checkpoint sizes that are only around 7% of the original size. This directly improves the performance of the checkpoint and roll-back operations.

5.3   Selective Checkpointing

Fault injection is a technique used to cover test cases that occur only rarely during normal operation. Those cases contain mainly code paths used for exception handling that are never executed, if the correlating fault is not present. Normally a debugger can be used for fault injection, but in sensor networks debuggers are usually not available. Checkpointing provides the possibility to create arbitrary states and transfer them to sensor nodes and can therefore be used to inject faults for testing purposes. In this case study, we inject faults into the routing table of a sensor node that uses the Rime communication stack. We use selective checkpointing and checkpoint inspection to create faulty states and upload them to the node.

The same application is possible using the checkpointing implementation by Österlind et al. [14]. Using their implementation, we need to replay a checkpoint on a simulated node where we can change the memory using debugging tools such as GDB. We then need to create a new checkpoint using the simulator. We believe that this procedure can be improved by using checkpoint inspection.

Scenario. To inject faults in the Rime routing table it is not necessary to transfer a complete state to the sensor node. We only need to transfer those segments, that contain the routing table itself. With the techniques introduced in Section 4.2 we are able to get the location and size of every symbol. With this information we are now able to create a new checkpoint containing only the memory segments for the Rime routing table using selective checkpointing. We measure the size of the selective checkpointing and it takes to transfer it to either a local node and or to the testbed.

Results. The memory footprint of one routing entry is 11 bytes. In our configuration, one routing table can hold up to 8 entries which results in a total memory of 88 bytes, which are allocated in one block. In addition to this, we also need to store the access pointer of the table which accounts another two bytes. We need to create headers for both memory sections, and for the checkpoint itself. The total checkpoint size that we upload to the nodes is 99 bytes. We did not compress the file because of the small size.

The times for injecting the fault are given in Figure 6. The average upload time of this checkpoint to the TWIST testbed this fault is 4.78 seconds. The rollback operation took 0.42 seconds in average. For the local case we measured 1.06 seconds for the upload and 0.02 seconds for the rollback operation. We observe in both cases, that the delay between initiating the upload and the start of the data transfer took the dominant part of the upload operation. Without selective checkpointing, we would need to upload a full checkpoint. Compared to the rollback operation of a full checkpoint, we reduce the time elapsed by 182 seconds on the TWIST testbed. This is a reduction of 98%. We reduce the time for local nodes by 35.3 seconds (86%).

Our experiments show that we can inject faults more efficiently using selective checkpointing and checkpoint inspection. We reduce the times to perform an injection by over 86% and avoid the need to replay an existing checkpoint on a simulated node to perform the operation.

6 Related Work

Testing and debugging software in sensor networks is notoriously difficult, and this circumstance has spurred a plethora of research. In controlled environments such as simulations and testbeds, the possibility of debugging greatly exceeds that of deployed network environments. Many techniques have been developed toward this end, including cross-layer simulation [9], symbolic execution [17], and pre-deployment modifications of the software to check more thoroughly for memory errors [5].

Once a network is deployed, however, other techniques are required to diagnose and mitigate system malfunction. Wachs et al. argued for designing protocols to have a high degree of *visibility* [19], meaning that the diagnosis of communication failures should have a low energy cost. This can greatly help software developers and network operators to understand why failures occur in deployed networks. However, when unforeseen failures occur in the protocol or other parts of the system, the originally designed visibility in a certain protocol may be insufficient to diagnose the error.

Clairvoyant allows source-level debugging in deployed wireless sensor networks networks [20]. This concept overlaps with parts of our work, since Clairvoyant makes it possible to read and write at arbitrary locations in system memory. However, Clairvoyant does not employ data compression to handle transfers of larger subsets of the system state, which is a gap that we fill for sensornet checkpointing in this paper. Checkpointing also operates on a larger scale than conventional debugging, making it practical to retrieve efficiently complete state of a node.

The technique we adopt and improve upon in this paper, sensornet checkpointing [14], offers full system visibility, allowing the inspection of errors unforeseen by protocol designers, and errors whose source are at other parts of the system than in the network stack. Moreover, sensornet checkpointing is not limited to diagnosis of errors alone; it also enables rollback of system state.

Plank et al.'s checkpointing library *Libchkpt* [16] offers checkpointing support for Unix applications. It includes incremental checkpointing and compression of checkpoints to make checkpointing more efficient. Inspired by their work we bring this functionality to resource-constrained networks and add the extended functionality of selective checkpointing.

7   Conclusions

To make sensornet checkpointing efficient and flexible enough to use for automated testing, network visualization, and software debugging, we have presented four improvements to the original checkpointing technique: compression, binary diffs, selective checkpointing, and checkpoint inspection. Through these improvements, we shrunk the file size of full checkpoints down to 7%-30% of the original size. This reduces the checkpointing and rollback operations time by at least 50%. We also made checkpointing more flexible with respect to the granularity of checkpointing, allowing one to checkpoint at any level from the full system down to individual variables. This allows testing of selected subsets of the system state with considerably lower transfer cost compared to sensornet checkpointing in its original form.

Acknowledgements. This work has been supported by SSF through the ProFUN and Promos projects; and by EIT ICT Labs, as part of the activity 12149, "From WSN Testbeds to CPS Testbeds". Thanks to Fredrik Österlind for providing the initial implementation of the TWIST plugin for Cooja.

References

1. Bell, T., Kulp, D.: Longest-match string searching for ziv-lempel compression. Software: Practice and Experience 23(7), 757–771 (1993)
2. Boano, C.A., Wennerström, H., Zúñiga, M.A., Brown, J., Keppitiyagama, C., Oppermann, F.J., Roedig, U., Nordén, L.-Å., Voigt, T., Römer, K.: Hot Packets: A systematic evaluation of the effect of temperature on low power wireless transceivers. In: Proceedings of the 5th Extreme Conference on Communication, ExtremeCom (August 2013)
3. Claessen, K., Hughes, J.: Quickcheck: a lightweight tool for random testing of haskell programs. SIGPLAN Not 46(4), 53–64 (2011)
4. Collette, A.: lzfx - a tiny, extremely fast compression library, https://code.google.com/p/lzfx/ (visited September 04, 2013)
5. Cooprider, N., Archer, W., Eide, E., Gay, D., Regehr, J.: Efficient memory safety for tinyos. In: Proceedings of the International Conference on Embedded Networked Sensor Systems (ACM SenSys), Sydney, Australia, pp. 205–218. ACM (2007)
6. Dunkels, A.: Full TCP/IP for 8-bit architectures. In: Proceedings of The International Conference on Mobile Systems, Applications, and Services (MobiSys), San Francisco, CA, USA (May 2003)
7. Dunkels, A., Österlind, F., He, Z.: An adaptive communication architecture for wireless sensor networks. In: Proceedings of the International Conference on Embedded Networked Sensor Systems (ACM SenSys), Sydney, Australia (November 2007)
8. Dunkels, A., Schmidt, O., Voigt, T., Ali, M.: Protothreads: Simplifying event-driven programming of memory-constrained embedded systems. In: Proceedings of the International Conference on Embedded Networked Sensor Systems (ACM SenSys), Boulder, Colorado, USA (November 2006)

9. Eriksson, J., Österlind, F., Finne, N., Tsiftes, N., Dunkels, A., Voigt, T., Sauter, R., Marrón, P.J.: Cooja/mspsim: Interoperability testing for wireless sensor networks. In: SIMUTools 2009, Rome, Italy (March 2009)

10. Gnawali, O., Fonseca, R., Jamieson, K., Moss, D., Levis, P.: Collection tree protocol. In: Proceedings of the International Conference on Embedded Networked Sensor Systems (ACM SenSys), Berkeley, CA, USA (2009)

11. Langendoen, K., Baggio, A., Visser, O.: Murphy loves potatoes: experiences from a pilot sensor network deployment in precision agriculture. In: Proceedings of the 20th International Parallel and Distributed Processing Symposium (IPDPS 2006). IEEE, Rhodes Island (April 2006)

12. Lim, R., Ferrari, F., Zimmerling, M., Walser, C., Sommer, P., Beutel, J.: Flocklab: A testbed for distributed, synchronized tracing and profiling of wireless embedded systems. In: Proceedings of the International Conference on Information Processing in Sensor Networks. ACM/IEEE IPSN (2013)

13. MacDonald, J.: xdelta http://xdelta.org/ (visited February 09, 2013)

14. Österlind, F., Dunkels, A., Voigt, T., Tsiftes, N., Eriksson, J., Finne, N.: Sensornet checkpointing: Enabling repeatability in testbeds and realism in simulations. In: Roedig, U., Sreenan, C.J. (eds.) EWSN 2009. LNCS, vol. 5432, pp. 343–357. Springer, Heidelberg (2009)

15. Percival, C.: Naive differences of executable code. Draft Paper (2003), http://www.daemonology.net/bsdiff

16. Plank, J.S., Beck, M., Kingsley, G., Li, K.: Libckpt: Transparent checkpointing under Unix. In: Usenix Winter Technical Conference, pp. 213–223 (January 1995)

17. Sasnauskas, R., Dustmann, O.S., Kaminski, B.L., Wehrle, K., Weise, C., Kowalewski, S.: Scalable symbolic execution of distributed systems. In: 2011 31st International Conference on Distributed Computing Systems (ICDCS), pp. 333–342. IEEE (2011)

18. Tsiftes, N., Dunkels, A., He, Z., Voigt, T.: Enabling Large-Scale Storage in Sensor Networks with the Coffee File System. In: Proceedings of the International Conference on Information Processing in Sensor Networks (ACM/IEEE IPSN), San Francisco, CA, USA (April 2009)

19. Wachs, M., Choi, J., Lee, J., Srinivasan, K., Chen, Z., Jain, M., Levis, P.: Visibility: A new metric for protocol design. In: Proceedings of the International Conference on Embedded Networked Sensor Systems (ACM SenSys), Sydney, Australia (2007)

20. Yang, J., Soffa, M., Selavo, L., Whitehouse, K.: Clairvoyant: a comprehensive source-level debugger for wireless sensor networks. In: Proceedings of the International Conference on Embedded Networked Sensor Systems (ACM SenSys), pp. 189–203 (2007)

21. Ziv, J., Lempel, A.: A universal algorithm for sequential data compression. IEEE Transactions on Information Theory 23(3), 337–343 (1977)

Towards Enabling Uninterrupted Long-Term Operation of Solar Energy Harvesting Embedded Systems

Bernhard Buchli, Felix Sutton, Jan Beutel, and Lothar Thiele

Computer Engineering and Networks Laboratory, ETH Zurich, Zurich, Switzerland
{bbuchli,fsutton,beutel,thiele}@tik.ee.ethz.ch

Abstract In this work we describe a systematic approach to power subsystem capacity planning for solar energy harvesting embedded systems, such that uninterrupted, long-term (*i.e.*, multiple years) operation at a predefined performance level may be achieved. We propose a power subsystem capacity planning algorithm based on a modified astronomical model to approximate the harvestable energy and compute the required battery capacity for a given load and harvesting setup. The energy availability model takes as input the deployment site's latitude, the panel orientation and inclination angles, and an indication of expected meteorological and environmental conditions. We validate the model's ability to predict the harvestable energy with power measurements of a solar panel. Through simulation with 10 years of solar traces from three different geographical locations and four harvesting setups, we demonstrate that our approach achieves 100% availability at up to 53% smaller batteries when compared to the state-of-the-art.

Keywords: Wireless sensor networks, energy harvesting, modeling, experimentation.

1   Introduction

Advances in miniaturization and low-power design of electronic devices have allowed Wireless Sensor Networks (*WSNs*) to reach a state at which they represent a feasible option for continuous observation of various processes, *e.g.*, industrial, agricultural, or environmental monitoring. Due to remote and inaccessible deployment sites, and the lack of power sources, the motes comprising a sensor network are usually battery powered devices [1]. However, the finite energy store imposed by non-rechargeable batteries severely limits the achievable performance level of application scenarios with increased energy demands, *e.g.*, [2]. Ambient energy harvesting, particularly in the form of solar energy harvesting [3, 4], has thus attracted much attention as a promising solution for enabling perpetual system operation.

The ultimate goal of an energy harvesting system is to enable uninterrupted long-term (*i.e.*, on the order of multiple years) operation at a defined minimum performance level (*i.e.*, sustained duty-cycle). However, simply enhancing an embedded system with energy harvesting capabilities may not suffice to achieve this goal [5, 6]. This is because solar energy harvesting opportunities depend both on static and dynamic factors, *e.g.*, efficiencies of the solar panel and energy storage element, solar panel installation

B. Krishnamachari, A.L. Murphy, and N. Trigoni (Eds.): EWSN 2014, LNCS 8354, pp. 66–83, 2014.

parameters [5], and time-varying meteorological conditions, and transient local obstructions. Despite the many design examples that can be found in literature describing solar energy harvesting systems specifically designed for long-term WSN applications, the problem of how to systematically sizing the energy store and solar panel capacities, such that uninterrupted, long-term operation at a defined performance level can be achieved, remains an open task. The work presented in this paper addresses this issue and provides a tool for design space exploration and identification of the smallest combination of battery and solar panel for a particular application.

The performance level achievable by an embedded computing system is ultimately limited by the available energy. Thus, the battery capacity must be large enough to cover the longest period without harvesting opportunities, and the panel must be able to generate sufficient amounts of energy to replenish the battery within an acceptable time frame. However, due to highly dynamic meteorological conditions, it may be difficult to define either of these periods without resorting to pessimistic assumptions [7]. In fact, literature review shows that most efforts attempt to mitigate the effects of improperly designed power subsystems with dynamic load scaling [8], which are based on expected harvesting opportunities predicted by an energy prediction scheme, *e.g.*, [9, 10].

While runtime energy awareness and reactivity is important for achieving improved system utility and energy efficiency, we argue that it can not replace appropriate design-time capacity planning of the power subsystem. Even a perfect, yet fictional energy predictor could achieve continuous operation only if the *entire* power subsystem is provisioned to support the given load. Hence, for application scenarios that require uninterrupted long-term operation at a pre-defined minimum performance level, the aforementioned approaches alone are unsatisfactory because they do not consider the effects of the power subsystem capacities.

To this end we propose a design-time, *i.e.*, offline power subsystem capacity planning algorithm for solar energy harvesting systems. The approach considers seasonal variations of the energy source, the sun, to approximate the harvestable energy and compute the required battery capacity given a panel size and deployment location information. Assuming that the modeled conditions reflect actual conditions, the power subsystem capacity obtained with this approach enables uninterrupted operation at a defined performance level, subject only to hardware failure, or environmental phenomena with a long-term effect on harvesting opportunities, *e.g.*, volcanic eruption.

The contributions of this work are summarized as follows. First, we propose a power subsystem capacity planning algorithm based on a modified astronomical model [11]. Second, we validate the modified model's ability to approximate the harvestable energy with power measurements of a solar panel. Thirdly, we evaluate the capacity planning approach through simulation, and show that it yields smaller batteries than the state-of-the-art (*SotA*) capacity planning algorithm [12]. We further show that our approach outperforms the *SotA* by achieving 100% availability over ten years for three different test datasets, while requiring up to 53% smaller batteries. In contrast to *SotA*, our approach does not rely on detailed power traces or calibration data, but only requires a crude estimate of average meteorological conditions at the intended deployment site.

Sec. 2 briefly reviews related work. *Sec. 3* introduces the high-level concept of the power subsystem capacity planning approach. *Sec. 4* provides a detailed discussion of the harvesting conditioned energy availability model that forms the basis of the capacity planning algorithm presented in *Sec. 5*. In *Sec. 6*, we evaluate the proposed method's ability to achieve uninterrupted long-term operation, and its sensitivity to parameter variations. Finally, *Sec. 7* concludes this work with a summary and brief discussion of future work.

2   Related Work

Many design examples of energy harvesting systems can be found in literature, *e.g.*, ZebraNet [13], Heliomote [14], Ambimax [15], Fleck [16], Rivermote [17], *etc.* However, they fail to provide systematic approaches for power subsystem capacity planning, and instead present anecdotal, application specific design choices that are based on simplified assumptions. Since the realization that energy harvesting is not necessarily sufficient to guarantee uninterrupted operation [7], efforts have primarily focused on mitigating the impacts of an inappropriately provisioned power subsystem with energy prediction schemes, *e.g.*, [18–20], and dynamic load scheduling based on short-term predictions [8–10, 21]. Three notable exceptions are [7, 12, 22], which are briefly discussed in the following.

In [12] an analytical model for long-term sustainable operation is presented. The authors consider battery capacity planning based on a representative power profile, inferring that the panel size is fixed. The approach is evaluated with a network of Heliomotes over two months during Summer in Los Angeles. To the best of our knowledge, this is the only approach that presents systematic guidelines for offline capacity planning. It will be discussed in more detail in *Sec. 6.3* and used as a baseline for evaluation.

Design experiences of the HydroSolar micro-solar power subsystem are presented in [7]. Despite leveraging the same astronomical model [11] used in this paper, the authors compute the panel size under the assumption that at most 30 minutes of daily charging would have to meet the daily energy requirements, essentially provisioning the solar panel for the worst case scenario (see *Sec. 5*). The battery is selected such that it can support 30 days of operation without harvesting opportunities. However, their deployment did not achieve uninterrupted operation despite seemingly overprovisioning the power subsystem. Interestingly, the authors mention that capacity planning for long-term operation is reasonable, if not necessary, and may be beneficial for improved system utility; however, they do not further investigate this insight.

Another closely related work that relies on the same astronomical model is presented in [22]. The authors empirically validate the model and show that it is, despite its low complexity, very applicable to real-world scenarios. However, the authors are not concerned with capacity planning, but rather focus on runtime prediction of harvesting opportunities with an extended astronomical model. The same battery and panel sizing guidelines as in [7] are used, which may result in an underprovisioned power subsystem.

3   Power Subsystem Design for Long-Term Operation

The ability to achieve uninterrupted long-term operation for solar energy harvesting systems depends on a properly dimensioned power subsystem that can support the expected load. *Fig. 1* shows the high-level design flow of the proposed capacity planning approach for enabling long-term, uninterrupted system operation. The dashed boxes represent user inputs that characterize the deployment setup, hardware technology employed, electrical load, and expected meteorological conditions. The capacity planning algorithm discussed in *Sec. 5* then computes the battery capacity required to support a user-specified performance level DC_{sys}.

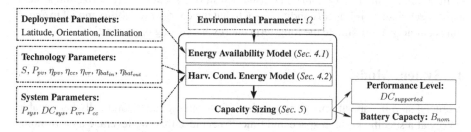

Fig. 1. Design flow for power subsystem capacity planning. Dashed boxes and arrows represent user inputs based on which the supported duty-cycle and required battery capacity are computed.

For estimating the theoretically harvestable energy, we leverage the fact that the energy source, the sun, follows both a diurnal and annual cycle. These cycles and the resulting solar energy can be approximated very well with an astronomical model [11]. This model requires deployment location and solar panel setup information as input, i.e. latitude of the deployment site, and orientation and inclination angles of the solar panel, to which we collectively refer as *deployment parameters*.

The astronomical model further depends on three parameters that account for the atmosphere's optical characteristics and the reflective properties of the ground. However, the exact values for these parameters are highly dependent on time-varying meteorological phenomena. In *Sec. 4.1* we explain how the model parameterization is reduced such that it takes a single input parameter to account for atmospheric and reflective properties. We call this parameter the *environmental parameter Ω*.

The energy that can effectively be harvested on a given day further depends on the *technology parameters*. These parameters characterize the technologies employed by specifying the solar panel's surface area A_{pv}, its conversion efficiency η_{pv}, and maximum power rating P_{pv}, the efficiencies of the power conditioning circuitry (η_{vr} and η_{cc}), and the charge and discharge efficiencies ($\eta_{bat_{in}}$ and $\eta_{bat_{out}}$) of the chosen storage element. In this work we are not concerned with the selection of optimal storage technology, as this is highly application specific. Note that we leave the selection of panel size to the designer and compute the battery capacity for the given panel. This is because solar panels are available in discrete sizes and scale linearly with output power rating. The capacity of a battery is somewhat less dependent on size. More importantly, however, the panel's maximum physical size is primarily limited by the form factor of the mote's enclosure and therefore considered a more sensitive design constraint.

Finally, the *system parameters*, i.e. power dissipation P_{sys}, and minimum expected duty-cycle DC_{sys}, and power conditioning circuitry, *i.e.*, voltage regulator P_{vr}, and charge controller P_{cc}, characterize the load imposed on the battery. The system's total energy requirement defines the performance level expected by the designer, while the supported duty-cycle $DC_{supported}$, computed by the capacity planning algorithm defines the fraction of the expected performance level that can be sustained with the computed battery capacity B_{nom}. Note that this work assumes constant power dissipation by the load; however, the model also applies to variable power profiles if the average load behavior can be approximated at design time.

In summary, the input parameters discussed in this section characterize the system and expected meteorological conditions such that the energy availability model in *Sec. 4* can accurately approximate the long-term energy harvesting opportunities.

4 System Model

A crucial step in capacity planning consists of estimating the theoretically harvestable energy at a specific point in space and time. To achieve this, we leverage an astronomical energy model [11]. *Sec. 4.1* discusses three modifications to this model such that varying environmental conditions can be taken into account. *Sec. 4.2* describes the harvesting conditioned model, which incorporates conversion and storage inefficiencies.

4.1 Energy Availability Model

According to [11], the total solar energy $E_{astro}(\cdot)$, incident on a flat surface located at latitude L, oriented at azimuth and inclination angles ϕ_p, and θ_p respectively. As shown in *(1)*, it is defined as the sum of the energy contained in direct solar radiation $E_{sun}(\cdot)$, the diffuse radiation by the sky $E_{sky}(\cdot)$, and the reflection of direct and diffuse radiation by the ground $E_{gnd}(\cdot)$, on a given day d, and time of day t [11]. The magnitude of $E_{astro}(\cdot)$, given in $Wh \cdot m^{-2}$, further depends on the distribution and optical characteristics of absorbent gases in the atmosphere, represented by diffuse sky radiation parameter k, optical thickness of the atmosphere τ, and the reflective properties of the ground R, all of which are unit-less. More details on this model and the impact of varying optical characteristics are given in [11], and [23, 24] respectively.

$$E_{astro}(\cdot) = E_{sun}(d, t, L, \phi_p, \theta_p, \tau) + E_{sky}(d, t, L, k, \theta_p, \tau) + E_{gnd}(d, t, L, k, R, \theta_p, \tau)$$
(1)

Local obstructions, such as trees, buildings, and meteorological factors (i.e. clouds, snow) also affect the solar energy incident on the panel. Accounting for these effects relies on extensive knowledge of the topographical and meteorological conditions at the deployment site, hence they are not directly considered by the astronomical model. As discussed later in this section, we account for these effects in the calculation of the environmental parameter Ω.

The astronomical model is further expressed in terms of k and τ, both of which are dependent on time-varying optical characteristics of the atmosphere that are difficult to predict [24]. The authors in [11] suggest values of $k = 0$ and $k = 1$ for absolute lower and upper bounds to obtain the contribution by diffuse sky radiation. For the atmosphere's optical thickness, τ, values between 0.1 and 0.4 are recommended, where the former represents a very clear sky, and the latter a very hazy sky [11,23]. However, for energy harvesting purposes, an upper bound of $\tau = 1$, *i.e.*, no solar harvesting is possible, can be assumed.

In an effort to quantify the parameters k and τ, we note that solar power traces (see *Sec. 6.1*) can be closely approximated with $E_{astro}(\cdot)$ by letting $k = 0.1$ and varying τ, such that $\sum^T E_{astro}(\cdot) \cong \sum^T E_{actual}(d)$. We leverage this observation and define the so called environmental parameter Ω in *(2)* to replace τ. The parameter δ_i represents the proportion of time during which the atmosphere exhibits the optical thickness τ_i.

$$\Omega = \sum_i^N \delta_i \tau_i, \quad where \quad \sum_i^N \delta_i = 1 \tag{2}$$

To obtain a representative indication of the atmosphere's long-term average optical property, the granularity of the weather conditions is represented by N. For example, for a particular geographical location, and with $N = 4$, we might let $\delta = [0.25, 0.35, 0.2, 0.2]$ to represent 25% of the time with clear sky conditions ($\tau_1 = 0.1$), 35% and 20% with light ($\tau_2 = 0.4$), and heavy ($\tau_3 = 0.7$) occlusions respectively, and 20% with no harvesting opportunities at all ($\tau_4 = 1$) (see also *Sec. 6.2* and *6.4*).

As is evident from *(1)*, τ appears in the expressions for E_{sun}, E_{sky}, and E_{gnd}. However, due to fixing k and varying τ, Ω may take values larger than the quantities recommended for τ in the original model. Hence, to minimize the error due to diffuse sky radiation [25], we replace τ with $min(\Omega, 0.4)$ in the expression for E_{sky}.

The astronomical model assumes a flat horizontal terrain, which, depending on the topography of the deployment site, may not be a valid assumption. The authors in [11] state that the magnitude of $E_{gnd}(\cdot)$ is subject to large error because of topographical variations. However, with a solar panel located at $40°N$, oriented due south (*i.e.*, $\phi_p = 180°$) with $40°$ inclination angle, and $\tau = 0.2$, $k = 0.3$, the total annual solar energy incident with $R = 0$ is only 2.94% lower than assuming ground reflectivity of bare ground, *i.e.*, $R = 0.3$ [11]. Therefore, unless the effects of ground reflection at a particular deployment site can be obtained through profiling or detailed surface models, it is reasonable to ignore the effect of ground reflection, and assume $R = 0$.

4.2 Harvesting Conditioned Energy Model

The model introduced in the previous section is used to compute the energy incident on a flat surface with a surface area of $1m^2$ for a given time of the year. However, when concerned with electrical energy as opposed to solar energy, various losses due to conversion inefficiencies and self-consumption must be considered [5]. This section discusses the effects of non-ideal harvesting and storage elements.

System Architecture. In this work, a harvest-store-use system architecture as defined in [4] is assumed. In such an architecture, the energy to operate the load is always supplied by the battery, and no bypass path exists that allows operating the load directly from the solar panel when the battery is full, and surplus energy is available. Since there is no dependence on the type of energy store employed, alternative harvesting architectures may also be used. We further assume a stationary solar harvesting installation without sun-tracking capabilities, i.e. orientation and inclination angles are fixed.

Panel Characteristics. Only a fraction of the solar energy incident on a solar panel is converted to electrical energy. Depending on technology, the conversion efficiency η_{pv} achieves a few percent for thin-film technologies, and exceeds 40% for high-end multi-junction cells [26]. Furthermore, a solar panel has a manufacturer specified maximum output P_{pv}. This is typically given for Standard Test Conditions (STC), hence the peak power output is not an optimal indication of maximum power. Nevertheless, we assume the maximum possible harvested energy over a time period δt to be limited by $\delta t \cdot P_{pv}$.

In the context of *WSN* application scenarios, it is desirable to keep the solar panel small in size so to match the mote's housing and meet low cost expectations [5, 6, 27]. Large-scale photo-voltaic installations are usually only used for *WSN* base stations and experimental units when mains power is not available. Since the energy model is defined in units of energy per square meter, we account for different solar panel sizes by scaling the total daily electrical energy output by the panel's surface area A_{pv}. Hence, the total harvested energy on a given day d is approximated with *(3)*, where η_{cc} represent the charge controller's efficiency.

$$E_{pv}(d, \Omega) = A_{pv} \cdot \eta_{cc} \cdot \eta_{pv} \sum_{t=0}^{t=23} min(1hr \cdot P_{pv}, E_{astro}(d, t, L, k, R, \theta_p, \phi_p, \Omega)) \quad (3)$$

Charge Controller Characteristics. Before the energy transformed by the solar panel can be stored in the battery, a fraction $1 - \eta_{cc}$ of the total energy is lost due to the conversion inefficiency imposed by the charge controller, hence the multiplicative factor η_{cc} in *(3)*. Depending on the chosen technology, the conversion efficiency η_{cc}, can range from 50% for low cost controllers, up to 95% for high-end, *i.e.*, Maximum Power-Point Tracking controllers [7]. The choice of technology is very application specific, and there are arguments advocating advanced charge controllers [28, 29], while others argue that, for micro-solar energy harvesting systems, the gain is dwarfed by the energy expenditure of the controller [7]. It is also possible to operate without a charge controller [15], but the lack of over-voltage protection may significantly reduce battery life [29].

Charge controllers often implement a battery protection mechanism, known as low-power load disconnect [30]. If the battery is fully depleted at any point in time, the load will only be re-connected after the battery state-of-charge has reached a certain percentage of B_{nom}. Prolonged downtime due to protection against deep discharge cycles can incur significant performance penalties. Furthermore, deep cycles severely affect the battery health and its expected lifetime, and should therefore be avoided.

Battery Characteristics. The purpose of the battery is to store harvested energy for supporting the electrical load during periods when harvesting is not possible. However, a battery is not a perfect energy storage element. It suffers from a variety of deficiencies that depend on the battery's chemistry, temperature, discharge rate, and fill-level [30] .

Hence, to account for charging and discharging inefficiencies of the battery during simulation, the energy flowing into and out of the battery is scaled by the respective efficiency factors $\eta_{bat_{in}}$ and $\eta_{bat_{out}}$, as shown in *(4)* and *(5)*. The loss in the charging process due to battery internal resistance and electrochemical processes is represented by $\eta_{bat_{in}}$.

The factor $1/\eta_{bat_{out}}$ accounts for the fact that only a fraction of the charge transferred into the battery during charging can be recovered when discharging the battery [30] .

$$E_{bat_{in}}(d) = min(\eta_{bat_{in}} \cdot E_{pv}(d, \Omega), min(0, \eta_{bat_{out}} \cdot B_{nom} - B(d-1) - E_{bat_{out}}(d))) \tag{4}$$

$$E_{bat_{out}}(d) = E_{load}(d)/\eta_{bat_{out}} + E_{leak} \tag{5}$$

Since a battery has a finite capacity, not all energy generated by the panel may actually flow into the battery, as indicated by the $min(\cdot)$ function in *(4)*. Similarly, to support the energy consumption $E_{load}(d)$, which represents all energy consumers regardless of function (see *(7)*), the current battery level and harvested energy must exceed the amount to be withdrawn from the battery, *i.e.*, $B(d-1) + E_{bat_{in}}(d) > E_{bat_{out}}(d)$. The battery specific leakage E_{leak} is assumed to be constant [12]. Then, with the battery characterized by *(4)* and *(5)*, the battery state-of-charge at the end of a given day is obtained with *(6)*. B_{nom} is the manufacturer rated nominal capacity converted to Watt-hours. For consistency, $B(d) \geq 0 \; \forall d$, which means that the expected load may not always be sustained. To circumvent this, the designer may overprovision the battery to enable minimal operation, *i.e.*, $B(d) \geq B_{min} \; \forall d$.

$$B(d) = min(\eta_{bat_{out}} \cdot B_{nom}, B(d-1) + E_{bat_{in}}(d) - E_{bat_{out}}(d)) \tag{6}$$

We ignore aging effects of the battery [30]. However, we note that our approach results in very shallow discharge cycles and so protects the expected battery lifetime [30]. In fact, our method results in one full discharge cycle per year; assuming a battery rated for a few hundred discharge cycles [31], the battery will clearly outlast the electronics.

Load Model. The electrical load on the battery consists of all energy consumers present in the system. In addition to the electronic system that performs a particular task, the consumers may include power conditioning, and other supervisory circuitry. For the purpose of capacity planning, the load is specified as the system's total average power dissipation that must be supported by the battery. It is obtained by summing the products of the M system components' duty-cycle (DC_i) and power dissipation (P_{sys_i}). The total daily energy required to operate at the expected performance level is then defined by *(7)*, where $\gamma = 24$ hours.

$$E_{load}(d) = \gamma \cdot \left[P_{cc} + P_{vr} + \sum_{i}^{M} (DC_{sys_i} \cdot P_{sys_i}) \right] \tag{7}$$

The power dissipation by the charge controller and input voltage regulator is represented by P_{cc} and P_{vr}, respectively. These are assumed to be always operational. Depending on design optimizations, however, both of them may be duty-cycled to reduce energy consumption. In that case, their average power dissipation is computed identically to that of the system components.

5   Capacity Planning for Long-Term Uninterrupted Operation

As discussed in *Sec. 4*, the harvestable energy can be closely approximated if setup and technology parameters are known. To account for the effects of meteorological conditions, and thus more closely approximate the long-term energy input, the environmental parameter Ω was defined. This parameter can be obtained with (2), or, if available, by profiling a representative dataset. The total energy consumption, defined in (5), completes the necessary information for long-term capacity planning.

Intuitively, a battery should be sized exactly such that (i) it can support the expected operation during periods of solar energy deficit, and (ii) be replenished by the panel during times of solar energy surplus. We consider the annual solar cycle to compute the power subsystem capacity such that uninterrupted long-term system operation with a minimum battery capacity and solar panel size can be achieved. Two such cycles are illustrated in *Fig. 2*, which shows the actual energy input $E_{actual}(d)$ of the CA dataset, the daily system consumption to be supported, and the model approximation $E_{bat_{in}}(d)$ such that $\sum^T E_{actual}(d) \cong \sum^T E_{bat_{in}}(d)$ over $T = 720$ days.

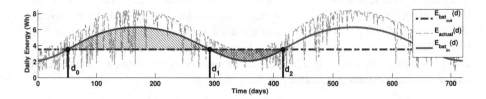

Fig. 2. Actual (E_{actual}), and modeled daily energy input ($E_{bat_{in}}$) and output ($E_{bat_{out}}$) for panel area $A_{pv} = 0.02m^2$ over two years of the CA dataset (see *Sec. 6.1*). Surplus energy is indicated with the hatched area. The cross-hatched area shows the required battery capacity.

The battery capacity, B_{nom}, required to operate the system during times of deficit, *i.e.*, $E_{bat_{out}}(d) > E_{bat_{in}}(d)$, $d \in [d_1, ..., d_2]$, is given in (8) and illustrated by the cross-hatched area in *Fig. 2*. Note that we assume the battery to be fully charged on day d_1. The first term on the left-hand side in (8) specifies the amount of energy that is necessary to support the system operation, while the second term represents the modeled energy input expectations. The difference is then the minimum required battery capacity B_{nom}.

$$\sum_{d_1}^{d_2} (E_{bat_{out}}(d) - E_{bat_{in}}(d)) \leq B_{nom} \tag{8}$$

Similarly, (9) specifies the amount of energy that is harvested in excess of what is required to sustain short term operation during periods of surplus, *i.e.*, over the interval $[d_0, ..., d_1]$ (hatched area in *Fig. 2*). As mentioned previously, the harvested energy during periods of surplus must be able to recharge the battery. To achieve perpetual operation over multiple years, the left-hand term in (9) must therefore be at least as large as the left-hand term in (8).

$$\sum_{d_0}^{d_1} (E_{bat_{in}}(d) - E_{bat_{out}}(d)) \geq B_{nom} \tag{9}$$

The required battery capacity B_{nom} can then be obtained by finding the intersections d_0, d_1, and d_2 between $E_{bat_{in}}(d)$ and $E_{bat_{out}}(d)$ such that inequalities (8) and (9) hold. For example, with the CA dataset shown in *Fig. 2*, and a panel size of $20cm^2$

and $E_{load} = 227.8mW$, the required battery capacity is approximately 68Wh (see *Sec. 6.3*). When reducing the panel size by 50%, the battery capacity must be increased by roughly 67% in order to achieve a performance level of 65% of the larger panel setup. This clearly shows the non-linear relationship between battery capacity and solar panel performance.

6 Evaluation

This section evaluates the proposed method's ability to yield a battery capacity that ensures uninterrupted long-term operation of solar energy harvesting systems.

6.1 Evaluation Methodology, Validation Data, and Performance Metrics

Methodology. To validate the modified astronomical model, we first compare its energy estimations to measurements performed with a solar panel. As a second step, we evaluate the model's ability to support long-term operation by simulating a system according to *Sec. 4* and *5*, and the simulation input data discussed in the following.

Table 1. Name, time-period, and location of NSRD[1] datasets used for evaluation of the proposed approach. Maximum, mean, minimum and variance of solar radiation are given in $Wh/0.01m^2$.

Name	Time Period	Latitude	Longitude	Maximum	Mean	Minimum	Variance
CA	01/01/99 – 12/31/09	34.05	-117.95	10.37	7.03	0.92	5.62
MI	01/01/99 – 12/31/09	42.05	-86.05	10.55	5.34	0.53	9.05
ON	01/01/99 – 12/31/09	48.05	-87.65	10.98	5.07	0.44	11.24

Model Validation Input Data. For validation of the modified astronomical model, we obtain ground-truth data by measuring the power generated by a $0.1725m^2$ monocrystalline solar panel (cleversolar CS-30) rated at 30 Watt over a period of 41 days (22/07/2013 - 08/31/2013). The power generated by the panel, and dissipated over a purely resistive load was sampled at $1Hz$ with a custom measurement circuit. The panel was placed on the roof-top of our university building at $47.37°N$, $8.55°E$, and oriented with azimuth, and inclination angles of $170°$ and $70°$ respectively. This particular location has clear view of the sky without any obstructions that could lead to shading, hence deviations from the model can be assumed to originate from weather effects only. Ground reflections are assumed to be negligible.

Simulation Input Data. For the simulation input data, we resort to the National Solar Radiation Database[1] (NSRD) from where we obtain hourly, global (i.e. direct and diffuse) solar radiation for three locations in California (CA), Michigan (MI), and Ontario (ON) (see *Table 1*). We use 11 years of data, from which the first year (*i.e.*, days 1-365) of each location is used as calibration data (see *Sec. 6.3*), while the data for the remaining 10 years is used as input for the simulation discussed in *Sec. 6.3*.

---

[1] http://rredc.nrel.gov/solar/old_data/nsrdb/1991-2010

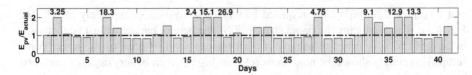

Fig. 3. Ratio of total daily energy predicted with our approach ($E_{pv}(d, \Omega = 0.51)$), and actual energy input ($E_{actual}(d)$) for each day. Note: bars are capped at 2, and labeled with actual value.

Table 2. Modified astronomical model validation statistics

(a) Statistics for 41 day experiment.

Min:	0.7947	Mode:	0.7947
Max:	26.87	St. Dev.:	5.737
Mean:	3.389	Range:	26.07
Median:	1.01		

(b) Weekly energy sums. E_{actual} refers to measurements with solar panel.

	Week						
	1	2	3	4	5	6	Total
E_{pv} [Wh]	4844	5646	5034	5109	5164	3706	29503
E_{actual} [Wh]	3773	5775	3155	4929	3605	3255	24492
E_{pv}/E_{actual}	1.28	0.98	1.6	1.04	1.43	1.14	1.20

The data traces from NSRD are given in $Wh \cdot m^{-2}$ of solar energy incident on a flat surface with zero inclination. To account for smaller panel sizes, inefficiencies of individual components, and losses in energy storage during simulation, the data is conditioned as explained in *Sec. 4.2*. For the technology parameters we assume $\eta_{bat_{in}} = 0.9$, $\eta_{bat_{out}} = 0.7$, $\eta_{cc} = \eta_{vr} = 1$, $\eta_{pv} = 10\%$, and zero inclination angle. The reconnect hysteresis (see *Sec. 4.2*) is set at 30% of battery capacity $B = \eta_{bat_{out}} \cdot B_{nom}$.

Performance Metrics. For performance comparison between the approach discussed in this paper and the state-of-the-art (*SotA*) [12], we define the following metrics. Since size and cost considerations play a major role in *WSN* scenarios, an optimal energy harvesting system is one with the smallest hardware configuration that is able to achieve the expected performance level, *i.e.*, when E_{load} is sustained over the entire simulation.

For evaluating the performance of the two approaches, we assume that the maximum feasible panel size is given, and wish to obtain the minimum battery capacity such that uninterrupted operation can be achieved. We report the computed battery capacities, and percentage of time spent with depleted battery for each configuration and dataset. Any set of input parameters that cannot support long-term operation at the expected performance level is considered invalid.

6.2 Modified Astronomical Model Validation

The measurement data described in *Sec. 6.1* is used as ground truth for validation of the modified astronomical model. Here we are concerned with how well the actual energy input can be approximated with a given Ω. We assume $\Omega = 0.51$ as per *(3)* with $\tau = [0.1, 0.4, 0.7, 1]$ and $\delta = [0.25, 0.35, 0.2, 0.2]$ to represent the expected weather condition. For the panel efficiency we use $\eta_{pv} = 21.5\%$ according to the specification, and the technology and deployment parameters from *Sec. 6.1*.

Table 3. Expected, and actual performance level achieved (in mW), and required battery capacity (*i.e.*, $B = \eta_{bat_{out}} \cdot B_{nom}$, in Wh) obtained from simulation of 4 panel sizes (in m^2) and the 3 datasets listed in *Table 1* for *SotA* and the method proposed in this work

	A_{pv}	MI Expected	Actual	B	CA Expected	Actual	B	ON Expected	Actual	B
SotA	0.005	55.73	52.32	42.51	73.17	73.17	61.48	56.75	51.04	56.96
This work			55.73	88.85		73.17	56.84		56.75	137.5
SotA	0.01	111.46	104.65	85.03	146.28	146.28	122.96	113.53	102.11	113.93
This work			111.46	168.39		146.28	113.5		113.53	275.1
SotA	0.015	157.54	148.34	106.44	197.85	197.85	133.89	159.1	145.19	171.42
This work			157.54	218.74		197.85	110.8		159.1	363.81
SotA	0.02	186.71	179.18	113.9	227.83	227.83	127.02	186.72	173.01	180.58
This work			186.71	216		227.83	67.59		186.72	381.6

As is evident from *Fig. 3*, which shows the ratio of estimated and actual energy input for each day, the model tends to significantly overestimate available energy for days with little, to no energy harvesting opportunities. *Table 2a* lists statistics for the same 41-day period. *Table 2b* shows the results when considering an estimation granularity of one week. Over the entire period, the actual conditions are overestimated by 20.04%. This is a good result, considering that even more elaborate models tend to suffer a great deal from uncertainties, particularly due to modeling of diffuse sky radiation [25].

6.3   Capacity Planning Performance Evaluation

The previous section showed that our energy availability model can closely approximate actual conditions. This section now demonstrates that our approach in fact supports uninterrupted long-term operation of a simulated system for a variety of input data. Aside from *SotA* [12], we are not aware of concrete algorithms for power subsystem capacity planning of energy harvesting systems. Thus, the method described in [12, 32, 33] is used as a baseline and briefly reviewed in the following.

Reference Model. In [12] the authors present a set of abstractions for capacity planning of energy harvesting systems that can be considered the state-of-the-art (*SotA*) in harvesting theory. The authors define Energy-Neutral Operation (ENO) as a performance metric, and formally state the conditions that must be met to achieve ENO. The authors argue that a system's total average power dissipation, ρ_c, must always be less than, or equal to the source's average power generation, ρ_s. If energy inefficiency is acceptable, *i.e.*, dissipating the power generated by the panel as heat when the battery is full, the minimum battery capacity is defined by the sum of the maximum negative deviation from ρ_s, and the maximum positive deviation from ρ_c. If wasting is not permitted, the battery capacity must be increased by the maximum positive deviation from ρ_s such that surplus energy can be buffered [32]. Despite defining a capacity for long-term continuous operation, the authors conclude that, for achieving ENO, the battery state-of-charge $B(d)$ on day d must be no less than $B(d-1)$. With this approach the benefits of capacity planning are not fully leveraged; the system must rely on a well performing energy prediction scheme to achieve acceptable long-term performance.

In order to extract ρ_s, the *SotA* algorithm requires a dataset that is representative of the conditions at the deployment site. However, when applying the method described in [32] to obtain this quantity, it is found that their approach yields significantly different performance levels depending on the particular time period used. In fact, even for datasets with little variance, *e.g.*, the CA dataset (see *Table 1*), ρ_s converges to its average value only after a few seasonal cycles. This exemplifies that, when attempting to achieve uninterrupted long-term operation at a predefined performance level, consideration of the source's longest cycle is necessary. In the case of solar harvesting, the period can generally be assumed to be one year. However, in areas where significant meteorological phenomena with a periodicity of multiple years occur, improved results may be obtained if the analysis is performed over the respective period.

Simulation. The *SotA* approach attempts to compute the supported performance level and required battery size based on a given power profile. Our approach, on the other hand, takes the expected performance level as input. Hence, to evaluate and compare the two approaches through simulation, we first obtain the respective performance levels and battery capacities as follows. With the setup and technology parameters defined in *Sec. 6.1*, we find the battery capacity and supported performance level with the *SotA* approach and one year of calibration data for all three datasets listed in *Table 1* and four panel sizes, *i.e.*, $5cm^2$, $10cm^2$, $15cm^2$, and $20cm^2$. The respective performance levels obtained with *SotA* are then used as input to our model to compute the minimal capacities required for each dataset. Once these quantities have been found for *SotA* and our approach, we run a simulation with the remaining 10 years of data.

Note that our approach does not require calibration data. However, since *SotA* relies on a representative power trace, we allow our approach to extract the weather conditions from the calibration data to compute Ω (see *Sec. 4.1*). We use $\tau = [0.1, 0.4, 0.7, 1]$ and $N = 4$ in *(2)* and let δ_i be the days with more than 75%, 50%, 25%, and 0% of the maximum expected energy, *i.e.*, $E_{astro}(\Omega = 0.1)$. Since meteorological conditions tend to follow a certain periodicity, Ω may be obtained with very little data. In fact, we did not find significant improvements when using more than half a year of calibration data, as long as the data is representative of the conditions during the critical periods of continuous solar energy deficit, *i.e.*, winter in the northern hemisphere.

Results. The results obtained from simulation are summarized in *Table 3*, and discussed in the following. As is evident, the *SotA* approach achieves an acceptable performance only for the CA dataset. As defined in *Sec. 6.1*, acceptable performance means that the battery can support the user-specified performance level indefinitely.

While the *SotA* approach yields smaller battery capacities for the MI and ON datasets compared to our approach, the configurations fail to sustain the expected performance level over the entire simulation period. Our approach, on the other hand, achieves the expected performance level with zero down-time for all configurations and simulations.

CA Dataset. With the CA dataset, *SotA* achieves the expected performance level for the entire 10 year period with all simulated panel sizes. This comes at no surprise; the authors of the *SotA* approach are located in Southern California and used locally measured data for design and verification of their approach. From *Table 1* we see that this particular dataset has the lowest input data variance, with roughly half of that of the other datasets. Nevertheless, with $A_{pv} = 0.005m^2$ and $A_{pv} = 0.01m^2$, the *SotA* approach yields a battery size that is about 1.48 times the size of the minimal capacity. For the other two panel sizes, the algorithm overestimates the absolute minimal possible capacity by a factor of 1.86, and 2.7, respectively.

For the same dataset, our approach yields smaller battery capacities that can sustain the expected performance level over the entire simulation period. When compared to *SotA*, a reduction of roughly 8% in capacities are obtained with $A_{pv} = 0.005m^2$ and $A_{pv} = 0.01m^2$. For $A_{pv} = 0.015m^2$ and $A_{pv} = 0.02m^2$ our approach yields 17.25% and 46.8% smaller capacities than *SotA*. This is an interesting result because it shows that average generation, ρ_s, is not a good indicator of the long-term sustainable performance level. With increasing panel size, ρ_s behaves in a manner that may not be representative of the long-term dynamics, causing the *SotA* model to assume an overly pessimistic negative deviation from ρ_s, and yield a larger capacity than necessary.

MI and ON Datasets. The results in *Table 3* show that *SotA* does not achieve satisfactory performance for the MI and ON dataset. Hence, we only focus on the results of our approach. For the MI dataset, the minimal possible battery capacity is overestimated by a maximum of 13.5%. For the ON dataset, our approach overestimates by up to 22.1%. This constant, but reasonable overestimate is due to assuming Ω larger than absolutely necessary. In fact, reducing Ω by 20% for ON leads to an overestimate of only 1.4%. For the MI dataset, Ω must be reduced by 7% to achieve the same result. However, doing so would result in dangerously low battery fill-levels during times of deficit, causing the system to become susceptible to low-power disconnect penalties.

When given the opportunity to analyze two full years of calibration data, the *SotA* approach fails to achieve the expected performance level only for one of the configurations of the MI dataset. With $A_{pv} = 0.015m^2$, the system spends 0.59%, or 21.5 days of the time with a drained battery. Considering that *SotA*'s performance depends on the closeness of ρ_s to actual average generation, longer data traces are expected to improve its performance. Interestingly, *SotA* overestimates the battery capacities for the CA dataset almost identically when only one year of data is available, which is due to the low variance in the energy input. For the other two datasets, both approaches yield comparable capacities, despite giving *SotA* the advantage of analyzing two years of calibration data, while our method only used one year of calibration data.

Energy Approximation. In this work we focused on long-term provisioning because short-term deviations from the model should be absorbed by a properly sized battery. Here we investigate how our model can cope with source variations that lead to energy deficit. *Fig. 4* shows the ratio of total energy approximated by the model, and effectively harvested energy for each year on the left, and the same for the periods of continuous deficit on the right. As is evident, with the largest panel size used ($A_{pv} = 0.02$), the model assumes on average around 95% of the actual annual energy input for the CA and MI datasets, and roughly 88% for ON. The ratios of approximated and actual energy input for the panels with area $0.005m^2$ and $0.01m^2$ are about 85% for CA and MI, and around 78% for ON.

For the periods of deficit, shown on the right hand graphs in *Fig. 4*, much more variation is evident from one year to the next. However, the approximations with different

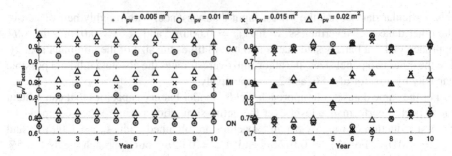

Fig. 4. Ratio of total energy E_{pv} approximated with our approach, and actual energy input (E_{actual}) for each year (left), and for each year's period of deficit (right). Note the scales.

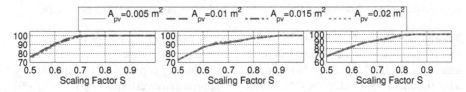

Fig. 5. Achieved performance level for CA (left), MI (middle), and ON (right) datasets and four panel sizes with down-scaled energy input

panel sizes are much less scattered, and the approximation with the larger panel size is not always best. Nevertheless, on average, the model underestimates actual conditions by roughly 20% for the CA and MI datasets, and about 25% for ON. This shows that the battery obtained is reasonably overprovisioned, and will be able to safely bridge short periods with energy input below modeled long-term expectations.

6.4 Sensitivity Analysis

In this section we investigate the model's sensitivity to the selection of the environmental parameter Ω. We further exemplify the importance of choosing inclination, and azimuth angles such that they are representative of the actual deployment setup.

Environmental Parameter. As is evident from *Sec. 6.2*, the model's ability to accurately estimate the long-term expected energy input depends on proper choice of Ω. This parameter is used to account for environmental effects due to *e.g.*, meteorological conditions and local obstructions. These cause the model to overestimate actual energy input, which is equivalent to assuming too low of a value for Ω.

Hence, to investigate these effects on the model's estimation accuracy, we scale Ω with a scaling factor S (*i.e.*, $E_{pv}(..., S \cdot \Omega)$ in (4)), and simulate the system as discussed in *Sec. 6.1*. The achieved mean duty-cycle over ten years for the three datasets are shown in *Fig. 5*. The results show that the expected duty-cycle can be achieved when the energy input is at least 75%, 85%, and 90% of the original magnitude for the CA, ON, and MI datasets respectively.

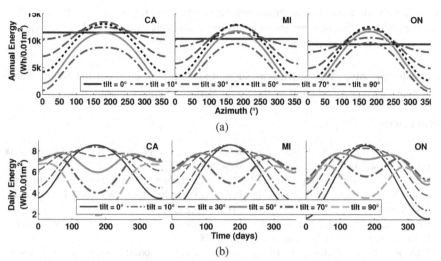

Fig. 6. (a) Total *annual* energy incident with inclination angles from $0°$ to $90°$ as a function of azimuth angle. (b) Total *daily* energy incident over one year for inclination angles ranging from $0°$ to $60°$ ($\tau = 0.1$, $k = 0.3$, $R = 0.3$, $\eta_{pv} = 0.1$).

Setup Parameters. The effects of varying the setup parameters, i.e. inclination and orientation angles, on the harvestable energy are illustrated in *Fig. 6a*. It shows the total *annual* energy incident on a panel with a surface area of $10cm^2$ over the course of one year for the three datasets in *Table 1* and various inclination angles as a function of panel orientation. As is intuitively clear, for an inclination angle of $0°$, i.e. the panel is placed parallel to the ground, the orientation has no effect.

Similarly, *Fig. 6b* shows the total *daily* energy incident on the same panel for various inclination angles. The effect on the harvestable energy due to setup parameters, and seasonal variations is clearly visible, solidifying our argument that the source's seasonal behavior must be considered when attempting to achieve uninterrupted long-term operation at a predefined performance level.

7   Conclusions

In this work we presented a systematic approach to offline capacity planning of the power subsystem for solar energy harvesting systems. The approach is based on a modified astronomical model and takes into account seasonal variations of the energy source to enable uninterrupted long-term operation. Solar power measurements of a real panel are used to validate the modified model. We further compared our approach to the state of the art (*SotA*) in harvesting theory through simulation with real-world input data, and showed that the proposed method achieves zero down-time (compared to up to 10% for *SotA*) for three different locations and four different panel sizes while requiring up to 53% smaller batteries. The results show that pre-deployment design considerations are absolutely inevitable for achieving long-term uninterrupted system operation. In order to enable the system to adapt to significant deviations from the model, and therefore improve the energy efficiency, we are currently extending this work with a low-complexity, power subsystem aware, dynamic duty-cycling scheme.

Acknowledgments. This work was supported with a grant from the Swiss Nano-Tera.ch initiative and evaluated by the Swiss National Science Foundation.

References

1. Mini, R.A., Loureiro, A.A.: Energy in wireless sensor networks. In: Middleware for Network Eccentric and Mobile Applications, pp. 3–24. Springer (2009)
2. Buchli, B., Sutton, F., Beutel, J.: GPS-equipped wireless sensor network node for high-accuracy positioning applications. In: Picco, G.P., Heinzelman, W. (eds.) EWSN 2012. LNCS, vol. 7158, pp. 179–195. Springer, Heidelberg (2012)
3. Chalasani, S., Conrad, J.M.: A survey of energy harvesting sources for embedded systems. In: IEEE Southeastcon, pp. 442–447. IEEE (2008)
4. Sudevalayam, S., Kulkarni, P.: Energy harvesting sensor nodes: Survey and implications. IEEE Communications Surveys & Tutorials 13(3), 443–461 (2011)
5. Hanssen, L., Gakkestad, J.: Solar Cell Size Requirement for Powering of Wireless Sensor Network Used in Northern Europe. In: Proceedings of the International Workshops on PowerMEMS, pp. 17–20 (2010)
6. Seah, W.K., et al.: Research in Energy Harvesting Wireless Sensor Networks and the Challenges Ahead (2012)
7. Taneja, J., et al.: Design, Modeling, and Capacity Planning for Micro-solar Power Sensor Networks. In: Proceedings of the 7th International Conference on Information Processing in Sensor Networks, IPSN 2008, pp. 407–418. IEEE Computer Society, Washington, DC (2008)
8. Le, T.N., et al.: Power Manager with PID controller in Energy Harvesting Wireless Sensor Networks. In: 2012 IEEE International Conference on Green Computing and Communications (GreenCom), pp. 668–670. IEEE (2012)
9. Vigorito, C.M., et al.: Adaptive control of duty cycling in energy-harvesting wireless sensor networks. In: 4th Annual IEEE Communications Society Conference on Sensor, Mesh and Ad Hoc Communications and Networks, SECON 2007, pp. 21–30. IEEE (2007)
10. Piorno, J.R., et al.: Prediction and management in energy harvested wireless sensor nodes. In: 1st International Conference on Wireless Communication, Vehicular Technology, Information Theory and Aerospace & Electronic Systems Technology, Wireless VITAE 2009, pp. 6–10. IEEE (2009)
11. Dave, J., et al.: Computation of Incident Solar Energy. IBM Journal of Research and Development 19(6), 539–549 (1975)
12. Kansal, A., et al.: Power management in energy harvesting sensor networks. ACM Transactions on Embedded Computing Systems (TECS) 6(4), 32 (2007)
13. Zhang, P., et al.: Hardware design experiences in ZebraNet. In: Proceedings of the 2nd International Conference on Embedded Networked Sensor Systems, SenSys 2004, pp. 227–238. ACM, New York (2004)
14. Raghunathan, V., et al.: Design considerations for solar energy harvesting wireless embedded systems. In: Proceedings of the 4th International Symposium on Information Processing in Sensor Networks, p. 64. IEEE Press (2005)
15. Park, C., Chou, P.H.: Ambimax: Autonomous energy harvesting platform for multi-supply wireless sensor nodes. In: 2006 3rd Annual IEEE Communications Society on Sensor and Ad Hoc Communications and Networks, SECON 2006, vol. 1, pp. 168–177. IEEE (2006)

16. Sitka, P., et al.: Fleck-a platform for real-world outdoor sensor networks. In: 3rd International Conference on Intelligent Sensors, Sensor Networks and Information, ISSNIP 2007, pp. 709–714. IEEE (2007)

17. Glatz, P.M., et al.: Designing perpetual energy harvesting systems explained with rivermote: A wireless sensor network platform for river monitoring. Electronic Journal of Structural Engineering, Special Issue: Wireless Sensor Networks and Practical Applications, 55–65 (2010)

18. Lu, J., Whitehouse, K.: SunCast: fine-grained prediction of natural sunlight levels for improved daylight harvesting. In: Proceedings of the 11th International Conference on Information Processing in Sensor Networks, pp. 245–256. ACM (2012)

19. Sharma, N., et al.: Predicting solar generation from weather forecasts using machine learning. In: 2011 IEEE International Conference on Smart Grid Communications (SmartGridComm), pp. 528–533. IEEE (2011)

20. Bacher, P., et al.: Online short-term solar power forecasting. Solar Energy 83(10), 1772–1783 (2009)

21. Kooti, H., et al.: Energy Budget Management for Energy Harvesting Embedded Systems. In: 2012 IEEE 18th International Conference on Embedded and Real-Time Computing Systems and Applications (RTCSA), pp. 320–329. IEEE (2012)

22. Jeong, J., Culler, D.: Predicting the Long-Term Behavior of a Micro-Solar Power System. ACM Transactions on Embedded Computing Systems (TECS) 11(2), 35 (2012)

23. Bohren, C.F., Clothiaux, E.: Atmospheric Optics. Wiley-VCH (2006)

24. Heinemann, D., et al.: Forecasting of solar radiation. Solar energy resource management for electricity generation from local level to global scale. Nova Science Publishers, New York (2006)

25. Gubler, S., Gruber, S., Purves, R.: Uncertainties of parameterized surface downward clear-sky shortwave and all-sky longwave radiation. Atmospheric Chemistry and Physics 12(11), 5077–5098 (2012)

26. Green, M.A., Emery, K., Hishikawa, Y., Warta, W., Dunlop, E.D.: Solar cell efficiency tables (version 39). Progress in Photovoltaics: Research and Applications 20(1), 12–20 (2011)

27. Pister, K.: Smartdust: Autonomous sensing and communication in a cubic millimeter

28. Brunelli, D., et al.: An efficient solar energy harvester for wireless sensor nodes. In: Proceedings of the Conference on Design, Automation and Test in Europe, pp. 104–109. ACM (2008)

29. Corke, P., et al.: Long-duration solar-powered wireless sensor networks. In: Proceedings of the 4th Workshop on Embedded Networked Sensors, EmNets 2007, pp. 33–37. ACM, New York (2007)

30. Buchli, B., Aschwanden, D., Beutel, J.: Battery state-of-charge approximation for energy harvesting embedded systems. In: Demeester, P., Moerman, I., Terzis, A. (eds.) EWSN 2013. LNCS, vol. 7772, pp. 179–196. Springer, Heidelberg (2013)

31. Bergveld, H.J.: Battery management systems: design by modelling. PhD thesis, Enschede (June 2001)

32. Kansal, A., Potter, D., Srivastava, M.B.: Performance aware tasking for environmentally powered sensor networks. In: ACM SIGMETRICS Performance Evaluation Review, vol. 32, pp. 223–234. ACM (2004)

33. Kansal, A., et al.: Harvesting aware power management for sensor networks. In: Proceedings of the 43rd Annual Design Automation Conference, pp. 651–656. ACM (2006)

Implementation and Experimental Validation of Timing Constraints of BBS

Markus Engel, Dennis Christmann, and Reinhard Gotzhein

University of Kaiserslautern, Germany
{engel,christma,gotzhein}@cs.uni-kl.de

Abstract. BBS (Black Burst Synchronization) is a synchronization protocol for multi-hop wireless ad-hoc networks providing deterministic upper bounds for tick offset and convergence delay. General bounds can be determined analytically, and depend on parameters such as maximum network diameter and maximum clear channel assessment delay. From the general bounds, concrete bounds can be derived by inserting hardware-specific values. Certainly, it is crucial that the platform-specific values are accurate, and that all sources of delay are considered.

In this paper, we report on the experimental validation and derivation of timing constraints of BBS for an implementation on the Imote 2 platform, using a Software Defined Radio (SDR) for some measurements. In particular, we identify sources of delay that have an impact on the upper bounds for tick offset and convergence delay, and devise and conduct experiments to measure these delays. As it turns out, the timing constraints for BBS reported in the original work need several refinements. Also, the jitter introduced by optimization techniques of the hardware platform like instruction and data caches needs careful consideration. We have applied these insights gained from the experiments to improve the design and implementation of BBS.

1 Introduction

Synchronization is a core functionality in many distributed systems. Two kinds of synchronization can be distinguished. Time synchronization has the objective to synchronize the clocks of a set of nodes by agreeing on common reference points in time and associated time values. Tick synchronization is concerned with establishing common reference points in time only. This is sufficient, e.g., for communication based on time division multiple access (TDMA) schemes.

In a research project together with industrial partners, we apply a TDMA scheme in a communication system for wireless networked control systems used in production automation. In this project, it is crucial that deterministic guarantees for packet delays and transfer reliability can be given, which we want to achieve by collision-free medium access in exclusively reserved time slots. This, however, requires that an upper bound for tick offset, i.e., worst case synchronization inaccuracy, can be guaranteed.

To satisfy this requirement, we have identified Black Burst Synchronization (BBS) [1, 2] as a possible synchronization protocol. BBS is applicable in wireless

B. Krishnamachari, A.L. Murphy, and N. Trigoni (Eds.): EWSN 2014, LNCS 8354, pp. 84–99, 2014.
© Springer International Publishing Switzerland 2014

multi-hop networks and provides deterministic upper bounds for tick offset (synchronization accuracy) and convergence delay (duration of a resynchronization phase). This distinguishes BBS from most existing synchronization protocols in this domain, which can provide only average values obtained at runtime.

In [1, 2], general bounds for tick offset and convergence delay are determined analytically, using parameters such as maximum network diameter (in hops), maximum *Clear Channel Assessment* (CCA) delay, and transceiver switching times. To obtain concrete bounds, values of the particular network topology and of the specific hardware platform taken from data sheets are used. Certainly, it is crucial for the operation of BBS that these values are accurate. Furthermore, it is essential that all sources of delay are considered.

In this paper, we report on the experimental validation of timing behavior of BBS for our implementation on the Imote 2 platform. In particular, we reconsider the earlier findings on upper bounds for tick offset and convergence delay, and identify additional sources of delay mainly resulting from interaction between processor and transceiver. In our work, we have devised and conducted numerous experiments to measure these delays, and to validate values given in data sheets. For presentation in this paper, we have selected experiments that have provided us with important insights to improve the design and implementation of BBS.

The paper continues with a survey of related work. Afterwards, Sect. 3 outlines BBS. Section 4 presents the Imote 2 platform and a refined analysis of the BBS timing behavior for this hardware. Section 5 reports on experiments to measure and to derive platform-specific delays, and to validate values from data sheets. Finally, Sect. 6 summarizes our findings and outlines future work.

2   Related Work

While there are numerous papers investigating implications of wireless channels and different communication technologies such as IEEE 802.15.4 [3] and IEEE 802.11 [4], there is only little work on validation of transceiver properties and on derivation of additional hardware- and implementation-specific timing constraints. And indeed, for most protocols with the objective on improving average case, small deviations from data sheet values can actually be neglected.

This particularly holds for most synchronization protocols, which aim at highest synchronization accuracy and hardware independence. Examples are Reference Broadcast Synchronization (RBS) [5], Timing-Sync Protocol for Sensor Networks (TPSN) [6], and Gradient Time Synchronization Protocol (GTSP) [7]. In these protocols, exchange of synchronization messages is contention-based, thereby introducing risk of frame collisions and unpredictable delays. Because of this inherently integrated non-determinism, only average case instead of worst case analysis can be applied. A detailed discussion of BBS's advantages and a comparison with other synchronization protocols can be found in [1, 2].

However, deterministic protocols such as BBS require accurate consideration of all transceiver properties. Besides BBS, we found only few deterministic close-to-hardware protocols for sensor networks: In [8], the authors present BitMAC, a comprehensive MAC protocol for tree topologies, which are typical for wireless sensor networks. BitMAC covers several challenges of wireless networks like channel allocation (FDMA), reservations, and synchronization. To address these challenges, the authors of BitMAC introduce a new collision-resistant transmission scheme that is based on On-Off-Keying and similar to the black burst encoded transmission scheme of BBS. It was implemented on the BTnode3 platform [9] that is equipped with a CC1000 transceiver. Wireless Dominance (WiDom) [10, 11], is a binary countdown protocol for wireless networks and addresses sporadic message streams. An application of WiDom consists of a tournament phase that is preceded by a synchronization phase. WiDom has been implemented on MICAz sensor nodes [12] that are equipped with CC 2420 transceivers.

Though the authors of WiDom consider many hardware timing constraints, they do not scrutinize the data sheet values. Instead, the correctness of WiDom is ensured by large guard times. Thus, there is up to our knowledge no other work on the implementation of deterministic protocols dealing with timing constraints on such low abstraction level and with such high thoroughness.

3   Survey of BBS

Black Burst Synchronization (BBS) [1, 2] is a synchronization protocol for wireless multi-hop ad-hoc networks. Different from most existing synchronization protocols in this domain, BBS provides deterministic upper bounds for tick offset and convergence delay. Furthermore, BBS has low complexity regarding computation, storage, time, and structure, and is robust against topology changes due to node movement or node failure. The protocol is based on periodical resynchronization phases, in which all network nodes are synchronized by a round-based exchange of synchronization messages called *tick frames*. A tick frame consists of an SOTF bit (Start of Tick Frame) to mark the beginning of the frame, followed by the encoded round number k. Resynchronization is done as follows:

- Resynchronization is started by some master node V_m at a given local reference point in time called *local tick* and referred to by $t_{0,m}$. At $t_{0,m}$, V_m sends a tick frame with $k = 1$. This marks the beginning of synchronization round 1.
- All nodes V_i receiving the tick frame in round 1 record the start of reception as their local tick $t_{0,i}$ and send a tick frame d_{round} (the constant, and therefore pre-calculable, round duration) after $t_{0,i}$. This marks the beginning of synchronization round 2.
- Synchronization rounds continue until all nodes V_j have received a tick frame in some round k at $t_{k,j}$. Given the constant round duration, node V_j can compute its local tick $t_{0,j}$ as $t_{k,j} - (k-1) \cdot d_{round}$.
- The number of rounds equals $n_{maxHops}$, which represents an upper bound of the network diameter in hops.

In any round $k > 1$, it is possible that more than one node sends a tick frame, i.e., tick frames may collide. To render collisions non-destructive, BBS uses a black burst encoding for tick frames. A black burst encodes a binary one of a tick frame. A binary zero is encoded by no transmission. A black burst can be characterized as a period of transmission energy of defined length on the medium. The only information derived from a black burst is its starting point and its duration. Therefore, if several black bursts sent (almost) simultaneously overlap, this information is not destroyed. To detect black bursts, the Clear Channel Assessment (CCA) mechanism of the transceiver is used.

In [1, 2], the upper bound for tick offset after resynchronization is determined as follows:

$$d_{maxOffset} = n_{maxHops} \cdot d_{maxCCA} \qquad (3.1)$$

where d_{maxCCA} is the maximum CCA delay to detect the channel as busy. In most cases, it is sufficient to not consider the network-wide worst case offset but the two-hop worst case offset, which is denoted by $d_{maxOffset,local} = 2 \cdot d_{maxCCA}$. Due to diverging local node clocks, the tick offset increases after a synchronization phase, which is bounded by periodic resynchronizations.

Furthermore, the convergence delay is given as $d_{conv} = n_{maxHops} \cdot d_{round}$ with a round duration d_{round} as follows:

$$d_{round} = (n_{bits} + 1) \cdot d_{bit} + d_{proc} \qquad \text{with} \qquad d_{bit} = d_{rxtx} + d_{bb} + d_{txrx} \quad (3.2)$$

Here, n_{bits} is the bit count to transfer the maximal round number $n_{maxHops}$. It is increased by one due to the additional SOTF bit. d_{bit} is the bit duration, and d_{proc} is a processing delay needed by the receiving node before the next round can be started. The bit duration is determined by delays to switch the transceiver from rx to tx mode (d_{rxtx}) and back (d_{txrx}), and the duration of a black burst d_{bb}.

4   Implementation of BBS on the Imote 2 Platform

In the course of a current industrial project, in which we apply a TDMA scheme in a wireless networked control system, we have implemented BBS on the Imote 2 platform. During the implementation, it turned out that the original formulas as given in Eqs. (3.1) and (3.2) need refinement, because some additional delays, which are not explicitly given by data sheets, were not considered. Please note that Eqs. (3.1) and (3.2) describe upper bounds. Thus, implementations based on the original formulas may work in most cases and [1] indeed reports on a working implementation. They are, however, error-prone when variable delays come close to their bounds.

In the following, we first outline the Imote 2 platform, because precisely knowing your hardware is a precondition to capture all delays. Then, we present an extension to improve BBS's robustness and a refinement of its formulas.

4.1   Description of the Imote 2 Hardware Platform

The Imote 2 sensor platform [13] (see Fig. 1a and 1b), initially developed by Intel, is equipped with the PXA 271 processor and the CC 2420 transceiver [14].

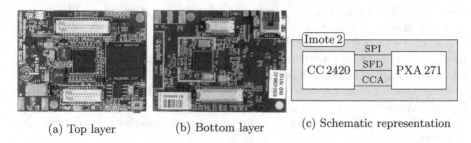

(a) Top layer   (b) Bottom layer   (c) Schematic representation

Fig. 1. Imote 2 hardware platform

The processor consists of an XScale core, which is based on the ARMv5TE processor architecture, 256 KiB SRAM, and numerous peripherals to interact with the environment, such as GPIO (General Purpose Input/Output), UART (Universal Asynchronous Receiver Transmitter), and SPI (Synchronous Peripheral Interface). Furthermore, the Imote 2 also includes 32 MiB SDRAM and 32 MiB Flash Memory stacked into the PXA 271 chip. The processor clock is configurable in fixed steps ranging from 13 MHz to 416 MHz.

The CC 2420 chip is an IEEE 802.15.4 compliant transceiver for the 2.4 GHz ISM band developed by Chipcon. Physical layer and parts of the IEEE 802.15.4 MAC layer are integrated into the chip. For the implementation of BBS, the MAC layer support is not needed, because IEEE 802.15.4 frames are sent only to generate energy on the medium. The digital interface of the CC 2420 consists of an SPI slave and several output pins. Figure 1c shows the interconnect of CC 2420 and PXA 271 schematically. The SPI bus is used to transfer commands to the transceiver, to read the transceiver's state, and to exchange payload of sent or received IEEE 802.15.4 frames. The output pins signal important events such as frame receptions (via Start-of-Frame-Delimiter (SFD) pin) and the current state of the medium (signaled by CCA pin). Each of these signals is connected to a GPIO pin of the PXA 271, thereby triggering interrupts at signal edges.

4.2   Improvement of the Robustness of BBS

In early experiments, we have encountered several problems with the robustness of BBS. We had, in particular, the problem that arbitrary communication patterns were interpreted as tick frames and that successive tick frames were merged, thereby leading to synchronization failures and a violation of the guaranteed tick offset. To solve this problem, we have changed the tick frame format of BBS. In our implementation, the tick frame is still composed of SOTF bit and round number, but the SOTF bit is now prolonged and distinguishably longer than the other bits of a tick frame. Thus, the probability of misinterpreting a medium occupancy as start of a tick frame is significantly reduced.

4.3   Refinement of BBS Timing Constraints

During the implementation of BBS on the Imote 2 platform and during experiments with first prototypes, we identified several sources of delays that have not been reported in [1, 2]. These delays are mainly because of poorly documented hardware latencies and have an impact on the convergence delay as well as the tick offset of BBS. In the following paragraphs, we provide an update of the original BBS formulas by considering additional delays.

Refinement of the Bit Duration d_{bit}. The bit duration d_{bit} describes the smallest interval to transmit consecutive black bursts. Comparing Eq. (3.2) with data sheets, we found that, on the one hand, some important constraints are not considered and, on the other hand, an unnecessary delay is listed. In the following, we derive three constraints for d_{bit}. The first constraint concerns sending nodes, the second and third constraints affect receivers.

To transmit a black burst, CPU and transceiver have to go through several steps. First, the transmission has to be set up, which means that hardware registers of the CC 2420 are reconfigured and the IEEE 802.15.4 payload is sent over the SPI bus. Since this delay, denoted by $d_{TX,pre}$, is variable in general, we investigate the worst case and consider the upper bound, referred to as $\widehat{d}_{TX,pre}$. After this preparation, a hardware timer of the PXA 271 processor is set in order to trigger the actual black burst transmission. When the timer fires, an STXON command is transferred to the transceiver. The duration between timer firing and STXON command reception by the CC 2420 is denoted by d_{TX}, and, according to our notation, its upper bound is called $\widehat{d}_{TX}$. Finally, there is a delay d_{rxtx} (with upper bound $\widehat{d}_{rxtx}$) to switch the transceiver from rx mode to tx mode. This delay results from recalibration of the frequency generator and adjustment of the power amplifiers. After switching to tx mode, the transceiver transmits the black burst, that has a constant duration d_{bb}.[1] Since one tick frame consists of several bits, black bursts may be sent in sequence and we have to sum up all delays and formulate the following constraint:

$$d_{bit} \geq \widehat{d}_{TX,pre} + \widehat{d}_{TX} + \widehat{d}_{rxtx} + d_{bb} \tag{4.1}$$

Note, that different from Eq. (3.2), d_{bit} does no longer depend on d_{txrx}, because according to the data sheet, the CC 2420 does not require to entirely switch back to rx mode between consecutive transmissions (see also verification in Sect. 5.2).

Besides the nominal duration of a black burst d_{bb}, receptions of black bursts are influenced by three factors: The first factor is due to the mode of operation of the CCA mechanism. Depending on the received signal strength, the detection of the actual medium state has a variable delay of up to $d_{maxCCA} = 128\,\mu s$. This implies that a perceived medium occupancy can be d_{maxCCA} longer than the actual transmission. The second factor is in the case of multiple senders transmitting black bursts simultaneously. Because these senders may have a worst case offset of $d_{maxOffset,local}$, the perceived medium occupancy can additionally be prolonged by $d_{maxOffset,local}$. In addition, the duration d_{RX} to signal the change of the medium state by the CCA pin to the PXA 271 processor and to trigger execution of the interrupt routine has to be considered. Because in

---

[1] The duration d_{bb} is actually configurable and must be larger than d_{maxCCA}.

general d_{RX} is also variable, we investigate the upper bound $\widehat{d}_{RX}$. To receive several consecutive black bursts, we therefore formulate a second constraint:

$$d_{bit} \geq d_{bb} + d_{maxCCA} + d_{maxOffset,local} + \widehat{d}_{RX} \qquad (4.2)$$

Besides separating consecutive black bursts, a receiver must also be able to determine bit positions of black bursts inside tick frames unambiguously. Since all points in time are considered relative to the SOTF bit of the tick frame, subsequent black bursts can be received earlier as well as later than expected. The deviation of the actual reception timestamp from the expected timestamp is composed of all maximum jitters that can occur between sending a black burst and its corresponding reception and is called $\widehat{\delta}_{tr}$. Note, that only jitter has to be considered, since constant delays can be subtracted out. In particular, $\widehat{\delta}_{tr}$ consists of three factors: First, there is a jitter at sender side, which is essentially the variable part of d_{TX}. We refer to the maximum of this jitter as $\widehat{d}_{TX}^{V}$. Next, there is the delay introduced by the CCA mechanism, d_{maxCCA}. Last, there is a jitter at the receiver side between the signaling of the medium state change and the storage of the corresponding timestamp in an interrupt routine. The maximum jitter for this operation is denoted by $\widehat{d}_{RX,intr}^{V}$. In total, we have

$$\widehat{\delta}_{tr} = \widehat{d}_{TX}^{V} + d_{maxCCA} + \widehat{d}_{RX,intr}^{V} \qquad (4.3)$$

Let t_{bit} be the point in time when an arbitrary bit is expected by a receiver. Then, $t_{bit} + d_{bit}$ would denote the point in time, when the next bit is expected. Because both points can be shifted by $\pm\widehat{\delta}_{tr}$, the following constraint must hold in order to assign received black bursts correctly:

$$t_{bit} + \widehat{\delta}_{tr} < t_{bit} + d_{bit} - \widehat{\delta}_{tr} \qquad \text{,which leads us to} \qquad d_{bit} > 2 \cdot \widehat{\delta}_{tr} \qquad (4.4)$$

Refinement of Round Duration and Tick Offset. Because of the changed tick frame format (see Sect. 4.2), the duration of the SOTF bit d_{SOTF} has to be distinguished from the duration of other bits d_{bit} of a tick frame. The revised round duration is now given by

$$d_{round} = d_{SOTF} + n_{bits} \cdot d_{bit} + d_{proc}. \qquad (4.5)$$

Note that different to Eq. (3.2), d_{bit} is now set to a value fulfilling Eqs. (4.1), (4.2), and (4.4). d_{SOTF} is derived similar to d_{bit}.

Different from the original definition of the tick offset $d_{maxOffset}$ in Eq. (3.1), we additionally have to consider variable processing delays at sender and receiver nodes as described in Eq. (4.3). Thus, the upper bounds for network-wide and two-hop tick offset after resynchronization are now refined as

$$d_{maxOffset} = n_{maxHops} \cdot \widehat{\delta}_{tr} \qquad (4.6)$$

$$d_{maxOffset,local} = 2 \cdot \widehat{\delta}_{tr} \qquad (4.7)$$

5 Experimental Validation and Derivation of Timing Constraints

In this section, we present selected results from numerous experiments that have provided insights into the Imote 2 platform and all variable delays from Sect. 4.3, thereby leading to an improved design and implementation of BBS. We want to point out that the objective of this section is to determine upper bounds for variable delays and to validate timing constraints from data sheet values and *not* to evaluate our entire BBS implementation against the original implementation. In particular, a comparison would not reveal practical insights, because BBS aims at worst case bounds, and producing identical worst case evaluation scenarios for both implementations is hardly possible. However, results from functional evaluations of our BBS implementation can be found in [15].

To measure timing constraints, we intercept SPI bus, CCA pin, and SFD pin between CC 2420 and PXA 271 processor (see Fig. 1c) with an ASIX Sigma 2 logic analyzer.[2] Thus, we can monitor actual timestamps of events (such as transfers of commands) and deduce relevant delays with high accuracy. Most measured delays are subject to variation. To capture these variations, each experiment was repeated between 100 and 1000 times, depending on the objective. In all presented experiments, which ran in a laboratory, we have used the Imote 2 with 104 MHz. To mitigate interference from other networks, TX power and CCA threshold were tuned appropriately.

5.1 Maximum Switching Delay $\widehat{d}_{rxtx}$

The reliable operation of BBS requires an accurate calculation of d_{bit}. Regarding the constraint in Eq. (4.1), an upper bound of the switching delay $\widehat{d}_{rxtx}$ must be known. In the CC 2420 data sheet, the nominal default value for d_{rxtx} is given as 192 μs, but the chip can be reconfigured to use 128 μs. In the experiment presented below, we configured the chip to use 128 μs, validated the given switching delay, and determined the upper bound $\widehat{d}_{rxtx}$.

The events that are used to measure the actual switching delay are sketched in Fig. 2. During the experiment's run, these events are monitored by the logic analyzer. While the transceiver is in RX mode, switching is started at t_{STXON} when the transmission command STXON is received via the SPI bus by the CC 2420. After switching is finished, a sync header consisting of preamble (set to 8 symbols in the experiment) and SFD field (2 symbols) is transmitted. A rising edge on the SFD pin signals the end of this transmission at $t_{\ulcorner\text{SFD}}$. The actual measured switching delay, which we call Δ_{rxtx}, can now be calculated as follows:

$$\Delta_{rxtx} = t_{\ulcorner\text{SFD}} - t_{\text{STXON}} - d_{syncHdr} \tag{5.1}$$

where $d_{syncHdr} = (8 + 2) \cdot d_{sym} = 10 \cdot 16\,\mu s = 160\,\mu s$ is a constant delay, and $d_{sym} = 16\,\mu s$ is the symbol duration.

---

[2] The analyzer supports sampling frequencies of up to 200 MHz. Due to technical limitations, we had to reduce the sampling frequency in some experiments. Concrete measurement errors are provided for each experiment.

Table 1. Δ_{rxtx}: Summary of measuring results to switch from rx to tx mode

	Δ_{rxtx}	Measurement error
Minimum	128 860 ns	±10 ns
Maximum	129 000 ns	±10 ns
Range	140 ns	±20 ns
Deviation	36.91 ns	

The results of the experiment are shown in Tab. 1 and Fig. 3. The maximum switching delay $\widehat{d}_{rxtx}$ including the maximal measurement error is 129.01 µs, which is slightly higher than the data sheet value. All measured delays lie within a small range of 140 ns, thereby arguing for a high quality of $\widehat{d}_{rxtx}$. By considering the maximal observation error, we get an upper bound of the variable part of $\widehat{d}^{V}_{rxtx}$ = 160 ns. The difference between the data sheet and the measured values ($\sim$ 1 µs) was analyzed in further experiments in more detail. In these experiments, the deviation could be traced back to variable delays of processing SPI frames by the CC 2420.

5.2 Transmission of Multiple Frames in Sequence

The experiment in this section examines if the CC 2420 transceiver is able to cancel automatic transitions from tx to rx mode. This would shorten bit duration d_{bit} and improve convergence delay d_{conv}. In our setup, we use two Imote 2. The first one sends two consecutive frames. The second one tries to receive both frames and signals success. In this experiment, we used a Software Defined Radio (SDR) to record and compare the signal strength of both transmissions.

In Fig. 4, the sender's signals between CC 2420 and PXA 271, which were monitored during the experiment's runs, as well as the signal strength on the medium are shown. The end of the first transmission is detected by a falling edge of the SFD signal. This triggers an interrupt, in which the second STXON command is sent to the transceiver. This interrupt processing induces a small

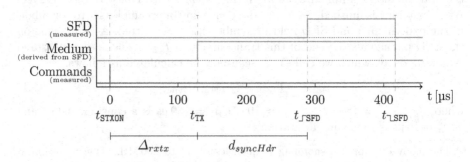

Fig. 2. Δ_{rxtx}: Measuring points and observed signal behavior

delay Δ_{proc}, which is far less than $\widehat{d}_{txrx}$. The second transmission is initialized right after the second STXON command, i.e., the transceiver does not entirely switch to rx mode, but cancels this step.

In all repetitions of our experiment, both frames could be received and decoded properly. In addition, the SDR did not show any differences in the received signal strengths. These results allow us to skip the switch back to rx mode when transmitting multiple black bursts in sequence. Therefore, our hypothesis in Sect. 4.3 is valid and we are allowed to drop d_{txrx} from the bit duration d_{bit}.

5.3   CCA Delay d_{maxCCA}

The upper bound of the CCA delay, given by d_{maxCCA}, affects bit duration d_{bit} as well as maximum tick offsets $d_{maxOffset}$ and $d_{maxOffset,local}$ of BBS. For the correct and reliable operation of BBS, it is therefore crucial that d_{maxCCA} is an upper bound and that the actual CCA delay never exceeds d_{maxCCA}.

In the following, we present results of an experiment with the focus on CCA delay. The experiment consists of two nodes: A sending node transmitting black bursts and a corresponding receiving node. The timestamps of several important events are captured by the logic analyzer, which is in this experiment connected to both nodes. In particular, we have recorded the point in time when the transmission is started by the sending node, t_{TX}, as well as the points in time when the CCA mechanism of the receiver claims the medium to be occupied or clear again, $t_{\urcorner\mathsf{LCCA}}$ and $t_{\mathsf{\Gamma CCA}}$, respectively.

From these timestamps, we derive the difference between start of a black burst transmission and its perception $\Delta_{TX\to\urcorner\mathsf{LCCA}} = t_{\urcorner\mathsf{LCCA}} - t_{TX}$. Furthermore, we calculate the perceived black burst duration $\Delta_{\urcorner\mathsf{LCCA}\to\mathsf{\Gamma CCA}} = t_{\mathsf{\Gamma CCA}} - t_{\urcorner\mathsf{LCCA}}$ and the difference between end of the black burst transmission and medium is reported clear again, $\Delta_{TXEND\to\mathsf{\Gamma CCA}} = t_{\mathsf{\Gamma CCA}} - t_{TXEND}$, where $t_{TXEND} = t_{TX} + d_{bb}$. The duration of black bursts d_{bb} is fixed to 288 µs in this experiment. The measurement is repeated over varying distances between sender and receiver.

The results are shown in Fig. 5 and allow following conclusions: First, there is no correlation between CCA delays and distance. This result can be traced back to a highly uncorrelated relation between RSSI value and distance, and

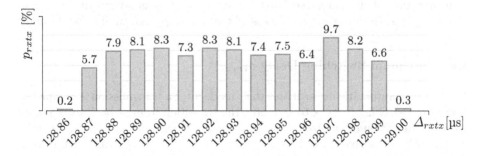

Fig. 3. Relative frequency p_{rxtx} of switching delays from rx to tx mode

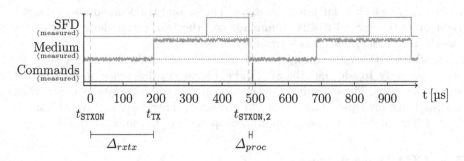

Fig. 4. Signal behavior and perceived signal strength as a function of time when transmitting two frames consecutively

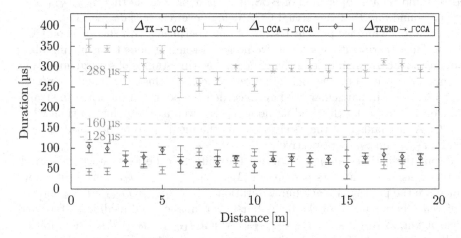

Fig. 5. Minimal, average, and maximal CCA delays as functions of distance

confirms previous work reporting on a large RSSI variability in indoor environments with multi-path fading and reflections (e.g., in [16–18]). Second, the CCA delays $\Delta_{TX \to \llcorner CCA}$ and $\Delta_{TXEND \to \ulcorner CCA}$ are always below d_{maxCCA}, and the maximum duration of the perceived black burst $\Delta_{\llcorner CCA \to \ulcorner CCA}$ is always in the range $d_{bb} \pm d_{maxCCA}$. In summary, we can assert that d_{maxCCA} is a valid upper bound.

5.4 Maximum Switching Delay $\widehat{d}_{txrx}$

The CC 2420 automatically switches to rx mode after a transmission is complete. Similar to switching from rx to tx mode, the transition from tx back to rx mode needs recalibration of the frequency generator. For this task, the data sheet of the CC 2420 transceiver gives 12 symbol durations, i.e., $d_{txrx} = 192\,\mu\text{s}$. However, since switching from rx to tx mode can be shortened to $128\,\mu\text{s}$ by configuration, it seems likely that $128\,\mu\text{s}$ are also sufficient for switching from tx to rx mode.

To check this hypothesis, we came up with an experiment, in which one node occupies the medium with a continuous signal[3] while a second node sends a regular black burst. The pin behavior of the CC 2420 transceiver of the second node was observed while and after transmission and is given in Fig. 6: At $t_{\llcorner SFD}$, the SFD pin level goes low. According to the data sheet, this denotes the end of the transmission. Shortly after, at $t_{\ulcorner CCA}$, the CCA signal is driven high which means that the transceiver claims to sense a clear medium, albeit the medium is occupied by our continuous signal. It is likely that at this point in time, the switch to rx mode is finished and the transceiver is capable of receiving data again. At $t_{\llcorner CCA}$, there is a falling edge on the CCA signal, i.e., the transceiver eventually detects the continuous medium occupancy.

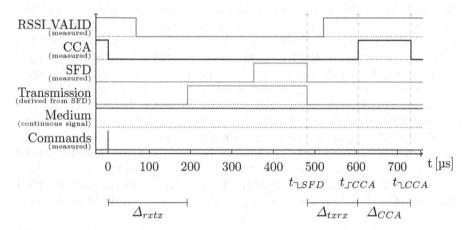

Fig. 6. Δ_{txrx}: Measuring points and observed signal behavior at the sender

To prove the hypothesis that the transceiver is ready to receive at $t_{\ulcorner CCA}$, we maximized the duration $\Delta_{CCA} = t_{\llcorner CCA} - t_{\ulcorner CCA}$ by minimizing the signal strength of our continuous signal. Thereby, we forced the CCA mechanism to exploit all eight symbol durations in d_{maxCCA} to detect the continuous signal. Thus, we can state that $t_{\ulcorner CCA}$ denotes the point in time when switching is completed and the transceiver is able to receive again, if the following observations are made:

$$\Delta_{CCA} \approx d_{maxCCA} \tag{5.2}$$

Finally, we can evaluate the switching duration from tx to rx mode as follows:

$$\Delta_{txrx} = t_{\ulcorner CCA} - t_{\llcorner SFD} \tag{5.3}$$

The results are given in Tab. 2 and show that our precondition in Eq. (5.2) is satisfied. Next, it can be seen that Δ_{txrx} is about 123.75 µs, thereby providing evidence that 128 µs are sufficient to switch from tx to rx mode. In summary, we

---

[3] We also used a CC 2420 transceiver in test mode to generate a continuous carrier.

Table 2. Δ_{txrx}: Summary of measuring results for switching from tx to rx mode

	Δ_{txrx}	Δ_{CCA}	Measurement error
Minimum	123 750 ns	128 120 ns	±5 ns
Maximum	123 755 ns	128 125 ns	±5 ns
Range	5 ns	5 ns	±10 ns
Deviation	1.614 ns	2.454 ns	

recommend to use $\widehat{d}_{txrx} = 128\,\mu s$ as upper bound, since the measured 123.75 µs are subject to component tolerance and environmental influence.

Another lesson learned from this experiment is regarding the RSSI_VALID signal, which was also captured and is shown in Fig. 6. According to the data sheet, this signal denotes whether the RSSI (Received Signal Strength Indication) value, which can be read by an SPI transfer, is valid. Since the CCA mechanism compares the RSSI value against a threshold, the RSSI_VALID signal also indicates whether the level on the CCA pin is valid. The RSSI_VALID signal is not exposed via a physical pin but must be read from an internal CC 2420 register via SPI. Though the signal is delayed, because we had to poll the state of RSSI_VALID continuously, we gain an important insight from our experiments: The RSSI_VALID signal is, as expected, driven low while transmitting, but has a rising edge already before $t_{\lceil CCA}$. This means that the signal indicates a valid RSSI value, though the transceiver is not yet ready to receive. As a resulting note, we recommend to ignore the RSSI_VALID signal and to not interpret RSSI value and CCA signal for at least $\widehat{d}_{txrx} + d_{maxCCA} = 256\,\mu s$ after a transmission.

5.5   Processing Delays

In order to guarantee reliable operation of BBS on the Imote 2 platform, we have to consider that the PXA 271 processor also induces hardware latencies. In Sect. 4.3, we refer to the upper bounds of these latencies by $\widehat{d}_{TX,pre}$, $\widehat{d}_{TX}$, $\widehat{d}_{RX}$, $\widehat{d}_{TX}^{\mathcal{V}}$, and $\widehat{d}_{RX,intr}^{\mathcal{V}}$. It is crucial that these upper bounds are not underestimated, because this would break constraints and render BBS unreliable. If, on the other hand, bounds are overestimated, we can classify the delays with respect to their consequences into two groups.

- If a delay of the first group is overestimated, this will have a negative impact on the convergence delay d_{conv}, because the bit duration d_{bit} is greater than actually needed. In particular, this is $\widehat{d}_{TX,pre}$, $\widehat{d}_{TX}$, and $\widehat{d}_{RX}$.
- If a delay of the second group is overestimated, this will have a negative impact on synchronization accuracy, i.e., the tick offsets $d_{maxOffset}$ and $d_{maxOffset,local}$. This is particularly $\widehat{d}_{TX}^{\mathcal{V}}$ and $\widehat{d}_{RX,intr}^{\mathcal{V}}$.

Since our implementation aims at robustness and accuracy (and not efficiency), we overestimated delays of the first group based on empirical data of some simple measurements and concentrated on tighter bounds for the second group.

Both quantities ($\widehat{d}^{\mathcal{V}}_{TX}$ and $\widehat{d}^{\mathcal{V}}_{RX,intr}$) include the variable delay of the processor when an interrupt is raised. We call the upper bound of the variable part of this delay $\widehat{d}^{\mathcal{V}}_{intr}$. To measure $\widehat{d}^{\mathcal{V}}_{intr}$, we conducted an experiment with one Imote 2, where we triggered an interrupt by creating an edge to a GPIO pin. The interrupt handler on the PXA 271 answers this interrupt request by generating an edge on another GPIO pin. Thus, we can monitor the input and output event with a logic analyzer and measure the reaction delay (denoted by Δ_{intr}). Note, that the duration to emit the output edge is also included in the measured duration by this approach.

The measurement results are shown in Tab. 3. The overall reaction delay is approx. 4.1 µs which is quite long compared to a CPU clock cycle of just 9.62 ns. The range, which is essentially the variable part of Δ_{intr}, is however only 80 ns with a maximum observation error of 10 ns. From this, we can deduce

Table 3. Δ_{intr}: Measuring results for interrupt reaction delay

	Δ_{intr}	Measurement error
Minimum	4 075 ns	±5 ns
Maximum	4 155 ns	±5 ns
Range	80 ns	±10 ns

$$\widehat{d}^{\mathcal{V}}_{RX,intr} = \widehat{d}^{\mathcal{V}}_{intr} = 90\,\text{ns}$$

$$\widehat{d}^{\mathcal{V}}_{TX} = \widehat{d}^{\mathcal{V}}_{intr} + \widehat{d}^{\mathcal{V}}_{rxtx} = 90\,\text{ns} + 160\,\text{ns} = 250\,\text{ns},$$

where $\widehat{d}^{\mathcal{V}}_{rxtx}$ is the variable part of Δ_{rxtx} as determined in Sect. 5.1.

Further experiments revealed that $\widehat{d}^{\mathcal{V}}_{intr}$ highly depends on processor workload. For example, if software on the PXA 271 has periodic bursty workloads, the range is increased up to 10.4 µs. Therefore, we identified sources of jitter and elaborated on countermeasures to keep the variable delay low:[4]

- If an interrupt request is raised, while an older interrupt is being served, the later one will be deferred until the first one is completely handled. Since we roughly know the points in time when black bursts are expected (namely during synchronization phases), we can assure that only relevant interrupts are handled during this time by simply masking all uninvolved interrupts.
- Whenever an interrupt is raised, the CPU instruction currently in execution stage must be completed. Depending on the type of the instruction, the duration until completion can vary significantly. This especially holds for memory operations. To counteract this, we make sure that there is no such instruction executed when a black burst is expected by taking control over the processor in advance.
- When finally the CPU begins serving the interrupt, it is critical whether the code and data of the interrupt routine is already available in the cache or if it must be transferred from backing memory first. Due to PXA 271's cache eviction strategy, it is unpredictable in practice, whether a specific datum is held in cache after executing arbitrary program code. As a countermeasure, we used the cache locking feature of the PXA 271 core, thereby guaranteeing that required instructions and data are always held in cache.

---

[4] The evaluation of these proposals can be found in [15].

6   Conclusions and Outlook

For the implementation of deterministic protocols, knowledge about timing constraints and hardware platform is crucial. In this paper, we have presented our Imote 2 implementation and experimental validation of BBS, a deterministic synchronization protocol for ad-hoc networks with bounded tick offset and convergence delay. During our work, we have identified additional sources of delay that have an impact on the offset and delay bounds of BBS, but have not been considered in the original papers [1, 2]. We have analyzed these sources of delay and refined the original formulas to include hardware latencies. In numerous experiments, we have quantified these delays and used the obtained values to improve the robustness of our implementation.

During the implementation of BBS, we gained the experience that implementing deterministic protocols requires a holistic approach taking all characteristics of the underlying hardware into account. Due to optimization techniques in modern hardware tackling the improvement of the average case, many delays can only be determined empirically. Therefore our results can not easily be transferred to other hardware. However, the approach to deal with hardware characteristics and additional delays may be helpful for implementations on other platforms and/or of other protocols.

Regarding the Imote 2 platform, an important finding was the inaccuracy or even incorrectness of data sheet values. This particularly holds for the CC 2420 transceiver, for which we found that switching to rx mode requires less time than stated in the data sheet (about 128 μs instead of 192 μs). On the other hand, additional jitter has to be considered, which is introduced by the transceiver to process commands received via SPI and during interrupt handling. To cope with these problems, validation experiments are indispensable. Though our discussion and evaluation mainly concentrate on BBS for Imote 2, the results also show that other protocols can benefit from attentive considerations of hardware characteristics. This holds particularly for all protocols relying on correct transceiver behavior. In this regard, our experiments revealed a crucial problem of the CC 2420's RSSI_VALID signal, which may lead to a misinterpretation of the current channel state, and may be a problem for CSMA-based protocols.

Albeit we have a working BBS implementation, we are looking for more efficient and accurate implementations with dedicated hardware and Software Defined Radios (SDRs). Such hardware can be customized for transmission of black bursts, thereby considerably improving convergence delay as well as offset.

References

1. Gotzhein, R., Kuhn, T.: Black Burst Synchronization (BBS) - A Protocol for Deterministic Tick and Time Synchronization in Wireless Networks. Computer Networks 55(13), 3015–3031 (2011)
2. Gotzhein, R., Kuhn, T.: Decentralized Tick Synchronization for Multi-Hop Medium Slotting in Wireless Ad Hoc Networks Using Black Bursts. In: 5th Annual

IEEE Communications Society Conference on Sensor, Mesh and Ad Hoc Communications and Networks, SECON 2008, pp. 422–431. IEEE, San Francisco (June 2008)

3. Institute of Electrical and Electronics Engineers: IEEE Standard 802 Part 15.4: Low-Rate Wireless Personal Area Networks (LR-WPANs). IEEE Computer Society, New York (June 2011)

4. Institute of Electrical and Electronics Engineers: IEEE Standard 802 Part 11: Wireless LAN Medium Access Control (MAC) nad Physical Layer (PHY) Specifications. IEEE Computer Society, New York (February 2012)

5. Elson, J., Girod, L., Estrin, D.: Fine-Grained Network Time Synchronization Using Reference Broadcasts. In: OSDI, Proceedings of the Fifth Symposium on Operating Systems Design and Implementation (OSDI 2002), Boston, MA, USA (2002)

6. Ganeriwal, S., Kumar, R., Srivastava, M.B.: Timing-sync protocol for sensor networks. In: Akyildiz, I.F., Estrin, D., Culler, D.E., Srivastava, M.B. (eds.) SenSys, pp. 138–149. ACM (2003)

7. Sommer, P., Wattenhofer, R.: Gradient clock synchronization in wireless sensor networks. In: Proceedings of the 2009 International Conference on Information Processing in Sensor Networks, IPSN 2009, pp. 37–48. IEEE Computer Society, Washington, DC (2009)

8. Ringwald, M., Römer, K.: BitMAC: A Deterministic, Collision-free, and Robust MAC Protocol for Sensor Networks. In: Proceedings of Second European Workshop on Wireless Sensor Networks (EWSN 2005), Istanbul, Turkey, pp. 57–69 (2005)

9. Texas Instruments: BTnodes - A Distributed Environment for Prototyping Ad Hoc Networks (web page), http://www.btnode.ethz.ch/

10. Pereira, N., Andersson, B., Tovar, E.: WiDom: A Dominance Protocol for Wireless Medium Access. IEEE Trans. Industrial Informatics 3(2), 120–130 (2007)

11. Pereira, N., Andersson, B., Tovar, E., Rowe, A.: Static-Priority Scheduling over Wireless Networks with Multiple Broadcast Domains. In: RTSS 2007: Proceedings of the 28th IEEE International Real-Time Systems Symposium, pp. 447–458. IEEE Computer Society, Washington, DC (2007)

12. MEMSIC Inc.: MICAz datasheet, http://www.memsic.com/support/documentation/wireless-sensor-networks/category/7-datasheets.html?download=148 (2013); Revision B

13. MEMSIC Inc.: Imote 2 datasheet, http://www.memsic.com/support/documentation/wireless-sensor-networks/category/7-datasheets.html?download=134%3Aimote2 (2013)

14. Texas Instruments: CC2420 datasheet, Revision SWRS041c (2013)

15. Engel, M.: Optimierung und Evaluation Black Burst-basierter Protkolle unter Verwendung der Imote 2-Plattform. Master's thesis, TU Kaiserslautern (2013)

16. Vanheel, F., Verhaevert, J., Laermans, E., Moerman, I., Demeester, P.: Automated linear regression tools improve RSSI WSN localization in multipath indoor environmentlymbero. EURASIP Journal on Wireless Communications and Networking 2011(1), 1–27 (2011)

17. Lymberopoulos, D., Lindsey, Q., Savvides, A.: An Empirical Characterization of Radio Signal Strength Variability in 3-D IEEE 802.15.4 Networks Using Monopole Antennas. In: Römer, K., Karl, H., Mattern, F. (eds.) EWSN 2006. LNCS, vol. 3868, pp. 326–341. Springer, Heidelberg (2006)

18. Azenha, A., Peneda, L., Carvalho, A.: Error analysis in indoors localization using ZigBee wireless networks. In: IECON 2010 - 36th Annual Conference on IEEE Industrial Electronics Society, pp. 2193–2197 (2010)

SOFA: Communication
in Extreme Wireless Sensor Networks

Marco Cattani*, Marco Zuniga, Matthias Woehrle, and Koen Langendoen

Delft University of Technology, Delft, The Netherlands
{m.cattani,m.zuniga,matthias.woehrle,k.g.langendoen}@tudelft.nl

Abstract. Sensor networks can nowadays deliver 99.9% of their data
with duty cycles below 1%. This remarkable performance is, however,
dependent on some important underlying assumptions: low traffic rates,
medium size densities and static nodes. In this paper, we investigate the
performance of these same resource-constrained devices, but under scenarios that present extreme conditions: high traffic rates, high densities
and mobility. To cope with these stringent requirements, we propose a
novel communication protocol named SOFA (Stop On First Ack). SOFA
utilizes opportunistic anycast to drastically reduce the rendezvous times
of asynchronous duty cycled nodes –long rendezvous times are the key
limitation of protocols operating under high densities and high traffic
conditions. SOFA is also stateless, which makes it resilient to mobility.
We implemented SOFA in the Contiki OS and tested it both in simulation and on a 100-node testbed. Our results show that SOFA reliably
communicates in mobile networks with extreme densities (hundreds of
nodes) and higher traffic rates (packets per second) while maintaining
a low duty cycle ($\approx$2%). Under these extreme conditions, current duty
cycled protocols collapse.

1 Introduction

Hitherto, the protocol stack of wireless sensor networks has been mainly designed
and optimized for applications satisfying one or more of the following conditions:
(i) low traffic rates (a packet per node every few minutes), (ii) medium sized densities (tens of neighbors), and (iii) static topologies. There are, however, many
scenarios where these relatively mild network conditions do not hold and traditional protocol stacks simply collapse. We consider mobile networks consisting of
hundreds of thousands of nodes with hundreds of neighbors that need to disseminate information at a relatively high rate (a packet per node every few seconds,
instead of every few minutes).

Our work is motivated by a scenario related to public safety: the need to
monitor crowds in open-air festivals. SOFA is part of the EWiDS project aimed at
providing attendees with coin-size devices that can actively monitor the density
of their surroundings and issue alerts when crossing dangerous thresholds.

---

* Marco Cattani was supported by the Dutch national program COMMIT\.

B. Krishnamachari, A.L. Murphy, and N. Trigoni (Eds.): EWSN 2014, LNCS 8354, pp. 100–115, 2014.
© Springer International Publishing Switzerland 2014

From a networking perspective, communication in mobile scenarios with high traffic rates and high densities poses several non-trivial technical challenges. First, similar to traditional WSN, these Extreme Wireless Sensor Networks (EWSN) also work with devices with limited energy resources and need to rely on radio duty-cycling techniques to save energy. Second, due to the network scale and node mobility, we cannot rely on methods that combine duty cycling techniques with central coordinators [8] or that require some level of synchronization between the wake up periods of a given node and its neighbors [7,17]. The system must be asynchronous and fully distributed. Third, due to their inefficient bandwidth utilization, traditional unicast and broadcast primitives –which are asynchronous, distributed and built on top of duty cycling techniques [3,16]– simply collapse under the traffic-demands of EWSN.

Henceforth, providing an energy-efficient communication primitive in EWSN requires a careful evaluation of the following problem: in asynchronous duty cycling techniques, much of the bandwidth is wasted in coordinating the rendezvous of the (sleeping) nodes. In EWSN, nodes need to reduce this overhead to free up the channel's bandwidth for actual *data* transmissions.

To tackle this problem, SOFA (*Stop on First Ack*) introduces a bi-directional communication primitive called *opportunistic anycast*. This primitive establishes a data exchange with the *first* neighbor to wake up. In this way, SOFA avoids the need for neighborhood discovery and minimizes the inefficient rendezvous time typical of asynchronous MAC protocols.

By selecting opportunistically the next neighbor to communicate with, SOFA provides a perfect building block for gossiping algorithms [2,14,13]. Gossiping techniques have been proven to be particularly suitable to disseminate information in large-scale distributed systems. Overall, SOFA offers an alternative to the traditional protocol stack, that cannot operate in extreme sensor networks.

We implemented SOFA in Contiki and evaluated it through a series of experiments on a 100-node testbed, and with Cooja simulations (considering mobility and densities of up to 450 nodes). Overall, our study makes the following three key contributions:

- We introduce EWSN and the problem of communicating in such networks.
- We present the design, implementation and evaluation of SOFA, a communication protocol that utilizes *opportunistic anycast* to overcome the limitations of inefficient rendezvous mechanisms. SOFA combines the energy efficiency typical of low-power MAC protocols with the robustness and versatility of gossip-like communication.
- We show that SOFA can successfully deliver messages, regardless of mobility, in networks with densities of hundreds of nodes while maintaining the duty cycle at approximately 2%.

2   Related Work

The constrained energy resources of WSN led to a first generation of protocols that traded bandwidth utilization for lower energy consumption. Such protocols are based on asynchronous radio duty-cycling methods, which implies that senders need to wait for their receiver to wake up (to rendezvous), before sending their data. While in low power listening (LPL) [3] nodes send a beaconing sequence until the receiver wakes up, in low power probing (LPP) [5,16], the sender waits for a wakeup beacon from the receiver.

The WSN community is well aware of the limitations of the first generation of low-power protocols and several notable contributions have improved their performance. To reduce the overhead of the rendezvous phase, protocols such as WiseMAC [7] keep track of the wakeup periods of their neighbors and use this information to wakeup just a few instants before the intended receiver. This type of protocols works very well on stable networks, where the overhead of estimating the wake periods is seldom done. Highly mobile scenarios, however, prevent the use of these methods.

Another efficient way to disseminate information has been recently proposed by Ferrari et al. [8]. By using a finely synchronized TDMA mechanism, together with extremely efficient network-wide floods, the authors are able to disseminate information irrespective of mobility. However, their low-power wireless bus requires a central coordinator and a network with limited diameter (the synchronization degrades as the number of hops increases). The wide scale (graph diameter) of EWSN prevents the use of this approach, and the central coordinator exposes a single point of failure.

2.1   The Need for Opportunistic Communication

Several notable studies have identified the important role that opportunistic communication has on improving the performance of low-power WSN. In essence, the key idea of these studies is the following: instead of waiting for a predefined node to wake up, opportunistically transmit to who is available now. In ORW [10], the authors propose to use anycast communication to improve the performance of CTP [9], the de-facto data collection protocol in WSN. In Backcast [6], the authors show that by using anycast communication, the capture effect can be leveraged to increase the probability of receiving an ack from a viable receiver. While SOFA is motivated and inspired by these studies, there is an important difference. We do not use opportunistic anycast to improve the performance of traditional network protocols under mild conditions, but to enable a new communication protocol that scales to EWSN. To summarize we make the following observations:

- Basic asynchronous low-power MAC protocols collapse under the densities and traffic demands of extreme wireless sensor networks.
- Mobility prevents the use of more complex and efficient low-power MACs.
- Opportunistic behaviors are needed to scale to EWSN.

3   SOFA Mechanism

The design of SOFA follows two main goals: reduce the inefficient rendezvous phase of low-power MAC protocols, and guarantee that the dissemination of

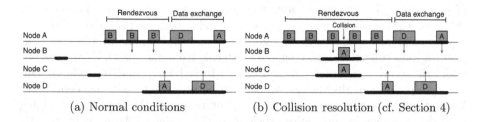

(a) Normal conditions   (b) Collision resolution (cf. Section 4)

Fig. 1. SOFA mechanism

data is performed in an efficient and reliable way. To satisfy these goals, SOFA implements an efficient communication primitive, called *opportunistic anycast*, that minimizes the rendezvous overhead and natively supports Gossip, a robust data dissemination technique created for large-scale networks.

Before proceeding it is important to remark that SOFA focuses on maximizing the messages exchanged locally among neighbors (1-hop), leaving the multi-hop dissemination and aggregation of information to the Gossip layer.

3.1   The Basic Idea

The general idea of SOFA can be applied to any asynchronous duty cycled MAC protocol. Due to space constraints, we focus our analysis on the LPL version of SOFA. The reason is that this implementation performs better in extreme densities, especially in terms of reliability. Nevertheless, in Appendix A, we will provide some insight on the LPP implementation.

Rendezvous Phase: In traditional LPL protocols [3], when a sender wakes up, it transmits a series of short packets –called beacons– and waits for the receiver to wake up. When the intended receiver wakes up, it hears the latest beacon and sends an acknowledgement back. SOFA follows a similar mechanism: the sender, node A in Figure 1(a), also broadcasts a series of beacons but only waits until *any* neighbor wakes up. The main difference between the two mechanisms lays in the selection of the destination. While in LPL the destination is chosen by the upper layers in the stack, in SOFA the MAC protocol opportunistically chooses the destination that is most efficient to reach: the first neighbor to wake up. If nodes B or C were to be chosen, node A would need to send beacons (jam the channel) until these nodes wake up again. By sending its data to the first neighbor that wakes up (node D), SOFA reduces the nodes' rendezvous time, allowing low-power MAC protocols to efficiently scale to EWSN. We call this communication primitive *opportunistic anycast*.

Data Exchange Phase: Selecting the first (random) neighbor that wakes up as *the* destination, has a strong relation with a family of randomized networking algorithms called gossiping [2,14]. *Gossip algorithms do not aim for traditional end-to-end communication* (where routes are formed and maintained ahead of time), instead they exchange information randomly with a neighbor (or subset of neighbors). The relation between SOFA and Gossiping is fundamental for the practical impact of our work. Unicast and broadcast primitives allow the development of a wide-range of algorithms and applications in WSN such as routing, data collection, querying and clustering (to name a few). Unfortunately, under the stringent characteristics of EWSN these basic primitives collapse. Our aim is to provide an alternative communication protocol for extreme conditions. We hope that this effort will allow the community to use SOFA as a basic building block for other gossip applications such as routing in delay tolerant networks [15] and landscaping of data [11].

We will now describe the design of the three key characteristics of SOFA: *short rendezvous phase, reliable push-pull data exchange,* and *random peer sampling.* The design of a short rendezvous phase was influenced by the limitations of asynchronous duty cycled protocols. The push-pull data exchange and the random peer sampling were designed to satisfy the needs of general gossiping applications.

3.2   Short Rendezvous Phase

Stopping at the first encounter, instead of searching for a specific destination, has two important consequences on the performance of SOFA. First, and most importantly, it eliminates the main limitation that LPL has under extreme networking conditions: channel inefficiency. By drastically reducing the length of the rendezvous phase, the channel no longer gets easily saturated by medium/high traffic demands or medium/high node densities. A short rendezvous phase also reduces the duty cycle of the radio, which in turn, increases the lifetime of the node. Second, increasing the network's density (up to a point) improves the performance of SOFA. With more neighbors, the probability that one will soon wake up is higher.

To quantify the benefits of a short rendezvous phase, we present a simple model that captures the expected duration of the rendezvous phase as a function of the neighborhood size and the wakeup period (the time elapsed between two consecutive wake-ups of a node). Since nodes wake up periodically in a completely desynchronized way, we can model the inter-arrival times of the nodes' wake-ups as a set of independent random variables with uniform distribution. The first order statistic U_1 can then be used to estimate the length of the rendezvous phase. The expected length $E[U_1]$ of N uniform random variables (neighbors) is given by the Beta random variable with parameters $\alpha=1$ and $\beta=N$

$$U_1 \sim B(1, N), \quad E[U_1] = \frac{1}{1 + N}$$

Given a wakeup period W and a neighborhood size N, the expected length of the rendezvous phase of SOFA can be computed as follows:

$$E[s] = \frac{W}{1 + N} \qquad (1)$$

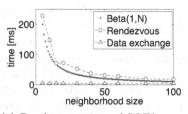

(a) Rendezvous time of SOFA compared to the Beta model

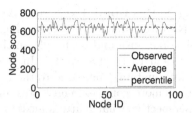

(b) Node selection. The score shows how many times each node is selected (cf. Section 3.4)

Fig. 2. SOFA rendezvous phase (testbed results)

Considering that the expected rendezvous time of unicast $E[u]$ is $W/2$ [3,12] and that the time spent for the data exchange phase is negligible compared to the rendezvous (see Figure 2(a)), we can model the gain G of SOFA compared to unicast as the following:

$$G = \frac{E[s]}{E[u]} = \frac{W}{1+N}\frac{2}{W} = \frac{2}{1+N}$$

For a node with 99 neighbors, this means that the expected rendezvous times of SOFA is 50 times smaller than the one using unicast. Figure 2(a) compares the expected length of the rendezvous phase using the proposed model with values observed in testbed experiments. In this example, $W=1$ s and the neighborhood size ranges from 5 to 100 nodes. The slight underestimation is mainly due to collisions, which delay the detection of the first node by the sender.

It is important to highlight three key points about the impact of density on SOFA. First, since the performance of SOFA is not significantly affected by changes in medium/high densities, SOFA does not need to adapt to this type of density fluctuations in mobile networks. Second, to reduce the duration of the rendezvous phase in low density networks, the wakeup period can be reduced (at the cost of increasing the duty cycle). This trade-off is studied in more detail in Section 5.3. Finally, in case the network switches from an extreme condition to a normal one (low density), the protocol stack can switch to the use of standard broadcast and unicast messages. To detect the density of the network, SOFA can exploit the tight correlation between the number of neighbors and the expected length of the rendezvous phase (Equation 1).

3.3   Reliable Push-pull Data Exchange

To exchange data efficiently and reliably, SOFA has two phases: a 2-way rendezvous phase and a 3-way data exchange phase. These phases are shown in Figure 1(a) and their design is driven by two factors: (i) the high relative cost of the rendezvous phase compared to the data-exchange phase, and (ii) the effect of unreliable and asymmetric links on the *constant mass* requirement of gossip's *data-aggregation* algorithms. The effect of these factors is explained below.

Using a Push-pull Exchange Amortizes the High Relative Cost of the Rendezvous Phase. Gossiping algorithms have two types of data communication: push and push-pull. In the push method, only the sender transfers information to the receiver(s). In the push-pull method, two nodes exchange their information. Compared to the latter, push-pull allows gossip algorithms to compute more complex aggregates and converge faster [4]. Nevertheless, from our perspective what matters most is the relative cost of the rendezvous phase. Given that the cost of this phase is high compared to the data exchange phase, it is beneficial to exchange as much information as possible once two nodes rendezvous. For this reason, SOFA implements a push-pull approach. A push approach would double the overhead of the rendezvous phase, making SOFA less resilient to extreme conditions.

The 2-way Rendezvous Phase Filters Out Asymmetric and Unreliable Links, While the 3-way Handshake Reduces the Probability of Losing "Gossip Mass". Losing messages has a particularly detrimental effect on the accuracy of gossiping. For example, when two nodes agree to swap half their value (mass), the loss of a message results in a too low value on the node that missed it, which influences the outcome of all the other nodes as the error propagates in consecutive rounds. The conservation of mass is, thus, an important issue in gossiping algorithms. From a design perspective, this means that we need to consider two important points. First, nodes should avoid the use of unreliable and asymmetric links (which have been shown to be commonplace in WSN [18]). Second, if a packet is lost, we have to reduce the chances of losing mass.

The 2-way rendezvous phase reduces the chance of using unreliable and asymmetric links. Several studies have shown that unreliable links are usually asymmetric (and vice versa) [18]. On the other hand, bidirectional links are usually characterized by being more reliable. By performing a 2-way exchange before transmitting the actual data, SOFA increases the chances of using a reliable link. It is important to remark that some LPL methods do not follow this approach [12]. These methods piggyback the data on the beacons and acknowledgement packets, that is, they transmit information without checking first if the link is reliable and symmetric or not.

The 3-way data exchange phase reduces the chance of losing mass in the event that a packet is lost. In spite of our efforts to filter out unreliable and asymmetric links during the rendezvous phase, the high temporal variability of low-power links can cause a reliable link to become momentarily unreliable. In the event that a packet is lost, the worst situation for two nodes is to disagree on the outcome of an event. That is, two nodes should either agree that the message exchange was successful (both nodes received the mass) or agree that no message was exchanged (aborting the exchange). If only one node deems the event as successful, then the mass of the other is lost. The latter situation happens when the last packet of an n-way handshake is lost. This (dis)agreement problem is discussed in depth in [1], and the authors prove that in WSN the best strategy to reduce disagreements is to use a 3-way handshake.

3.4   Random Peer Sampling

Most gossip algorithms rely on the selection of a *random* neighbor (or subset of neighbors) at each round. Having a good random selection leads to a faster convergence. To ensure a proper random selection, SOFA introduces random values to the wakeup periods of each node. For a wakeup period of W seconds, nodes wake up uniformly at random between $[0.5W, 1.5W]$.

To validate the effectiveness of our approach, we performed an experiment on a 100-node testbed. For 10 minutes nodes exchange messages and count the number of times they are selected by their neighbors (their *score*). Figure 2(b) shows that the distribution of the scores is close to uniform, with the [5, 95] percentiles close to the average value. It is important to remark that this evaluation was performed on a static testbed. Mobility would further randomize the selection of neighbors, facilitating the dissemination of data, and drastically reducing the convergence time of Gossip [13].

4   Implementation

We implemented SOFA on the Contiki OS based on X-MAC [3]. Nodes were configured to wakeup every second for 10 ms. If a beacon is received within this 10 ms period, the node sends an acknowledgement and starts the data exchange phase. Otherwise, the node goes back to sleep. Notice that these parameters set a minimum duty cycle of 1 %, hence, any extra activity beyond this point is part of the overhead caused by the rendezvous and data exchange phases. Below we describe the implementation of the most important features of SOFA.

Transmit Back-off. In traditional MAC protocols, before sending a packet, a transmitter first checks the signal level of the channel (CCA check) to see if there is any activity. If no activity is detected the packet is sent. In SOFA, we do not perform a CCA check. Instead, a potential sender listens to the channel for 10 ms acting, practically, as a receiver. If after this period no packet is detected, the node starts the rendezvous phase. If the node detects a packet that is part of an on-going data exchange, it goes back to sleep (collision avoidance). However, if the detected packet is a beacon, the node changes its role from sender to receiver. By performing a transmit back-off instead of a CCA check, *SOFA transforms a possible collision between two senders into a successful message exchange with a very low rendezvous cost.*

Collision Avoidance. One of the key challenges of operating under extreme density conditions is the higher likelihood of collisions due to higher traffic demands. SOFA follows a simple guideline to reduce the frequency of collisions: if a sender detects a packet loss –for instance, by not receiving an ack–, instead of attempting a retransmission, the node goes back to sleep. This *conservative approach* reduces the traffic in highly dense networks. The main caveat of this approach is when the lost packet is the last data ack. In this case, the two parties will disagree on the data delivery, causing an information (*mass*) loss. Fortunately, our testbed results show that this is not a frequent event.

There is a collision event that is not avoided by the above mentioned approach and has a higher probability of occurrence in SOFA. When two or more active receivers detect a beacon, their ACKs are likely to collide (cf. nodes B and C in Figure 1(b)). The sender will receive neither of the ACKs and will consequently continue transmitting beacons. Upon receiving a subsequent beacon (not the expected data packet), the two colliding receivers infer that a collision has occurred and both will go back to sleep. The first node to wake up after the collision (node D) will acknowledge the beacon and exchanges its data. Finally, randomizing the wake up periods of nodes helps in reducing the chances that this type of collisions occurs repeatedly among the same couples of nodes.

Packet Addressing. SOFA uses two main types of data packets. For the rendezvous phase, the beacons have no destination address, any node can receive and process the information. For the data exchange phase, the packets contain the destination address of the involved parties. The beacon packets were as small as possible (IEEE 802.15.4 header + 1 byte to define the packet type and 1 byte when addressing is needed).

5 Results

To evaluate the effectiveness of SOFA we ran an extensive set of experiments and simulations. Our testbed has 108 nodes installed above the ceiling tiles of an office building. The wireless nodes are equipped with a MSP430 micro-controller and a CC1101 radio chip. To reach the highest possible neighborhood size, we set the transmission power to +10 dBm. With these settings, the network is almost a clique. For our simulations we used Cooja, the standard simulator for Contiki. We tested network densities of up to 450 nodes and different mobility patterns. Simulations beyond this density value are not possible with normal cluster computing facilities. For both experiments and simulations, the baseline scenario was configured to have a wake up period $W=1$ s and a transmission period $T=2$ s. That is, nodes wake up every second to act as receivers and every two seconds to act as senders. Considering that nodes listen for packet activity at each wakeup for 10 ms, the baseline duty-cycle is $\approx 1\%$. Any extra consumption beyond 1 % is caused by SOFA. The evaluation results presented in this section consider also other values for W and T, but unless stated otherwise the experiments are carried out using the baseline parameters. The results are averaged over 20 runs of 10 minutes each.

5.1 Performance Metrics

The evaluation of SOFA focuses on three key areas: energy consumption, bandwidth utilization and *mass* conservation. To capture the performance of SOFA in these areas, we utilize the following metrics:

Duty Cycle. The percentage of time that the radio is active. Duty-cycle is a widely utilized proxy for energy consumption in WSN because radio activity accounts for most of the energy consumption in WSN nodes.

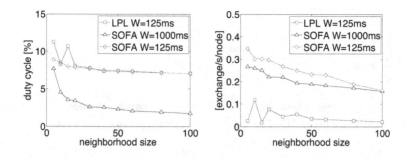

Fig. 3. SOFA compared to LPL (testbed results)

Exchange Rate. The number of successful data-exchanges (3-way handshakes) in a second. This is a per-node metric. If, instead, we count the total number of data exchanges in a second over the entire network we refer to the *global exchange rate*.

Mass Delivery Ratio. The percentage of times that the data-exchange phase ends up without any information loss. Recall that if the ack of the data phase is lost, the receiver deems the exchange as successful, but the sender deems the exchange as unsuccessful and ignores the previously received packet (mass loss). The *mass delivery ratio* is a metric focused on evaluating the viability of SOFA as a basic communication primitive to general gossip algorithms.

5.2   The Need for a Novel Approach

Previously in this paper, we argued that traditional low-power methods collapse under the stress imposed by extreme networking conditions. This subsection quantifies this claim. We compare SOFA with the standard Contiki implementation of LPL on our testbed. To provide a fair comparison, LPL chooses a random neighbor from a pre-computed list of destinations at every transmission request. That is, we do not enforce on LPL the necessary neighbor discovery process that would be needed to obtain the destination address (SOFA does not need an address to bootstrap the communication).

Figure 3 compares the duty cycle and the exchange rate of SOFA and LPL in our testbed. For LPL, the evaluation shows only the result for $W=125\,ms$ because LPL collapses with the baseline $W=1\,s$. This collapsing occurs because, with $W=1\,s$, the rendezvous phase of LPL requires on average $0.5\,s$. Hence, 5 nodes require on average a 2.5-seconds window to transmit their data, but the transmission period is $2\,s$, which leads to channel saturation. Comparing the best parameter for LPL ($W=125\,ms$) with the best parameter for SOFA ($W=1\,s$) shows that SOFA widely outperforms LPL. For most neighborhood sizes (30 and above), SOFA uses four times less energy and delivers five times more packets for the same T.

It is important to remark that SOFA is not a substitute for traditional low power methods, as they aim at providing different services. SOFA cannot provide

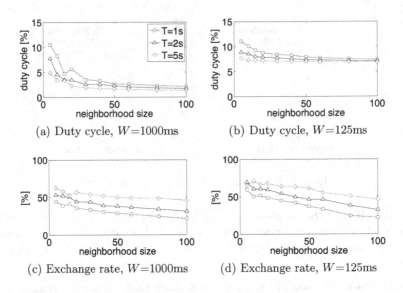

(a) Duty cycle, $W=1000$ms   (b) Duty cycle, $W=125$ms

(c) Exchange rate, $W=1000$ms   (d) Exchange rate, $W=125$ms

Fig. 4. Testbed performance for different wake-up times W and transmission periods T. Note that the *exchange rate* is normalized to T.

several of the functionalities required by applications relying on unicast and broadcast primitives. Most WSN applications are designed for data gathering applications sending a few packets per minute. In these scenarios, the state-of-the-art in WSN research performs remarkably well. The aim of our comparison is to highlight that traditional methods were not designed to operate under extreme conditions neither to efficiently support Gossip applications. We will now analyze the performance of SOFA based on different parameters and scenarios.

5.3   Exploring SOFA Parameters

SOFA is a simple protocol with only two parameters available for fine-tuning: the wakeup period W and the transmission period T. We now evaluate the performance of SOFA as a function of these parameters. The results of this subsection are all based on testbed experiments. Figure 4 shows the performance of SOFA for two different wakeup periods (125 and 1000 ms), and for three different transmission periods (1, 2 and 5 seconds).

The Impact of the Transmission Period T. Let us start by analyzing the impact of T on the duty cycle. Figure 4(a) shows two important trends. First, beyond a certain neighborhood size (≈ 30), T does not have a significant impact on the duty cycle. Decreasing the transmission period certainly increases the duty cycle of the node, but not by much. Second, in low/medium dense networks (below 30 neighbors), increasing T has a more significant effect on the duty cycle, but it is still a sub-linear relation. An increment of T by a factor of five, increases the duty cycle by only a factor of two. The reason for the difference in duty cycle between low/medium and high density networks, is that at lower densities, SOFA spends more time on the rendezvous phase. This implies a higher overhead at each transmission attempt. Conversely, increasing the density increases the likelihood of finding a receiver sooner.

Note that, thanks to the *transmit back-off mechanism* (which changes the role of senders to receivers to reduce collisions), increasing the transmission rate decreases the length of the rendezvous phase. With nodes sending data more often, the probability that two senders are active at the same time is higher. While in a normal MAC protocol this would lead to collisions, in SOFA it translates into an efficient message exchange (the rendezvous time is minimal) among the two senders. As for the impact of T on the relative exchange rate, SOFA behaves as most protocols do when they work under high traffic demands: the higher the traffic rate, the more saturated the channel, and the lower the probability to exchange information. This trend is observed in Figure 4(c). It is important to notice, however, that the exchange rate decreases in a gentle manner.

The Impact of the Wake Period Period W. Intuitively, reducing the wakeup period should reduce the rendezvous time (because nodes wakeup more frequently), which in turn should free up bandwidth and allow a higher exchange rate. However, the trade-off for a more efficient use of bandwidth would be a higher duty cycle. Figures 4(b) and (d) show the performance of SOFA with a wakeup period W=125 ms. With this value, the baseline duty cycle is 8%. The figures show that reducing W does increase the relative exchange rate, but mainly on low/medium dense networks (by $\approx 50\%$). Therefore, it is possible to improve the performance of SOFA in low density networks at the cost of increasing the energy consumption. For high density networks, however, we have a similar throughput but with a duty cycle that is four times higher.

5.4 SOFA under Extreme Densities and in Mobile Scenarios

The previous testbed results show that SOFA performs well in densities as high as 100 neighbors. However, from a practical perspective it is important to determine (i) the saturation point of SOFA, i.e., how many nodes SOFA can handle before saturating the bandwidth, and (ii) the impact of mobility. Unfortunately, there are no large-scale mobile testbeds available in the community, and hence, we rely on the Cooja simulator to investigate these aspects.

SOFA Shows a Strong Resilience to Extreme Densities. Figures 5(a) and (c) show the prior testbed results together with the simulation results. These results consider clique networks for both the testbed and simulation results. First, it is important to notice that Cooja captures, in a pretty accurate way, the trends observed on the testbed. Figure 5(a) shows that the duty cycle continues to decrease (almost monotonically) and stabilize after a density of more than 100 neighbors. Figure 5(c) shows that the exchange rate degrades monotonically but in a graceful manner (notice that the x-axis is in a log scale).

There is, however, a more important question to answer about SOFA: *at what density does it saturate?* The clique curves (bottom two curves) in Figure 5(d)

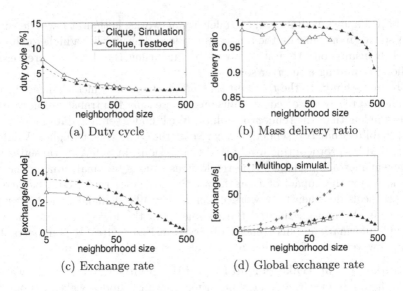

(a) Duty cycle

(b) Mass delivery ratio

(c) Exchange rate

(d) Global exchange rate

Fig. 5. SOFA's performance in extreme network conditions (testbed and simulation results)

provide some insight into this question. In these experiments, we evaluated the global exchange rate at different densities. For the tested parameters, SOFA saturates when the density approaches 200 neighbors per node. Note that these are clique scenarios. In multi-hop networks, SOFA can exploit the well known spatial multiplexing effect (parallel data exchanges) and achieve higher global exchange rates. The top curve in 5(d) depicts this behavior. The highest point represents a network with 450 nodes and an average density of 150 neighbors.

The Performance of SOFA Remains the Same in Static and Mobile Scenarios. By being a stateless protocol, with nodes acting independently in an asynchronous and distributed fashion, SOFA does not require spending energy on maintaining information about the node's neighborhood and it is independent from the network topology and mobility.

To test SOFA with dynamic topologies, we simulated an area of 150x150 meters where nodes moved according to traces generated by the BonnMotion's random waypoint model. We tested three speeds: 0 m/s (static), 1.5 m/s (walking) and 7 m/s (biking). The radio range was set to 50 meters, with every node being connected, on average, to one third of the network. The maximum density was 150 nodes in a 450-node network. The resulting multi-hop networks had an effective diameter of just below three hops, which ensures that hidden terminal effects are taken into consideration. Figure 6 shows the duty cycle and the exchange rate of SOFA under the patterns *static*, *walking* and *biking*. We can see that the speed of the nodes does not influence neither the energy consumption nor the delivery ratio and the exchange rate.

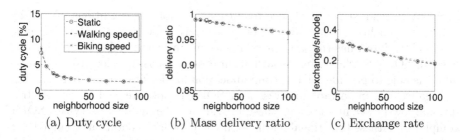

(a) Duty cycle   (b) Mass delivery ratio   (c) Exchange rate

Fig. 6. SOFA performance under different mobility scenarios (simulation results)

5.5 Gossip Support

As mentioned before, one the goals of our study is to develop a communication primitive that is useful for general gossip applications. In gossip, it is important to conserve mass. Our 3-way handshake phase guarantees that, unless the last ack is lost, the two nodes will reach either a positive agreement (both nodes exchange their mass) or a negative agreement (both nodes keep their mass). Clearly, a positive agreement is the most desirable outcome, but both outcomes guarantee that no mass is lost during the exchange. The most important issue is to reduce the possibility of disagreements (when only one node, the sender, deems the transaction as successful).

To evaluate SOFA's ability for mass conservation, we compute the mass delivery ratio. This metric represents the fraction of data exchanges that end up successfully. Figure 5(b) depicts the *mass delivery ratio* of SOFA under different densities. The figure shows that even under extreme densities (450 neighbors) SOFA is able to achieve a high percentage of successful exchanges (above 90 %). This is an important result. In the previous subsection, we found that SOFA saturates at approximately 200 nodes, beyond this point the exchange rate decreases monotonically. But, Figure 5(b) shows that the few exchanges that are able to occur beyond this point are able to be completed successfully. In other words, even under extremely demanding conditions SOFA has a remarkable ability to conserve mass. This feat is due to the careful design of SOFA aimed at (i) selecting reliable links (rendezvous phase), (ii) implementing a transmit back-off instead of a CCA (to avoid sender-based collisions), (iii) avoiding the use of retransmissions (which would jam the channel) and (iv) providing a method to reduce mass losses due to packet drops (3-way handshake).

6 Conclusions

In this study we define the concept of Extreme Wireless Sensor Networks and propose SOFA, a communication protocol that can operate efficiently and reliably under EWSN's stringent conditions. To the best of our knowledge, this is the first effort aiming at mobile sensor networks with high densities and high traffic rates. Traditional low-power protocols, which were not designed with these requirements in mind, simply collapse under such circumstances.

SOFA shows a strong resilience to extreme networking conditions. First, the stateless, asynchronous and distributed characteristics of SOFA make it immune to mobility. SOFA has the same performance in static and mobile environments. Second, SOFA reaches a bandwidth saturation at densities close to 200 nodes and it is able to provide reliable communication for densities of up to 450 nodes.

Finally, it is important to stress that SOFA is not intended to replace traditional low-power methods, as these provide a different set of services. SOFA complements these traditional methods. If the network's conditions change (to a milder state), the network stack can switch to unicast and broadcast primitives.

References

1. Boano, C., Zuniga, M.: JAG: Reliable and Predictable Wireless Agreement under External Radio Interference. In: IEEE 33rd Real-Time Systems Symposium (RTSS), pp. 315–326 (2012)
2. Boyd, S., Ghosh, A.: Gossip algorithms: Design, analysis and applications. In: 24th Annual Joint Conf. of the IEEE Computer and Communications Societies, IFOCOM 2005, pp. 1653–1664 (2005)
3. Buettner, M., Yee, G., Anderson, E.: X-MAC: a short preamble MAC protocol for duty-cycled wireless sensor networks. In: Sensys 2006 4th Int. Conf. on Embedded Networked Sensor Systems, pp. 307–320 (2006)
4. Demers, A., Greene, D., Hauser, C.: Epidemic algorithms for replicated database maintenance. In: Sixth ACM Symposium on Principles of Distributed Computing, pp. 1–12 (1987)
5. Dutta, P., Dawson-Haggerty, S., Chen, Y., Liang, C.-J.M., Terzis, A.: Design and evaluation of a versatile and efficient receiver-initiated link layer for low-power wireless. In: Sensys 2010 8th ACM Conference on Embedded Networked Sensor Systems, pp. 1–14. ACM Press (2010)
6. Dutta, P., Musaloiu-E, R., Stoica, I., Terzis, A.: Wireless ACK collisions not considered harmful. In: HotNets-VII The Seventh Workshop on Hot Topics in Networks (2008)
7. El-Hoiydi, A.: WiseMAC: an ultra low power MAC protocol for the downlink of infrastructure wireless sensor networks. In: ISCC 2004 Ninth Int. Symp. on Computers and Communications, pp. 244–251 (2004)
8. Ferrari, F., Zimmerling, M., Thiele, L., Mottola, L.: The low-power wireless bus. In: 10th Conf. on Embedded Networked Sensor Systems (Sensys), pp. 1–14 (2012)
9. Gnawali, O., Fonseca, R., Jamieson, K.: Collection tree protocol. In: Sensys 2009 7th ACM Conf. on Embedded Networked Sensor Systems, pp. 1–14 (2009)
10. Landsiedel, O., Ghadimi, E., Duquennoy, S., Johansson, M.: Low Power, Low Delay: Opportunistic Routing meets Duty Cycling. In: IPSN 2012 11th Int. Conf. on Information Processing in Sensor Networks, pp. 185–196 (2012)
11. Loukas, A., Zuniga, M., Woehrle, M., Cattani, M., Langendoen, K.: Think globally, act locally: on the reshaping of information landscapes. In: IPSN 2012 12th Int. Conf. on Information Processing in Sensor Networks, pp. 265–276 (2013)
12. Moss, D., Levis, P.: Box-MACs: Exploiting physical and link layer boundaries in low-power networking. Computer Systems Laboratory Stanford University (2008)
13. Sarwate, A.D., Dimakis, A.G.: The Impact of Mobility on Gossip Algorithms. IEEE Transactions on Information Theory 58(3), 1731–1742 (2012)
14. Shah, D.: Gossip algorithms. In: Found. and Trends in Networking, pp. 1–125 (2009)

15. Spyropoulos, T., Psounis, K., Raghavendra, C.S.: Spray and Wait: An Efficient Routing Scheme for intermittently connected mobile networks. In: SIGCOMM 2005 Workshop on Delay-tolerant Networking, pp. 252–259 (2005)
16. Sun, Y., Gurewitz, O.: RI-MAC: a receiver-initiated asynchronous duty cycle MAC protocol for dynamic traffic loads in wireless sensor networks. In: SenSys 2008 6th ACM Conf. on Embedded Network Sensor Systems, pp. 1–14 (2008)
17. Tang, L., Sun, Y., Gurewitz, O., Johnson, D.B.: EM-MAC: a dynamic multichannel energy-efficient MAC protocol for wireless sensor networks. In: Twelfth Int. Symp. on Mobile Ad Hoc Networking and Computing (MobiHoc), vol. 11, pp. 23:1–23:11 (2011)
18. Zuniga, M., Krishnamachari, B.: An analysis of unreliability and asymmetry in low-power wireless links. ACM Trans. on Sensor Networks 3(2), 7 (2007)

Appendix A: SOFA and LPP

SOFA is a generic mechanism that can be applied to any low power duty cycled protocol. In this appendix we briefly explore SOFA in combination with low power probing (SOFA-LPP). The main difference with SOFA-LPL resides in the rendezvous mechanism. While in SOFA-LPL the initiator actively probes the channel with beacons, in LPP the initiator passively listens to the channel until a neighbor sends out his wake-up beacon signaling it is ready for communication.

LPP can lead to collisions when two nodes target the same destination, as they will both respond to the wake-up beacon of that node. For unicast this is unlikely (nodes target specific neighbors), but for opportunistic anycast senders in close proximity target the same (first to wake-up) node. Similar to SOFA-LPL's transmit back-off, we can remedy this by having an initiator first act as a receiver (by sending out a beacon of its own) before turning into a sender (passively listening for beacons); this way two initiators engage in an effective communication with each other instead of ending up with a collision.

Figure 7 shows that SOFA-LPP performs worse than SOFA-LPL. In particular, SOFA-LPP suffers in terms of mass delivery ratio and exchange rate. This is largely due to the periodical wakeup beacons, which saturate the channel for medium to highly-dense networks.

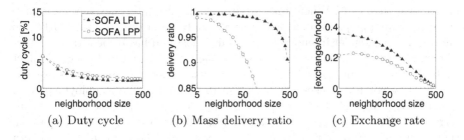

Fig. 7. SOFA-LPP compared to SOFA-LPL (simulation results)

All Is Not Lost:
Understanding and Exploiting Packet Corruption in Outdoor Sensor Networks

Frederik Hermans, Hjalmar Wennerström, Liam McNamara,
Christian Rohner, and Per Gunningberg

Uppsala Universitet, Sweden

Abstract. During phases of transient connectivity, sensor nodes receive a substantial number of corrupt packets. These corrupt packets are generally discarded, losing the sent information and wasting the energy put into transmitting and receiving. Our analysis of one year's data from an outdoor sensor network deployment shows that packet corruption follows a distinct pattern that is observed on all links. We explain the pattern's core features by considering implementation aspects of low-cost 802.15.4 transceivers and independent transmission errors. Based on the insight into the corruption pattern, we propose a probabilistic approach to recover information about the original content of a corrupt packet. Our approach vastly reduces the uncertainty about the original content, as measured by a manifold reduction in entropy. We conclude that the practice of discarding all corrupt packets in an outdoor sensor network may be unnecessarily wasteful, given that a considerable amount of information can be extracted from them.

Keywords: wireless, transmission errors, packet corruption, outdoor sensor networks, robustness, 802.15.4.

1   Introduction

Outdoor sensor networks experience significant variations in radio link performance over time [1,2]. When links are in a transient state, they receive a large amount of corrupt packets, which are commonly discarded. Consequently, the information the sender intended to transmit is lost and has to be retransmitted. Therefore, corrupt packets incur a cost on the networks' limited energy budget for both transmitting and receiving the corrupt packet, and for retransmission.

We study corrupt packets from an 802.15.4-based outdoor deployment in a remote area. We find that corruption occurs to a non-negligible degree on intermediate links. It emerges that corruption follows a distinct, stable pattern that holds over various time scales and across links. We explain this pattern by considering an implementation aspect of low-cost 802.15.4 transceivers, the tie resolution strategy in coding, and a channel model in which errors occur independently. While corruption in packets has been studied recently in outdoor

B. Krishnamachari, A.L. Murphy, and N. Trigoni (Eds.): EWSN 2014, LNCS 8354, pp. 116–132, 2014.

networks [3] and earlier in the case of interference [4,5], we are the first to explain the occurence of the observed pattern.

Some earlier work has also addressed how to make use of corrupt packets. Apart from forward error correction, the approaches either selectively retransmit parts of a packet that are suspected to be corrupted [6,7], or aim to reconstruct a correct packet from multiple corrupt packets [8].

We take a novel path to handling corrupt packets. We note that data in sensor networks is often inherently uncertain, e.g., due to limited accuracy of sensor readings. We therefore propose an approach that—rather than trying to exactly reconstruct a corrupt packet—probabilistically infers the packet's original content by exploiting the pattern in corruption. In combination with application knowledge, our approach enables recovery of information from corrupt packets. In contrast to earlier work, our approach does not need retransmissions of corrupt packets and hence does not incur an additional communication cost.

The evaluation of our approach shows that the uncertainty associated with a corrupt packet can be reduced significantly, as measured by an up to eight-fold reduction in entropy. We further validate our approach by applying it to data collected from a second deployment in another location, and find that it enables recovery of information from corrupt packets.

In summary, this paper makes the following core contributions:

- By analyzing data from a long-term outdoor deployment, we describe the distinct pattern of how 802.15.4 packets are corrupted. Crucially, we can explain the pattern by considering implementation aspects of low-cost 802.15.4 transceivers and a simple radio channel model.
- Based on our insights, we describe an approach that probabilistically infers the original content of a corrupt packet. We evaluate this approach on a data set from a separate deployment, and find that it enables recovery by correctly assigning high probabilities to the original content. We also achieve a manifold reduction in the uncertainty associated with a corrupt packet.

To ensure that this paper is focused and self-contained, we have decided to leave out certain systems aspects, which we will address in future work.

The rest of the paper is organized as follows. We describe our deployment and data collection in Sec. 2, and briefly recap the IEEE 802.15.4 standard in Sec. 3. We analyze packet corruption in our deployment in Sec. 4, and describe our recovery approach in Sec. 5. Section 6 evaluates the approach, followed by a brief discussion of practical aspects in Sec. 7. We then survey related work in Sec. 8 and conclude the paper in Sec. 9.

2   Deployment and Data Collection

We deployed a sensor network at the outskirts of Uppsala, Sweden. The network is located in an open field with no trees or bushes in the surroundings, in a remote location that very few people have access to. The deployment is therefore not affected by man-made radio interference, e.g., from WiFi or Bluetooth.

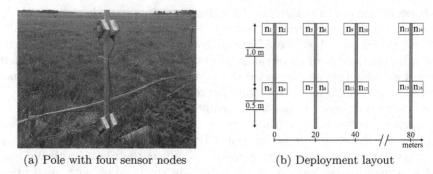

(a) Pole with four sensor nodes   (b) Deployment layout

Fig. 1. Outdoor deployment. Sensor nodes are labeled 1–16 in the right figure.

The network is comprised of 16 TelosB sensor nodes, which are equipped with 802.15.4-compatible CC2420 radio transceivers that operate in the 2.4 GHz ISM band [9]. The nodes are attached to four poles, with four nodes per pole (Fig. 1a). The poles are aligned along a straight line with a distance of 20 m between consecutive poles, as shown in Fig. 1b. On each pole, two nodes are mounted at 0.5 m above the ground and two nodes are mounted at 1.5 m.

The purpose of the network is to study radio links in 802.15.4 outdoor networks. Therefore, nodes take turns in sending 34-byte long probing packets every 500 ms. Whenever a node receives a packet, it logs the received packet content and the signal-to-noise ratio and Link Quality Indication (LQI) associated with the packet. Rather than discarding corrupt packets, nodes are programmed to also log corrupt packets. For power supply and log data collection, all nodes are connected via 5 m long RF-shielded USB cables to low-power Linux machines, which in turn are connected via Ethernet to a regular desktop PC that acts as a central experiment monitor.

By analyzing the log files, which contain all sent and received packets (both correct and corrupt), we can determine which parts of a corrupt packet have suffered corruption. We use this information to analyze corruption in Sec. 4.

3   Recap of IEEE 802.15.4

We briefly recapitulate the aspects of the IEEE 802.15.4 standard that are relevant to this paper. IEEE 802.15.4 is a standard for low-rate, low-power wireless communication [10], which has found wide-spread adoption in sensor networks.

A transmitted byte is represented by two four-bit *symbols*. 802.15.4 employs a direct sequence spread spectrum (DSSS) technique, in which each of the 16 possible symbols is represented by one *code word*. A code word, in turn, is represented by a 32-bit long pseudo-noise *chip sequence*.

We clarify the operation of 802.15.4 with an example. A sender wants to transmit a packet with n bytes of payload to a receiver. The sender translates each byte to two symbols. For each symbol, it determines the corresponding code word. The code words' chip sequences are then modulated onto a carrier

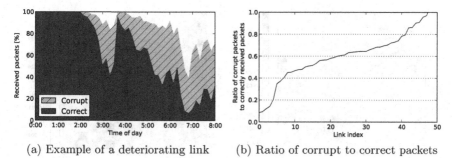

(a) Example of a deteriorating link   (b) Ratio of corrupt to correct packets

Fig. 2. The left figure exemplifies the amount of corrupt packets received for a specific link. The right figure shows that almost all intermediate links receive a substantial amount of corrupt packets.

frequency. The receiver demodulates the incoming chip sequences and matches them to the known code words. In this way, the receiver decodes $2n$ symbols, from which it can construct the n payload bytes.

Synchronization is required to detect packet boundaries. A sender starts each packet with a predefined preamble, followed by a start frame delimiter and a length field. Upon decoding a preamble and start frame delimiter, a receiver knows that a packet is being transmitted. If the receiver fails to decode the preamble, the packet is lost.

Due to noise on the radio channel, a receiver's demodulated chip sequence may differ from the chip sequence transmitted by the sender. In this case, the incoming chip sequence is matched to the closest code word. DSSS thereby achieves resilience against noise, since there is a many-to-one mapping between chip sequences and code words. If sufficiently many chips are demodulated incorrectly [11], the receiver matches the incoming chip sequence to an incorrect code word, and hence decodes the wrong symbol. In this case, packet corruption occurs. To detect corruption, 802.15.4 packets end with a two-byte cyclic redundancy check (CRC) field. A receiver computes the CRC for the incoming packet and compares it against the received trailing CRC field. If they mismatch, the receiver knows that corruption has occurred.

4   Packet Corruption in an Outdoor Sensor Network

In this section, we analyze corrupt packets that were received by nodes in our deployment over the course of one year, from June 2012 to June 2013. We begin by briefly quantifying the amount of corruption occurring in the deployment. Then, we describe how corruption affects individual transmitted symbols, followed by a characterization of the effect of corruption on whole packets. Our analysis is focused on the regularities in corruption that enable the probabilistic recovery of information, as described in Sec. 5.

Because corrupt packets are usually discarded, the degree to which packet corruption occurs is unknown for most sensor networks. From our log data we

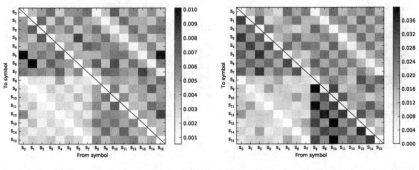

(a) Symbol mutations in data set   (b) Symbol mutations in simulation

Fig. 3. Symbol mutations as observed in the data set and in simulation. Our simulation model produces the same core pattern as the empirical measurements.

observe that *intermediate links* (links that have a PRR between 10% and 90% [12,13]) experience a substantial amount of packet corruption. Figure 2a shows a representative example of such an intermediate link. The depicted link initially has a high PRR, but deteriorates over time. As PRR falls, the amount of corrupt packets, indicated by the hatched gray area, grows.

Next we look at the amount of corruption over all intermediate links from the duration of the deployment. We observe that about 80% of intermediate links have a ratio of corrupt packets to correctly received packets of at least 0.5. That is, for every two correctly received packets, they receive one corrupt packet on average. Figure 2b illustrates this ratio of corrupt packets to correctly received packets for intermediate links for a time span of two weeks in March 2013.

We conclude that packet corruption occurs at a non-negligible scale on intermediate links. Because intermediate links are the best candidates for improving network performance, this initial observation motivates us to understand packet corruption in more detail.

4.1 Corrupt Symbols

We now consider corruption at the finest level of granularity at which it can be observed in our deployment: the symbol level. If a node sends a packet containing a symbol s_i and due to corruption a receiver decodes the symbol incorrectly, which symbol s_j will the receiver likely decode?

Figure 3a shows how often each possible mutation $s_i \rightarrow s_j$ is observed over all links from the span of twelve months. The figure is a visual representation of the *mutation matrix*. An entry (j, i) of the mutation matrix denotes the frequency with which we observed a sent symbol s_i to be received as s_j. The matrix diagonal describes how often a symbol was decoded correctly. We omit the diagonal in the figure to focus on corruption. The darker the color in the figure, the higher the frequency. A distinct visual structure emerges in the figure, which leads us the following three observations:

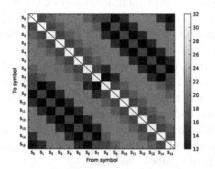 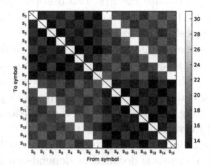

(a) Hamming distances between code words of the 802.15.4 standard

(b) Hamming distances between MSK-transformed code words

Fig. 4. Hamming distances for 802.15.4 code words (left) and MSK-transformed code words (right). The MSK transformation explains observations 1 and 2.

Observation 1: Mutations are not uniformly distributed. If corruption occurs to a sent symbol, the received symbol depends on which symbol was sent. For example, if a node sends symbol s_0 which suffers corruption, the receiver most commonly decodes it as a s_5 (see column 0). Conversely, if a node receives a corrupt symbol as s_5, it is least common that s_{13} was sent (see row 5).

Observation 2: The most significant bit of a symbol is more stable than other bits. Note that the subdiagonal $(8,0)$ to $(15,7)$ and the superdiagonal $(0,8)$ to $(7,15)$ are lighter than the rest of the plot. For each column, the corresponding entry on these diagonals represents the symbol which differs from the sent symbol in only the most significant bit. For example, the sent symbol $s_0 = 0000_2$ is least commonly decoded as $s_8 = 1000_2$. This leads to the most significant bit of a symbol being more stable on average in our deployment.

Observation 3: Symbols s_0 to s_7 are more stable than other symbols. Consider the bottom left quadrant in Fig. 3a. It is significantly lighter than the other quadrants. This reflects the fact that in our data, the symbols s_0 to s_7 are unlikely to be decoded as s_8 to s_{15}. The converse is not true. Consequently, symbols s_0 to s_7 are less commonly corrupted than symbols s_8 to s_{15}.

The pattern shown in Fig. 3a represents mutation frequencies aggregated over all links over the whole time span of the deployment. We confirmed that the pattern also holds for individual links, and at various time scales. An independent research group has recently observed a similar pattern in an outdoor environment [3], which suggests the observations to be general.

To the best of our knowledge, no explanation has been offered so far as to why the pattern emerges. As Schmidt et al. point out [3], the pattern is surprising because it shows a negative correlation to the pairwise hamming distances of the code words defined in the 802.15.4 standard (see Fig. 4a). For example, the hamming distance between the code words for s_0 and s_8 is low, yet this mutation is among the least common in our deployment.

We attribute the first two observations to an implementation aspect of low-cost 802.15.4 transceivers. Rather than implementing an O-QPSK demodulator, as suggested in the 802.15.4 standard, many low-cost transceivers use an MSK demodulator instead [14]. While an MSK demodulator can correctly receive a chip sequence sent by an O-QPSK modulator, the received chip sequence will be transformed. Therefore, MSK-based 802.15.4 transceivers use a transformed set of code words to ensure compatibility with other 802.15.4 transceivers. The hamming distances between the transformed code words are shown in Fig. 4b.

Observation 1 can be explained by considering that each code word varies in its hamming distances to other code words. Therefore, the symbol that a corrupt chip sequence is decoded as depends on which symbol was sent.

Next, observation 2 follows directly from the observation that the MSK-transformed code word for symbol s_i has the highest hamming distance to the MSK-transformed code word for the symbol which differs from s_i only in the most significant bit. This is visualized by the light sub- and superdiagonals in Fig. 4b. Therefore, the most significant bit is more stable on average.

It remains to explain observation 3, which states that symbols s_0 to s_7 are more stable than the other symbols. This observation does not follow from the use of transformed code words, because code word distances are of course symmetric. We can explain the observation by considering how ties are resolved. A tie occurs if a received chip sequence matches two or more code words equally well. In this case, the transceiver must resolve the tie by choosing one of the matching code words. In a simple simulation, we found that if ties are resolved in a specific order[1], a pattern very similar to the empirically observed mutation matrix emerges (Fig. 3b). With the found order, a tie between two code words $s_{0 \leq i \leq 7}$ and $s_{8 \leq j \leq 15}$ will always be resolved in favor of the first symbol. Consequently, symbols s_0 to s_7 are more stable, as stated by observation 3.

Our simulation assumed one sender and one receiver, a fixed signal-to-noise ratio (SNR) at the receiver, and a channel model in which chip errors are independent, as would be expected in an additive white Gaussian noise channel, for example. Fixing the SNR implies a fixed chip error probability at the receiver.

We draw another useful conclusion from the similarity of the empirical and the simulated mutation matrix. The similarity suggests that the radio channel in the deployment can be modeled by a channel in which errors are independent, as assumed in our simulation. Note that differences in absolute values in Fig. 3a and Fig. 3b can be explained by considering that the simulated mutation matrix is based on a fixed SNR, whereas the empirical mutation matrix is based on packets received at various SNR levels. Nonetheless, the similarity holds.

In summary, we conclude that corruption follows a distinct pattern, which we attribute to MSK-transformed code words, the tie resolution strategy and a radio channel with independent chip errors.

---

[1] The order is $s_7, s_6, \ldots, s_0, s_{15}, s_{14}, \ldots, s_8$.

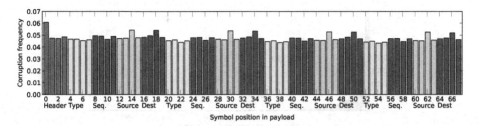

Fig. 5. Symbol error frequency over positions of the payload. Error frequencies are roughly uniform. Variations can be attributed to payload structure and content.

4.2 Errors in Packets

In the previous section, we considered the effect of corruption on individual symbols. We now shift our focus one layer up in the network stack to the link layer and consider how corruption affects whole packets, i.e., sequences of symbols.

Distribution of Errors. How are symbol errors distributed within a packet? Figure 5 shows this distribution where for each position of the payload, the plot shows the frequency with which a symbol at this position was corrupt. The x-axis is annotated with the content of the payload. For example, the first four positions contain the packet header.

The error frequency is similar across all positions, ranging from 4.5% to 6%. Although the distribution is roughly uniform, there are notable deviations. First, the symbol at position 0 is most often corrupt. Second, there is a periodicity: the error frequencies for positions 4 to 19 are similar to the frequencies for positions 20 to 35, and so on. These deviations can be explained by the content of sent packets. For all packets sent in our deployment, position 0 always contains symbol s_8, which we know to be least stable. Furthermore, the payload of the probing packets sent in our deployment repeats itself after position 20, giving rise to the observed periodicity. Finally, because the sent packets contain structured rather than random content, some positions have slightly higher corruption frequencies than others. The observed deviations from uniformity are within range of the deviations we would expect due to the effects described in Sec. 4.1.

Correlation of Errors. Are errors correlated? I.e., does an error at position x tell us something about whether an error occurred at position y? We computed pairwise correlations between all positions over all corrupt packets. The maximum absolute correlation between any two symbol positions is less than 0.09. Considering that a value of 0 indicates no correlation at all, we conclude that there are no notable correlations between errors at different positions. This observation agrees with our assumption that the deployment's radio channel is well described by assuming independent chip errors, and thus independent symbol errors.

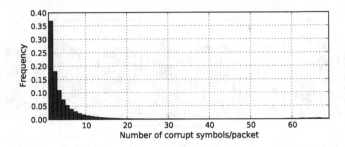

Fig. 6. Number of corrupt symbols per packet. Most suffer only little corruption.

Amount of Corruption in a Packet. Finally, we quantify how many symbols in a corrupt packet are incorrect. Figure 6 shows a normalized histogram of the number of symbol errors per corrupt packet. The figure shows that most packets have very few errors, and that the frequency of occurrence decreases with an increase in the amount of corruption.

5   Recovering Data from Corrupt Packets

We now describe how we use the observations from the previous section in an approach which for a given corrupt packet defines a probability distribution over the possible sent packets.

Computing a Probability Distribution over Possible Sent Packets. We consider how to infer the likely sent data from a received corrupt packet. Our goal is to assign probabilities to the possible sent data, given the data in a corrupt packet. Recall from Sec. 3 that corruption occurs if sufficiently many chips in an incoming chip sequences are decoded incorrectly and hence the chip sequence is matched to the wrong code word. For the remainder of this analysis, we denote the probability of an individual chip in a received chip sequence being flipped as p_{chip}. For now, assume that we know p_{chip} for each received packet. We will revisit this assumption in the next section.

For a given value of p_{chip}, we can compute through simulation a corresponding mutation matrix $M^{p_{chip}}$. For example, the mutation matrix shown in Fig. 3b describes the mutation probabilities for $p_{chip} = 0.3$. Most importantly to our approach, the matrix rows describe the mutation probabilities for a received symbol. Note that the matrix main diagonal describes the probabilities of a symbol being received correctly.

For a given received packet, we now want to infer the first symbol of the sent packet. Let the first symbol of the received packet be s_j, and consider the case in which we know the packet to be corrupt because the CRC failed. By considering row j of $M^{p_{chip}}$, we can assign a probability to each possible sent symbol that could have led to the receiver decoding s_j. More specifically, the probability that the sent symbol s_i is decoded as the received symbol s_j is given by the entry $M_{j,i}^{p_{chip}}$ of the mutation matrix. We write $p(s_i|s_j) = M_{j,i}^{p_{chip}}$. For example, the probability $p(s_5|s_{13})$ that symbol s_5 was sent when s_{13} was received is given by $M_{13,5}^{p_{chip}}$. This reasoning holds for all position of the packet.

Because symbol errors are independent, we can readily assign probabilities to sequences of sent symbols. Assume, for example, that a receiver decoded the sequence of symbols $r = (s_{13}, s_3, s_0, s_{11})$. What is the probability that the actual sent symbols were $t = (s_5, s_3, s_1, s_{11})$? Due to independence, this probability is given by the product of the individual mutation probabilities:

$$p(t|r) = p(s_5, s_3, s_1, s_{11}|s_{13}, s_3, s_0, s_{11})$$
$$= p(s_5|s_{13}) \cdot p(s_3|s_3) \cdot p(s_1|s_0) \cdot p(s_{11}|s_{11})$$
$$= M_{13,5}^{p_{chip}} \quad \cdot \quad M_{3,3}^{p_{chip}} \quad \cdot \quad M_{0,1}^{p_{chip}} \quad \cdot \quad M_{11,11}^{p_{chip}}$$

In the manner we just outlined, a probability can be assigned to every possible sent symbol sequence for a given received symbol sequence and a given value of p_{chip}. This conceptually simple idea comprises our recovery approach. For each received, corrupt packet, we can compute a probability distribution over the possible sent packets. To compute the distribution, all we need to know is the chip error probability p_{chip} during packet reception.

To summarize, our approach determines a probability distribution over the possible sent data for given received data in a corrupt packet and a given p_{chip}. This concludes our description of recovery. We deliberately do not specify how the probability distribution is to be used by an application, because we believe that application knowledge should drive this process.

Estimating p_{chip}. To assign probabilities to possible sent data, we need an estimate of the chip error probability p_{chip} for each corrupt packet. Unfortunately, low-cost transceivers do not provide such an estimate directly. Although there is a well-defined relationship between SNR and the chip error probability [15], we found the resolution of SNR reported by low-cost transceivers too low for a meaningful p_{chip} estimate.

To overcome this obstacle, we estimate p_{chip} for each packet by considering the LQI value associated with the packet. In the case of CC2420 transceivers, LQI is reflective of the correlation of an incoming chip sequence to the matched code word over the first eight symbols of a packet [9]. Therefore, we expect it to reflect the chip error rate. We construct a mapping from LQI values to chip error estimates as follows: for each LQI value l, we determine the empirically observed symbol error probability for symbol s_0. We then calculate the chip error probability p_{chip}^l that yields the same symbol error probability for s_0. We then construct a mapping from LQI to chip error probability by interpolating a 3rd degree spline through the resulting (l, p_{chip}^l) tuples. Our mapping is defined on LQI values in the range from 32 to 90, which covers 98.5% of all corrupt packets in our data set. We constrain the mapping to this range because we observe only very few corrupt packets with LQI less than 32 or higher than 90, and we therefore have little support to construct a mapping for these values.

While we do not expect our LQI to p_{chip} mapping to be perfect, we note that given the information that low-cost transceiver usually provide about the channel, it is difficult construct with a more well-defined estimate. We are confident that if transceivers were to provide high-resolution SNR measurements, a more exact estimator of chip error probabilities can be designed.

6   Evaluation

Our proposed approach defines a probability distribution over the possible sent data for given received data in a corrupt packet. We now address two questions pertaining to the resulting distributions. First, to what extent does the approach reduce uncertainty about the original content of a corrupt packet? Second, is the resulting distribution for a given corrupt packet meaningful? I.e., does it assign probabilities in a way such that the actual sent data has a high probability?

6.1   Reduction in Uncertainty

Let us address the first question of how much our approach reduces the uncertainty associated with a received, corrupt packet.

We consider the case in which a node sends a packet containing a 16-bit word t that we are interested in. This word could, for example, encode a sensor measurement, but for the sake of this analysis, we assume that we do not have any application-specific knowledge about the likely content t. We assume that a corrupt packet is received that contains the 16-bit word r. Due to the corruption, we do not know whether $r = t$ or not.

As a base case, assume that the corrupt packet is simply discarded. In this case, we know nothing about t. It could have taken any of the $2^{16} = 65,536$ possible values with equal probability. We measure the uncertainty associated with the discarded, corrupt packet by considering the entropy of the probability distribution over all possible words t' that could have been transmitted. There are 16 bits of entropy:

$$H_{\text{discard}} = -\sum_{t'=0}^{65535} p(t') \log p(t')$$

$$= -\sum_{t'} 2^{-16} \log 2^{-16} = 16.$$

Next, we consider the case in which we do not discard the corrupt packet. The corrupt packet contains a word r, but we do not know if $r = t$. Using the approach described in Sec. 5, we can compute the probability $p(t'|r)$ for every possible 16-bit word t'. As in the case of the discarded packet, we can compute the entropy, which depends on the estimate of p_{chip} and on the received word r:

$$H_r = -\sum_{t'=0}^{65535} p(t'|r) \log p(t'|r).$$

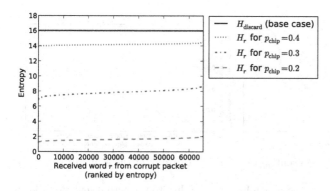

Fig. 7. Uncertainty associated with a corrupt packet in the case the packet is discarded, and when our proposed approach is used. Our approach significantly reduces the uncertainty, as measured by entropy.

Figure 7 depicts the entropy for both the base line case and our approach for different values of p_{chip}. The y-axis denotes the entropy. The x-axis relates to the received word r as described below.

In the base case, in which the corrupt packet is discarded, the entropy is 16 regardless of which word was received in the corrupt packet, and regardless of the chip error probability. With our approach, which assigns probabilities the possible sent words by considering which word r was received in the corrupt packet, the entropy depends on r. This is an effect of our observation that symbol mutations are not uniform. For a given chip error probability p_{chip}, the entropies H_r are plotted in increasing order along the x-axis.

The figure makes it clear that our approach significantly reduces the entropy associated with a corrupt 16-bit word. In the case of a chip error probability of 0.2, the entropy is reduced to less than 2 bits—an eight-fold reduction of the entropy of the base case. For a higher chip error probability of 0.3, the entropy is still halved in comparison to the base case. In the case of an extreme chip error probability of 0.4, the entropy is reduced by two bits. However, for such a high chip error probability, most packets will be lost rather than corrupt because the preamble is likely to be corrupt as well. We therefore conclude that for realistic chip error probabilities of 0.2 to 0.3, our approach vastly reduces the uncertainty associated with a corrupt packet.

6.2   Evaluation of Probability Assignment

We have shown how our probability assignment reduces the uncertainty associated with a corrupt packet. It remains to show that the probability assignment is sensible, i.e., that there is a meaningful relationship between the probability assigned to possible sent words t' and the word t that was actually sent.

To address this question, we consider corrupt packets from a deployment different from the one that provided the data for the analysis in Sec. 4. Evaluating our approach on data from a different deployment increases our confidence in the generality of our findings, and helps understand whether our approach is strongly tied to the observations from our deployment in Uppsala. The other deployment is located in the Abisko national park in northern Sweden, which lies above the polar circle (latitude of 66° 33′ 44″ N) in a climate that differs significantly from

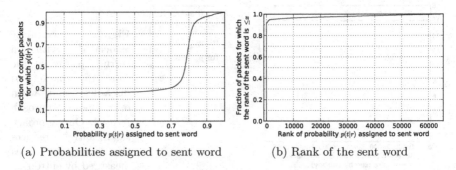

(a) Probabilities assigned to sent word   (b) Rank of the sent word

Fig. 8. Our approach correctly assigns a high probability to the actual sent word, both in absolute (left) and relative (right) terms

the climate in Uppsala. The Abisko deployment consists of 12 TelosB sensor nodes, and has a spatial layout similar to the Uppsala deployment. We consider corrupt packets from Abisko that were received during the first week of April 2013. We focus on this week because the deployment did not have any operational problems, such as failing nodes.

The data set of the Abisko deployment contains ca. 440,000 corrupt packets. We know the correct payload for each packet from our log data. We consider a 16-bit word t in these packets that describes the source address of the sender. We do not use any knowledge about the possible content of this word. For each corrupt packet, we estimate the chip error probability p_{chip} based on the packet's LQI measurement, as described earlier. We use the estimate to compute $p(t|r)$, which is the probability that is assigned to the sent word t when r was received. Clearly, it is desirable that a high probability be assigned to the sent word.

Figure 8a shows the empirical cumulative distribution function of the probability assigned to the sent word t for each corrupt packet. The x-axis shows the probability assigned to the sent word. The y-axis shows for how many of the packets this probability was below the corresponding x value. Note that for only 30 % of the corrupt packets, a probability of less than 0.7 is assigned to the sent word. For only 28 % of the corrupt packets, the probability assigned to the sent word is less than 0.5. It follows that for most corrupt packets, a high probability is assigned to the word that was actually sent. For these packets the probability assignment is sensible. However, a very low probability is assigned to the correct word for about 25% of the corrupt packets. Note that this does not imply that the assignment is wrong—in cases of a high chip error probability, there will be high uncertainty. High uncertainty means that the probability distribution will be more uniform across all possible sent words. The question thus is whether these low-probability assignments come from corrupt packets with high chip error probabilities. Before turning to this question, we conclude from Fig. 8a that for more than 70% of the corrupt packets, the probability assignment is sensible, because it assigns a high probability to the sent word.

We now order all possible sent words by decreasing order of assigned probability and determine the rank. E.g., the word t' that has been assigned the highest probability has rank one, the word with the second highest probability has rank two, etc. If two or more words have the same probability, they have the same rank. We are interested in the rank assigned to the sent word t.

The distribution of rank of the sent word is shown in Fig. 8b by an empirical cumulative distribution function. The figure shows that in 95% of the cases, the sent word is assigned a very high rank. I.e., the sent word is assigned a higher probability than most other possible candidates. We take this as an indication that even in cases where the highest probability is not assigned to the sent word, the sent word still takes a very high probability in comparison to other possible candidates. For the remaining 5% of corrupt packets, the rank is almost uniformly distributed up to the maximal rank of 65,536. We attribute this observation to misestimations of the chip error probability p_{chip}. Since we estimate p_{chip} from LQI, and LQI is only measured over the first eight symbols of a packet, it may by pure chance sometime misrepresent the chip error probability.

To summarize, we have shown in this section that for most corrupt packets, the sent word is assigned a high probability in comparison to other candidates. We conclude that the probability assignment we described in Sec. 5 indeed assigns probabilities in a meaningful manner. This observation suggests that our estimator of p_{chip} based on LQI is sufficiently accurate to enable recovery. Our approach thus enables sensor networks to infer the possible sent word corresponding to a corrupt packet.

7   Practical Considerations

We briefly discuss three aspects of practicality.

First, our approach determines a probability distribution over possible sent data. It does, by design, not produce a single value. When application knowledge about the likely content of a packet is available, this knowledge can be combined with our probability distribution to constrain the likely sent data even further. Application knowledge could be, for example, knowing the domain of a measured value from previous measurements. Such knowledge is often used to detect outliers, assess data quality, or handle missing data (e.g., see [11,16,17]). Such approaches are largely orthogonal to our proposal. Because the distributions computed by our approach are not centered around a single value, we believe that in combination with application knowledge, an even more exact inference of the content of corrupt packets is possible.

Second, a related question pertains to the complexity of our proposal. Note that the maths involved in determining the probability distribution is computationally very simple. Yet, for a received n symbol sequence, there are 16^n different possible sent values in the case of corruption. Enumerating all of them is infeasible for larger values of n. However, even for situations with moderately high chip error probabilities, many probabilities will be very close to zero. We envision that an application performing recovery will be interested in the top $k \ll 16^n$ possible sent sequences with the highest probabilities. These can be determined efficiently without enumerating all possible values. Therefore, we believe that recovery can be performed in-network by nodes that are slightly more powerful than the TelosB-type nodes.

Third, the packets we analyzed in this paper were all sent and received by Texas Instruments CC2420 transceivers. Although this particular chip has a very high prevalence in academic research, the question arises of how well our findings translate to other 802.15.4 radio chipsets. In part, the observed pattern is an effect of the use of MSK demodulators, which are cheap to implement [18]. Therefore, they are common in low-cost transceivers. Consequently, we expect the pattern to hold for other transceiver, too. Note that because the pattern emerges even on short time scales, its presence in a particular radio chipset can be readily verified in an anechoic chamber.

8   Related Work

Wireless channels are inherently unstable [19,12], causing errors in transmissions, and making mitigation strategies for these errors a wide field of research.

Schmidt et al. study corruption in an 802.15.4-based outdoor network and make observations similar to ours [3]. They point out that bit errors are not equally probable over all positions in the payload in 802.15.4 packets. They compare their empirical results to the expected values using code words as used with O-QPSK modulation. Han et al. identify patterns in the bit error probabilities of the payload in 802.11, which are not due to the channel conditions nor hardware-specific [20].

By using a software-defined radio, Wu et al. characterize the error patterns of individual 802.15.4 chip sequences in order to determine the channel conditions [21]. Similarly, Jamieson et al. implement a scheme in which they count the differences between the received and the known chip sequences to estimate the likelihood of a symbol being corrupt [6]. They then use this information, as part of a MAC protocol, to only re-transmit symbols that were likely corrupted. Dubois-Ferrière et al. combine successive alternating packets in order to infer the correct payload [8]. They show that this is feasible even when consecutive packets are broken, making the approach more robust than regular forward error correction. Hauer et al. propose to selectively retransmit parts of a packet during which there was a strong variation in received signal strength [7].

9   Conclusion

In this paper, we have described how corruption systematically affects symbols and packets in an outdoor 802.15.4 sensor network. We described a pattern in corruption that we attributed to the use of MSK demodulators, a specific tie resolution strategy when decoding, and a channel model with independent errors. These insights allowed us to formulate a novel probabilistic approach to recover information from corrupt packets. We showed that the approach reduces the uncertainty associated with a corrupt packet, and that it correctly assigns a high probability to the data that was actually sent. We will address systems aspects of our approach in future work and develop a concrete implementation of the proposed ideas. We specifically plan to investigate the trade-off between data quality and energy consumption, as well as the relationship of our proposed recovery mechanism to other approaches such as forward error correction.

We conclude that patterns in packet corruption in outdoor sensor networks can be understood, and that information may be recovered from some corrupt packets. All is not lost when it comes to corrupt packets, and therefore discarding all of them is unnecessarily wasteful.

References

1. Lin, S., Zhang, J., Zhou, G., Gu, L., Stankovic, J.A., He, T.: ATPC: adaptive transmission power control for wireless sensor networks. CM SenSys 2006 (2006)
2. Wennerström, H., Hermans, F., Rensfelt, O., Rohner, C., Nordén, L.A.: A Long-Term Study of Correlations between Meteorological Conditions and 802.15.4 Link Performance. In: IEEE SECON 2013 (2013)
3. Schmidt, F., Ceriotti, M., Wehrle, K.: Bit Error Distribution and Mutation Patterns of Corrupted Packets in Low-Power Wireless Networks. In: WiNTECH 2013 (2013)
4. Liang, C.J.M., Priyantha, N.B., Liu, J., Terzis, A.: Surviving Wi-Fi Interference in Low Power ZigBee Networks. In: ACM SenSys 2010 (2010)
5. Hermans, F., Rensfelt, O., Voigt, T., Ngai, E., Nordén, L.A., Gunningberg, P.: SoNIC: Classifying Interference in 802.15.4 Sensor Networks. In: IPSN 2013 (2013)
6. Jamieson, K., Balakrishnan, H.: PPR: partial packet recovery for wireless networks. In: ACM SIGCOMM 2007 (2007)
7. Hauer, J.-H., Willig, A., Wolisz, A.: Mitigating the Effects of RF Interference through RSSI-Based Error Recovery. In: Silva, J.S., Krishnamachari, B., Boavida, F. (eds.) EWSN 2010. LNCS, vol. 5970, pp. 224–239. Springer, Heidelberg (2010)
8. Dubois-Ferrière, H., Estrin, D., Vetterli, M.: Packet combining in sensor networks. In: ACM SenSys 2005 (2005)
9. Texas Instruments Inc.: CC2420 - 2.4 GHz IEEE 802.15.4, ZigBee-ready RF Transceiver, http://www.ti.com/lit/gpn/cc2420
10. IEEE Computer Society: 802.15.4: Wireless Medium Access Control (MAC) and Physical Layer (PHY) Specifications for Low-Rate Wireless Personal Area Networks (WPANs)
11. Wu, X., Liu, M.: In-situ soil moisture sensing: measurement scheduling and estimation using compressive sensing. In: ACM/IEEE IPSN 2012 (2012)
12. Srinivasan, K., Dutta, P., Tavakoli, A., Levis, P.: An empirical study of low-power wireless. ACM Trans. Sen. Netw. 6(2) (March 2010)
13. Baccour, N., Koubâa, A., Mottola, L., Zúñiga, M.A., Youssef, H., Boano, C.A., Alves, M.: Radio link quality estimation in wireless sensor networks: A survey. ACM Trans. Sen. Netw. 8(4) (September 2012)
14. Schmid, T.: GNU Radio 802.15.4 En- and Decoding. Technical report, Department of Electrical Engineering, University of California, Los Angeles 2006 (2006)
15. Xiong, F.: Digital Modulation Techniques, 2nd edn. Artech House (April 2006)
16. Kong, L., Xia, M., Liu, X.Y., Wu, M.Y., Liu, X.: Data loss and reconstruction in sensor networks. In: IEEE INFOCOM 2013 (2013)
17. Hasenfratz, D., Saukh, O., Thiele, L.: Model-driven accuracy bounds for noisy sensor readings. In: IEEE DCOSS 2013 (2013)

18. Notor, J., Caviglia, A., Levy, G.: CMOS RFIC Architectures for IEEE 802.16.4 Networks. Technical report, Cadence Design Systems, Inc. 2003 (2003)
19. Zúñiga Zamalloa, M., Krishnamachari, B.: An analysis of unreliability and asymmetry in low-power wireless links. ACM Trans. Sen. Netw. 3(2) (June 2007)
20. Han, B., Ji, L., Lee, S., Bhattacharjee, B., Miller, R.R.: Are All Bits Equal? Experimental Study of IEEE 802.11 Communication Bit Errors. IEEE/ACM Trans. Netw. 20(6) (2012)
21. Wu, K., Tan, H., Ngan, H.L., Liu, Y., Ni, L.: Chip Error Pattern Analysis in IEEE 802.15.4. IEEE Trans. Mob. Comp. 11(4) (2012)

Making 'Glossy' Networks Sparkle: Exploiting Concurrent Transmissions for Energy Efficient, Reliable, Ultra-Low Latency Communication in Wireless Control Networks

Dingwen Yuan, Michael Riecker, and Matthias Hollick

Secure Mobile Networking Lab, Technische Universität Darmstadt
`fistname.lastname@seemoo.tu-darmstadt.de`

Abstract. Wireless sensor networks (WSN) offer a promising engineering solution which brings deployment flexibility and saves wiring costs in industrial automation and control applications. However, utilizing this technology is still challenging due to the current low reliability of the standard WSN communication, e.g., large percentage of unreliable links, and the possibility of battery depletion and node failure. To overcome these difficulties we propose *Sparkle*, a WSN control network design based on concurrent transmission particularly oriented to periodic multi-loop control systems. It primarily draws on the Glossy protocol and inherits its advantages in high packet reliability, low latency and accurate time synchronization. The novelty of Sparkle is that it optimizes each end-to-end communication flow independently by performing "control" on the flow. Specifically, we show how to perform transmission power and topology controls. We introduce *WSNShape*, a unique topology control technique based on the capture effect, which drastically reduces energy while simultaneously improves packet reliability and latency, compared to Glossy. Finally, we design and implement *PRRTrack*, a component of Sparkle that can adaptively switch among various operation modes of different control strategies, thus trading-off reliability vs. energy consumption. Through evaluation on real-world testbeds, we demonstrate that Sparkle enables flows to satisfy the reliability requirement while reducing the energy consumption by in average 80% and the latency by a further 5% over the almost optimal latency of Glossy.

1 Introduction

Wireless sensor networks (WSN) with their very low power radio technology offer great potential in industrial automation and control applications by 1) cutting off huge cost of wiring, 2) offering high flexibility in deployment and 3) saving energy in communication and computation. However, the generally strict requirements on packet reliability and communication latency of these applications are especially challenging for the unreliable communication of WSN. Despite the fact that some pioneering works in academia and a few industrial

B. Krishnamachari, A.L. Murphy, and N. Trigoni (Eds.): EWSN 2014, LNCS 8354, pp. 133–149, 2014.

standards have appeared, to the best of our knowledge, no large scale application of WSN has yet taken place.

Recently, the Glossy protocol [1] showed the possibility of obtaining deterministic low latency, high reliability and high synchronization precision simultaneously by applying the technology of constructive interference (CI), i.e. a number of nodes transmit the same packet at roughly the same time so that the signals add up constructively at the receiver. These features match the requirements of control networks so good that Glossy can offer a sound basis for it. Based on Glossy, we design and implement *Sparkle*, a periodic multi-loop control network where each control loop is mapped into one or more communication flows. The novelty of Sparkle is that we perform "control" on each flow (say flow $a \to b$, a and b being two end nodes), with the goal that the QoS (quality of service) metrics of the flow satisfy given requirements or are optimized. For that purpose, we need the cooperation of the opposite flow (flow $b \to a$).

Specifically, we show that by effectively controlling the network topology and transmission power (tx power) of a flow, the QoS metrics of reliability, energy consumption and latency can be further improved simultaneously, compared to Glossy. We propose a novel technique for topology control, *WSNShape*, which uses the *capture effect* [2] to find a number of reliable paths between the source and the destination of a flow and then activate nodes on one or more of these paths. As shown by evaluation, it greatly reduces energy consumption and very probably also improves end-to-end reliability and latency. Additionally, we experimentally show that the tx power also affects the QoS metrics significantly and the Glossy protocol without WSNShape may not be reliable enough for control networks.

Based on these findings, we design and implement the "controller" of Sparkle, *PRRTrack*, which adaptively switches between operation modes of different tx powers and WSNShape levels. Experiments on two real-world testbeds show that the requirement on reliability is satisfied, the latency is reduced, and the energy consumption is greatly improved over today's state-of-the-art techniques.

2   Related Work

WSN-based networks for automation and control is a field under active research. Some industrial standards such as WirelessHART[1] and ISA100[2] have appeared. A few academic projects have also been reported, e.g. the GINSENG project for monitoring and control in oil refineries [3], and the TRITon project for lighting control in road tunnels [4]. All of them use static or semi-static routing for communication, which is inherently not robust to node or link failure.

Glossy [1] is a one-to-all flooding protocol based on the so-called constructive interference, i.e. the concurrent transmission of the *same* packets by multiple transmitters. It achieves almost optimal latency, high reliability and time synchronization of μs accuracy. Since these features match the requirements

---

[1] http://www.hartcomm2.org

[2] http://www.isa.org

of automation and control systems perfectly, we choose Glossy as the starting point to design our system Sparkle. When concurrent transmissions of *different* packets take place, one packet may overpower the others and be successfully received. This is called capture effect. The capture effect in WSN was first discussed by [2]. A recent work [5] shows the universality of the capture effect in WSN and employs it to implement an efficient all-to-all aggregative communication. WSNShape, the topology control technique of Sparkle, also makes use of the capture effect, and is therefore instantly reactive to node or link failure. A unified reception model for concurrent transmission in WSN is proposed in [6].

To optimize the energy efficiency of the end-to-end communication primitive implemented with the Glossy flooding technique, [7] uses the hop count from the source node as a metric for forwarder selection (topology control). It is shown to reduce the energy consumption by 30%. In contrast, we use the capture effect for forwarder selection, which leads to energy savings of about 80% to 90% together with better reliability and lower latency in networks of similar size. In addition, we assume nothing about the symmetry of the network (e.g. the hop count from node a to b is the same as from b to a), and the two directional flows between a pair of nodes are independently controlled.

In all, as far as we are aware of, Sparkle is the first wireless control network based on the technology of concurrent transmission [1][6], resulting in a system that has excellent performance in communication reliability, latency and energy consumption, as well as unprecedented robustness to node or link failure.

3   The Architecture of Sparkle

Sparkle employs a protocol similar to TDMA, which is normally used by wireless control networks, as it allows for deterministic scheduling and relatively deterministic QoS performance. The architecture makes independent QoS control for each end-to-end flow possible.

3.1   Mapping the Communication of Control Systems to Flows

Sparkle supports arbitrary communication requirements of periodic multi-loop control systems. For the simplest case of SISO (single input single output) control loop, it requires that a packet with sensor data is transmitted from the sensor to the controller, and a packet with actuation data is transmitted from the controller to the actuator periodically. If we implement the controller on any of the two end nodes, then we only need to maintain one QoS conformable flow from the sensor to the actuator node. On the other hand, if we implement the controller on a separate node, then two flows need to be maintained. For the more complex case of MIMO (multiple input multiple output) control loop, we need to maintain multiple flows from every sensor to the controller and from the controller to every actuator. Besides, Sparkle also supports the communication of data collection and dissemination commonly required by monitoring applications. As mentioned before, to control a flow, we need the cooperation of the opposite flow for delivering control commands.

3.2   Frame Structure

A Sparkle frame is composed of a *sync slot*, a number of *data slots* and zero or one *test slot* (Fig. 1). In each slot, a flooding is performed with different source node, different tx power and different set of participating nodes.

sync slot	data slot #1	data slot #2	...	test slot / idle

Fig. 1. A Sparkle frame

The purpose of the sync slot is to obtain network-wide time synchronization, in which an authority node (normally located in the network center) floods a short sync packet over the network with the Glossy protocol. Since the sync packet is very short (10 bytes in our implementation), it has a very high chance of being received correctly by each node, if we use a proper transmission power. The network-wide time synchronization is a prerequisite for the data communication in Sparkle. The next data slots are used for the communication of arbitrary flows. Different flows may have different period length, dependent on the requirement of the control systems. The test slot is used for the QoS control of the flows. Whether a set of flows (with arbitrary period length) is schedulable in Sparkle is determined by whether the total utilization of all slots is no more than 1.

3.3   Controlling the QoS Metrics of a Flow

Sparkle is capable of performing different QoS control for different flows. Generally speaking, the QoS controller of a flow is located at the destination node. It keeps track of the QoS metrics of the flow and sends out control commands to the source node or the whole network in the test slots of the opposite flow when necessary (e.g. setting tx power or activating/deactivating nodes for a flow). This design decision has the advantage of easy implementation and independent performance control for different flows, even for a pair of opposite flows. The detailed control scheme of Sparkle will be expounded later.

4   How Network Parameters Affect Performance

In this part, we investigate experimentally in real-world testbeds how the tx power and network topology affect the QoS metrics of reliability, latency and energy consumption. The so-called WSNShape technique is a novel topology control method which uses the capture effect to find the reliable paths from the source to the destination of a flow. It is very effective in finding reliable paths, compatible with the Glossy protocol as it requires no unicast transmission, and is much more lightweight and faster than ordinary routing protocols. Furthermore, it is resilient to node failure, which is not provided by the routing of existing control networks.

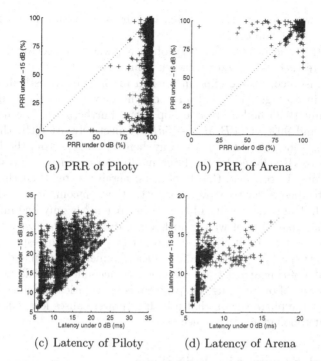

(a) PRR of Piloty   (b) PRR of Arena

(c) Latency of Piloty   (d) Latency of Arena

Fig. 2. The PRR and end-to-end latency at different tx powers. A point in the scatter plot is the metrics at $0dB$ and $-15dB$, for a given source and destination pair.

4.1   Different Transmission Powers

The evaluation results in the Glossy paper [1] show that a higher tx power gives lower latency and higher reliability. However, our evaluation on the two TUDμNet testbeds [8] shows that a higher tx power may lead to lower reliability when the network connectivity is very high.

TUDμNet includes two testbeds called Piloty and Arena respectively. The former has 63 telosB nodes [9] (n_1 to n_{63}, 55 are active), located in various offices on two floors of the CS building at TU Darmstadt, spanning a volume of $30 \times 20 \times 8\,m^3$. The latter has 60 telosB nodes (n_{1001} to n_{1060}, 42 are active), forming a 5×12 grid, located in a large room with line-of-sight between any two nodes, spanning a volume of $31 \times 7 \times 3\,m^3$. To compare different powers fairly, we let a source node perform Glossy flooding to all other nodes in the network, by setting the tx power of all nodes to $0dB$ and $-15dB$ alternately per second. In this way, we exclude the effect of the relatively slow channel variation of static WSN. Each active node acts once as the source.

Our results in Fig. 2 show that in the Piloty testbed, in almost all cases, the packet reception rate (PRR) is better when the higher tx power is chosen. However, in the Arena testbed, quite often the higher tx power gives lower reliability. The conclusion of the Glossy paper that the latency is lower under a higher tx power is generally supported by our experiments [1]. Intuitively, it is due to the smaller hop count.

We argue that the reason that very often a lower tx power improves PRR in the Arena testbed is a higher network connectivity than that in the Piloty testbed. For instance, in one experiment run in the Arena testbed, we found that at $0dB$, in average 33.04 nodes are one hop away from the source, while at $-15dB$, only 19.25 nodes are one hop away. Furthermore, one node has a PRR of 79% and 99% at $0dB$ and $-15dB$, respectively. At $0dB$, the node is for most of the time (62%) two hops away, hence it suffers from the low signal to noise ratio (SNR) caused by the large number of concurrently transmitting nodes at hop one. In contrast, that $0dB$ has generally better PRR than $-15dB$ in the Piloty testbed is due to a lower connectivity when compared to that of the Arena testbed. The node density of the former per m^3 is only one ninth of the latter, and the separation of walls and floors reduces the connectivity further. This brings to light that anticipating a proper tx power with respect to packet reliability is very hard. To do so, predicting the channel condition and taking the reception model of concurrent transmissions into account [6] would be required. One practical way of overcoming this problem is to empirically determine the tx power. Finally, the phenomenon that a high tx power causes low reliability also evidences that topology control is necessary.

4.2   Network Shaping with WSNShape

Control networks normally feature one-to-one communication, which is a special case of the one-to-all communication intrinsically supported by Glossy. If we could find a stripe of nodes between the source and destination for a flow, and only perform Glossy flooding among these nodes, energy consumption would be significantly reduced since lots of nodes are deactivated, and hopefully there would be still enough nodes in the stripe to take the advantage of the high reliability of constructive interference. However, we face two obstacles in *network shaping*, i.e. how to find the stripe: 1) Glossy is a routing free protocol and derives its advantages in reliability and latency from this feature. Therefore, network shaping with traditional routing protocols is not compatible with Glossy. 2) Since the channel condition is time-variant, we should continuously perform network shaping, which requires the process to be very lightweight and fast. Our novel WSNShape technique overcomes the two obstacles by effectively utilizing the capture effect.

Path Identification. The most important step of WSNShape is path identification, i.e. to find the reliable paths between the source and destination of a flow. We use the test slots of the flow for this purpose (Fig. 1). The process is as follows:

1. Activate all nodes in the network.
2. The source sets the bit corresponding to itself in the *path-ident* packet and broadcasts it. The path-ident packet contains basically a bit set of N bits where N is the number of nodes in the network[3].
3. Any node relays the packet exactly once in the way as Glossy. One difference is that instead of rebroadcasting the packet unmodified, the node sets the bit corresponding to itself in the path-ident packet before rebroadcasting.
4. If a packet is correctly received at destination, the packet can be used to reconstruct a path from the source to the destination.

Path Identification is Effective and Lightweight

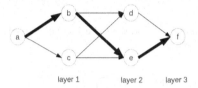

Fig. 3. An example of path identification. $a \rightarrow b \rightarrow e \rightarrow f$ is an identified path.

The capture effect implies that if a number of nodes transmit different packets concurrently and a packet is correctly decoded by the receiver, the packet should come from the node whose signal is the strongest at the receiver. Given that all nodes transmit with the same power, theoretically, we can infer that if a path is identified with the above process, then every link of the path, say $x \rightarrow y$, has the smallest signal loss among all links going into the node y, and the path has the shortest number of hops from the source to the destination.

Conceptually we build a network of K layers, where layer 0 only has the source node, and layer i contains all nodes that receive the packet after i relays. Each node in layer $i - 1$ has a directional link to each node in layer i. Fig. 3 shows a path identified from source a to destination f in an example network. Then, the signal loss of $b \rightarrow e$ is smaller than $c \rightarrow e$, because node b and c are both one hop away from a and transmit simultaneously. Similarly, the signal loss of $e \rightarrow f$ is smaller than $d \rightarrow f$. The shortest number of hops can be obtained taking into account the network is layered and directional. Although we cannot say that the identified path has the globally smallest cumulative path loss, as each link is locally optimal, practically, the path should be reliable and short.

To evaluate the quality of path identification, we test it on a number of flows with source and destination far apart on two floors in the Piloty testbed. A test slot is applied for each flow every 6s. The results for flows $n_{33} \leftrightarrow n_{60}$ are shown in Fig. 4, which are similar to that of the other flows. The path identification is very effective, both flows have a path identification rate P (the percentage of times that a path is successfully identified) of over 99%. This confirms that

---

[3] A control network normally has less than 100 nodes which takes only a dozen of bytes. If the network size is much bigger than the path length, we should enumerate the node ID of each hop rather than using a bit set.

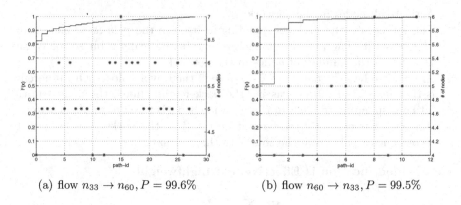

(a) flow $n_{33} \rightarrow n_{60}, P = 99.6\%$ (b) flow $n_{60} \rightarrow n_{33}, P = 99.5\%$

Fig. 4. The CDF and number of nodes in the identified paths, P is the path identification rate. Tx power $= 0dB$.

the capture effect is universal in WSN [5]. This has the advantage that the path identification is inherently resilient to node failure, which is not available in the routing of existing control networks. Since the capture effect is universal, as long as the network is connected, the sudden failure of a few nodes will not cause failure in path identification. The path identification is also lightweight and fast. For both testbeds, the size of the path-ident packet is rather small, of 16 bytes, which has both advantages of short radio-on time and high reception rate. However, the results also show the discrepancy between the experimentation and theory. In the testbed evaluation, we find that the distribution of the identified paths is concentrated on a few short paths (the most common 3 paths together have probability $> 90\%$), but has a long tail (29 and 12 paths are identified for both flows respectively). We argue that the reason that many paths of different length are identified is mainly due to the time variation of the channel. Yet it is favorable as it provides us with the chance to attain high reliability by combining multiple paths. Furthermore, despite the increase of path length, the path identification remains effective when we use a smaller tx power.

WSNShape Protocol. After we have identified the reliable paths, we are ready to utilize them to improve the QoS. The WSNShape protocol takes a parameter of *path count C*, which is the number of different paths we combine to form the stripe. C can be ∞, meaning that all paths should be combined. The WSNShape protocol performs the following steps for a flow continuously:

1. Path Identification. As described above, paths are identified in the test slots.
2. Path Combination. At the destination node we use a sliding window of size M, holding the most recent M paths identified ($M = 100$, keeping a history of 10 to 20 min). After a new path is put into the sliding window, we perform a sort on the paths in the decreasing order of path frequency. Then we combine the C most common paths to form a stripe[4].

---

[4] In our implementation, the statistics starts when 10 paths are identified.

3. Stripe Activation. If the nodes in the stripe have been changed, the destination node floods it in the form of bit map in the next test slot of the opposite flow. To guarantee a high probability of reception, the packet is flooded three times. When a node receives the stripe, it checks whether it is in the stripe or not. Based on that, it activates or deactivates itself (sleep) in the future data slots for the flow.

Since the WSN nodes are generally resource constrained devices with limited RAM and computational capability, we need to optimize the data structure of the sliding window. Although a relatively large number of path samples (up to 100) are preserved, normally the number of different paths is an order of magnitude less. Therefore, we use a linked list to keep these samples. A node in the linked list consists of a path and the number of occurrence of it. The data structure is efficient in terms of both storage and computation. In the next section, we will evaluate how the WSNShape performs compared to the baseline Glossy.

5   Performance Comparison of Different Sparkle Operation Modes

A Sparkle operation mode is a given combination of a tx power and a topology control. As shown by extensive evaluation in this section, different operation modes have different performance trade-offs in reliability, latency and energy consumption. Eight operation modes are investigated: 1) BL-HI, all nodes are active and have tx power of $0dB$. 2) BL-LO, all nodes are active and have tx power of $-15dB$. 3) NS-1, WSNShape with path count $C = 1$, which is basically single-path routing. 4) NS-2, WSNShape with $C = 2$.[5] 5) NS-3, 6) NS-4, 7) NS-5, and 8) NS-ALL, WSNShape with $C = \infty$. The evaluation gives insight into the performance of different operation modes, providing fundamentals for the design of an adaptive scheme.

5.1   Evaluation Setup

In the evaluation, the Sparkle frame has a period of $1s$. In each one-hour run, we evaluate 6 flows simultaneously. The 6 flows are 3 pairs of opposite flows (e.g. $a \leftrightarrow b$ is a pair). Each flow needs to transmit a packet per second (corresponding to a control system with period of $1s$). Thus, the frame is composed of 8 slots – one sync slot, 6 data slots, and one test slot which is circularly used by each flow to identify path and to broadcast the stripe of WSNShape for its opposite flow. To save energy, all packets except the stripe broadcast are transmitted only once. The stripe broadcast is transmitted 3 times. The stripe for a given path count is broadcast whenever it is updated. The data packet has a length of 126 bytes. Furthermore, in each slot, a node turns off the radio when it has transmitted for the given number of times (once or thrice) or it has been on for $40ms$. The same

---
[5] If there is in total one path, then this mode is same as NS-1.

Table 1. The statistical results of Sparkle modes. The column "adaptive" refers to the combination of BL-HI, BL-LO, NS-2 and NS-ALL. Good PRR means PRR $\geq$ 95%.

	BL-HI	BL-LO	NS-1	NS-2	NS-3	NS-4	NS-5	NS-ALL	adaptive
Good PRR Rate (%)	58.62	55.17	56.90	68.97	77.59	81.03	81.03	86.21	98.28
Normalized Latency (%)	100.00	169.26	91.81	92.91	93.13	92.79	93.06	93.93	-
Active Slot Rate (%)	100.00	100.00	6.66	9.14	11.62	13.28	14.58	18.23	-

as before, to fairly compare the different modes, the network circularly runs in each mode for $1s$. This is controlled by the *sync-seq*, a counter contained in the sync packet, incremented after each frame. After the network is bootstrapped, each node should share the same sync-seq. It also controls which flow should use a certain test slot. The program is implemented on the Contiki OS [10].

We evaluate two types of flows: 1) long flow, with end nodes far apart and 2) unreliable flow, where the flow itself or the opposite flow has low reliability ($< 90\%$) in the default BL-HI mode.[6] These flows represent the worst evaluation scenario since path identification should be relatively ineffective. However, for all flows, the path identification is successful. The long flow set includes 6 flows (3 pairs) for the Piloty and Arena testbeds respectively. The unreliable flow set includes 22 flows (11 pairs) for the Piloty testbed and 24 flows (12 pairs) for the Arena testbed.

5.2   Performance Comparison

The QoS metrics of a number of typical flows are depicted in Fig. 5 and the average values of the QoS metrics over all flows are shown in Tab. 1. We focus on the trade-off of 3 metrics: 1) PRR, the end-to-end reliability of packet delivery of a flow, 2) active slot rate (ASR), the number of active data slots over the number of all data slots for a flow and 3) normalized latency, the average end-to-end latency normalized over the value of the mode BL-HI. The active slot rate should be the same as the average percentage of active nodes, which is roughly proportional to the energy consumption.

Reliability. In average, the reliability of all WSNShape modes except NS-1 is better than that of the baseline modes BL-HI and BL-LO (Tab. 1). The mode NS-ALL is generally the best. The situation that NS-1 is significantly worse than the other WSNShape modes evidences the advantage of constructive interference of multiple transmitters in boosting reliability. It shows that the concurrent transmission based network with only a few concurrent transmitters is more reliable than the traditional network based on single-path routing, even if the path is reliable. On the other hand, if the number of concurrent transmitters is very high (mode BL-HI), the reliability may decrease. Furthermore, there is at least one flow for which a certain mode is better than all the others (Fig. 5). Thus, there is no winner in all cases and the relative performance among various

---

[6] These pairs of flows are identified by the experiments in Sec. 4.1 for evaluating the effects of tx power.

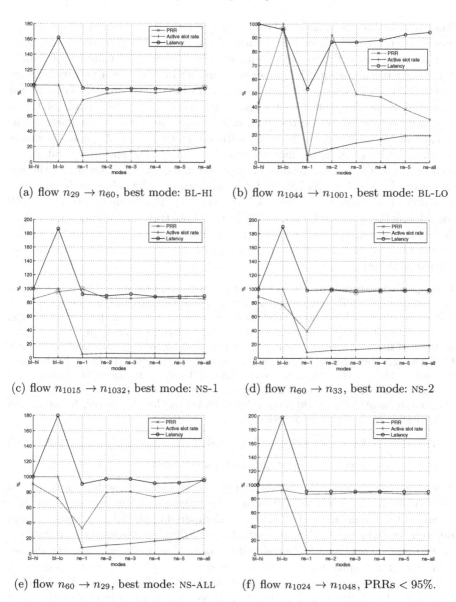

(a) flow $n_{29} \to n_{60}$, best mode: BL-HI   (b) flow $n_{1044} \to n_{1001}$, best mode: BL-LO

(c) flow $n_{1015} \to n_{1032}$, best mode: NS-1   (d) flow $n_{60} \to n_{33}$, best mode: NS-2

(e) flow $n_{60} \to n_{29}$, best mode: NS-ALL   (f) flow $n_{1024} \to n_{1048}$, PRRs < 95%.

Fig. 5. Some typical results from the evaluation of Sparkle modes. The points highlighted have good reliability (PRR $\geq$ 95%). Latencies are normalized to that of BL-HI.

modes can be chaotic. But if we can always choose the best mode among BL-HI, BL-LO, NS-2 and NS-ALL, over 98% of the cases, we can obtain good reliability ($\geq$ 95%, sufficient for most control systems). The only case that good reliability is unattained is shown in Fig. 5(f) where only one path can be identified for the flow and none of the modes reaches good reliability. This motivates us to design an adaptive scheme which can choose among the four modes.

End-to-end Latency. As listed in Tab. 1, the average latency of the WSNShape modes are 6% to 8% shorter than that of the BL-HI, and generally the latency increases slightly with the path count C. This shows the advantage of limited concurrent transmissions. The moderate number of concurrent transmitters increases SNR and thus the PRR in comparison to the large number of concurrent transmitters in the mode BL-HI. Therefore, statistically less rounds of transmissions are needed before the destination successfully receives a packet. The latency of the BL-LO mode is about 69% longer than that of the BL-HI mode, because the lower tx power increases the hop count. The end-to-end latency is near optimal. The largest average latency and hop count of a flow under the low tx power of $-15dB$ are $33.7ms$ and 7.0, respectively. The values under the high tx power of $0dB$ are $18.9ms$ and 3.7, respectively. The latencies are very small considering the large packet size of 126 bytes whose transmission takes more than $4ms$. In addition, Sparkle can provide the hard deadline guarantee by turning off the radio after the slot duration has finished (slot duration $= 40ms$ in our implementation).

Energy Consumption. The actual energy consumption should be roughly proportional to the ASR. Obviously ASR $= 100\%$ in the baseline modes because all nodes are active. The various WSNShape modes NS-1 to NS-ALL save as much as 93% to 82% of energy compared to the baseline modes. This is due to the large amount of inactive modes. Intuitively, the saving decreases with the path count C. Although the ASR value of the two baseline schemes is 100% in both cases, we expect that BL-LO consumes more energy than BL-HI, since the former has a much longer latency which increases the listen time significantly. This more than compensates the slight saving brought by the low tx power. In summary, we can give an energy consumption model:

$$E(\text{BL-LO}) > E(\text{BL-HI}) \gg E(\text{NS-ALL}) > \cdots > E(\text{NS-}i) > E(\text{NS-}j) > \cdots > E(\text{NS-1}) \quad (1)$$

where $E(\cdot)$ is the energy consumption of a mode, and $i = j + 1$.

Summary. In general, the reliabilities of the WSNShape modes improve with the path count C. The trade-off is that the latencies and energy consumptions (ASR) of them increase with C (Tab. 1). Compared to the Glossy protocol (with different tx powers), WSNShape with $C \geq 2$ brings improvement in reliability, latency and energy consumption simultaneously. The energy saving is significant, over 80%. The improvement in latency is slight, only a few percent. Regarding reliability, NS-ALL is generally the best mode. But the relative reliability can be chaotic for different flows. However, if we can adaptively choose the most reliable mode among BL-HI, BL-LO, NS-2 and NS-ALL, far better performance can be achieved than sticking to any specific mode, which is the main topic of the next section.

6   PRRTrack: Adaptively Minimizing Energy Consumption while Meeting Reliability Requirement

A useful control system must be stable and have a satisfactory performance, which normally requires that each flow has latency below and reliability above

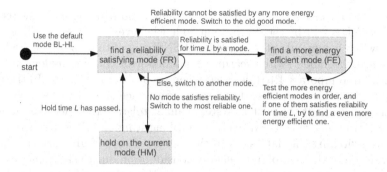

Fig. 6. The mode switch process of PRRTrack

preset values, respectively [11]. In this section, we design and evaluate an automatic scheme, PRRTrack, a component of Sparkle that adaptively switches between different operation modes, with the goal of minimizing energy consumption while meeting the reliability requirement. In case the reliability requirement cannot be satisfied by any of the modes, PRRTrack achieves the best-effort performance by keeping a flow operate in the most reliable mode for most of the time. The testbed evaluation shows that PRRTrack effectively achieves its design goal together with the advantage of improving latency.

6.1   The Design of PRRTrack

The main idea of PRRTrack is simple: if the current mode satisfies the reliability requirement, it tries to find a more energy-efficient one, otherwise it tries to find one that satisfies the reliability requirement. Given the model of relative energy efficiency of our various modes, the process to find a more energy-efficient mode is straightforward. But on the other hand, since no model of the relative reliability is available, the process to find a mode satisfying the reliability requirement is basically trial-and-error.

The control logic of PRRTrack is realized at the destination node of a flow. It performs two activities: first, it maintains the recently identified 100 paths for WSNShape; second, it keeps track of the *current PRR* by calculating the reception rate of the recent 100 data packets of a flow. Also, in the manner of feedback control, it gives proper commands of mode switch based on the difference between the current PRR and the reliability set-point.

The mode switch process of PRRTrack is illustrated in Fig. 6. We only switch among the four modes BL-HI, BL-LO, NS-2 and NS-ALL. Since we prefer to minimize mode switches, we revise our energy model from (1): $E(\text{BL-LO}) = E(\text{BL-HI}) > E(\text{NS-ALL}) > E(\text{NS-2})$.

6.2   Implementation

The implementation details of PRRTrack are as follows. The test slots are used for path identification and mode switch commands. The path-ident packets are sent by the source node once every $10s$ if there is no pending mode switch command, which is sent by the destination node whenever necessary. Included in the mode switch command is the stripe for WSNShape, if the mode is a WSNShape one. Since the mode switch features trial-and-error, in our implementation it may lead to temporary PRR decrease when we probe a new mode. In the chosen configuration, this may cause decreased performance of about $100s$ (the test duration, Fig. 7(c)). If the control system cannot tolerate that, we can implement the PRRTrack more conservatively by probing a mode in the test slots before actually switching the data slots to that mode. This will give better reliability performance at the cost of more energy consumption due to the higher overhead of test slots and slower mode switch reaction. Whenever we switch to a different mode, we flush the sliding window for PRR re-calculation.

6.3   Evaluation

For the evaluation of PRRTrack, we compare the performance of Sparkle with PRRTrack to that of Sparkle with the fixed mode BL-HI. In each round of the evaluation, we run both programs for 3 hours each. Similar to Sec. 5.1, 3 pairs of opposite flows are evaluated in each round. For each of the Piloty and Arena testbeds, we evaluate 12 random pairs of opposite flows.

The evaluation results of two representative flows in the Piloty testbed are shown in Fig. 7. We show the averaged PRR from the program start. From Figures 7(a) and 7(b) we observe that if we stick to the BL-HI mode, neither of the two flows can satisfy the reliability requirement PRR $\geq R$ with $R = 90\%$. Furthermore, the PRR values are not stable. There are long periods in which the PRR goes up or down steadily. From Figures 7(c) and 7(d) we see that if PRRTrack is applied, the reliability requirement can be satisfied and the PRR values are much more stable.

In the case of Fig. 7(c), we observe that after the PRRTrack starts, we transition immediately into the state FR. Then we test the modes NS-2, NS-ALL, BL-HI and BL-LO one by one, in the decreasing order of energy efficiency, to find a reliable one, but none of them satisfies PRR $\geq 90\%$ for $1000s$ ($L = 1000s$). Therefore, we switch to the most reliable mode at that time, BL-HI, and hold on it for $1000s$. After the hold time, we transition back to the state FR. But now BL-HI can meet R for over $1000s$, therefore we later transition to the state FE, to find a more energy-efficient mode. Now we land in the mode NS-ALL, which is not only more energy-efficient, but also reliable enough. But from time to time (after about every 1000 sec), we try the more efficient NS-2 for $100s$, to find a potentially reliable and more energy-efficient mode. However, until the end of the program, this probing is unsuccessful. The situation in Fig. 7(d) is much simpler. After we switch to the mode NS-2, the reliability requirement can always be satisfied, therefore we stay in the mode as it is the most energy-efficient one.

To measure the energy consumption of the radio component, which accounts for the predominant part of energy consumption of our system, we use Energest, a software-based method for energy measurement provided in Contiki [12]. For higher precision, we consider the different current consumptions of listen mode

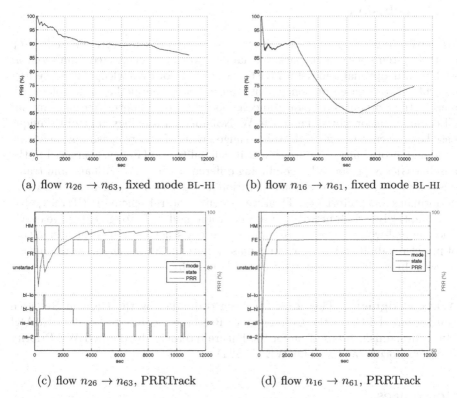

(a) flow $n_{26} \rightarrow n_{63}$, fixed mode BL-HI

(b) flow $n_{16} \rightarrow n_{61}$, fixed mode BL-HI

(c) flow $n_{26} \rightarrow n_{63}$, PRRTrack

(d) flow $n_{16} \rightarrow n_{61}$, PRRTrack

Fig. 7. The reliability of PRRTrack vs fixed mode. Reliability requirement $R = 90\%$.

Table 2. The energy consumption and latency of PRRTrack vs. fixed mode. Energy$_d$ is the energy consumption of data slots. Energy$_t$ is that of test slots.

	Fixed mode BL-HI (3 hours)			PRRTrack (3 hours)		
	Energy$_d(J)$	Energy$_t(J)$	Latency(ms)	Energy$_d(J)$	Energy$_t(J)$	Latency(ms)
flow $n_{26} \leftrightarrow n_{63}$	1008.27	0	18.09	196.21	24.11	16.15
flow $n_{16} \leftrightarrow n_{61}$	1009.68	0	16.11	109.21	23.17	14.45

and transmit mode with various tx powers. As listed in Tab. 2, the energy saving of the PRRTrack is huge. For two pairs of flows $n_{26} \leftrightarrow n_{63}$ and $n_{16} \leftrightarrow n_{61}$, including the control overhead (that of test slots), it uses only 22% and 13% of that of the fixed mode BL-HI, respectively[7]. The control overhead amounts for about 1/5 of the energy consumption. Additionally, PRRTrack also improves the average end-to-end latency by about 10%. Over all 24 pairs of flows, the average energy saving is 84% and the latency improvement is 5%.

---

[7] We look at the energy consumption of a pair of opposite flows together instead of separately because to achieve reliable transmission on one flow, we need the cooperation of some test slots of its opposite flow.

7   Conclusion

We have presented Sparkle, a communication network for periodic multi-loop control systems with high packet reliability, very low energy consumption, as well as near-optimal and deterministic latency. To our knowledge, it is the first control network based on concurrent transmission. Sparkle has a flexible architecture that supports arbitrary and independent QoS control mechanisms for all communication flows. The novel WSNShape is a topology control technique based on the capture effect. It leads to huge saving of energy consumption as well as to high probability of improvement in reliability and latency, compared to the baseline Glossy protocol. By combining different levels of WSNShape and transmission power, we derive various operation modes featuring different energy and performance characteristics. Then we design a control scheme PRRTrack, that can adaptively switch between these operation modes. Through extensive evaluation on real-world testbeds, we confirm that our scheme satisfies the design goal of preset reliability while in average massively reducing the energy consumption by 84%. In addition, it also reduces the latency by 5%.

Acknowledgment. This work has been co-funded by the German Research Foundation (DFG) in the Collaborative Research Center (SFB) 1053 "MAKI Multi-Mechanism-Adaptation for the Future Internet", by the LOEWE Priority Program Cocoon and by LOEWE CASED.

References

1. Ferrari, F., Zimmerling, M., Thiele, L., Saukh, O.: Efficient network flooding and time synchronization with glossy. In: IPSN, pp. 73–84 (2011)
2. Whitehouse, K., Woo, A., Jiang, F., Polastre, J., Culler, D.: Exploiting the capture effect for collision detection and recovery. In: EmNetS, pp. 45–52 (2005)
3. O'Donovan, T., et al.: The ginseng system for wireless monitoring and control. ACM Transactions on Sensor Networks 10(1) (2014)
4. Ceriotti, M., et al.: Is there light at the ends of the tunnel? wireless sensor networks for adaptive lighting in road tunnels. In: IPSN, pp. 187–198 (2011)
5. Landsiedel, O., Ferrari, F., Zimmerling, M.: Chaos: a versatile and efficient communication primitive for all-to-all data sharing and in-network processing at scale. In: SenSys (November 2013)
6. Yuan, D., Hollick, M.: Let's talk together: Understanding concurrent transmission in wireless sensor networks. In: LCN (2013)
7. Carlson, D., Chang, M., Terzis, A., Chen, Y., Gnawali, O.: Forwarder selection in multi-transmitter networks. In: DCOSS, pp. 1–10 (2013)
8. Guerrero, P.E., Gurov, I., Santini, S., Buchmann, A.: On the Selection of Testbeds for the Evaluation of Sensor Network Protocols and Applications. In: SPAWC, pp. 490–494 (June 2013)
9. Polastre, J., Szewczyk, R., Culler, D.E.: Telos: enabling ultra-low power wireless research. In: IPSN, pp. 364–369 (2005)

10. Dunkels, A., Grönvall, B., Voigt, T.: Contiki - a lightweight and flexible operating system for tiny networked sensors. In: LCN, pp. 455–462 (2004)
11. Zhang, W., Branicky, M.S., Phillips, S.M.: Stability of networked control systems. IEEE Control Systems Magazine 21, 84–99 (2001)
12. Dunkels, A., Österlind, F., Tsiftes, N., He, Z.: Software-based on-line energy estimation for sensor nodes. In: EmNets, pp. 28–32 (2007)

Energy Consumption of Visual Sensor Networks: Impact of Spatio-Temporal Coverage Based on Single-Hop Topologies

Alessandro Redondi[1], Dujdow Buranapanichkit[2],
Matteo Cesana[1], Marco Tagliasacchi[1], and Yiannis Andreopoulos[3]

[1]Electronic, Information and Bioengineering Department, Politecnico di Milano, Italy
{redondi,cesana,tagliasa}@elet.polimi.it
[2]Department of Electrical Engineering, Prince of Songkla University, Thailand
dujdow.b@psu.ac.th
[3]Electronic and Electrical Engineering Department, University College London, UK
i.andreopoulos@ucl.ac.uk

Abstract. Wireless visual sensor networks (VSNs) are expected to play a major role in future IEEE 802.15.4 personal area networks (PAN) under recently-established collision-free medium access control (MAC) protocols. In such environments, the trade-off between the number of camera sensors to deploy (spatial coverage) and the frame rate to use for each camera sensor (temporal coverage) plays a major role in the VSN energy consumption. In this paper, we address this aspect for *single-hop* VSNs, i.e. networks comprising independent and identical wireless visual sensor nodes connected to a collection node via a star topology. We derive analytic results for the energy-optimal spatio-temporal coverage parameters of such VSNs under *a-priori* known bounds for the minimum frame rate per sensor and the minimum and maximum possible number of nodes to deploy. Our results are parametric to the probability density function characterizing the data-production rate per node and the energy consumption parameters of the system of interest. Experimental results using TelosB motes under: a collision-free transmission protocol, the IEEE 802.15.4 PAN physical layer (CC2420 transceiver) and Monte-Carlo–generated data sets, reveal that our analytic results are within 7% of the energy consumption measurements for a wide range of settings. In addition, results obtained via a multimedia subsystem performing visual feature extraction in video frames show that the optimal spatio-temporal settings derived by the proposed framework allow for up to 48% of reduction of energy consumption in comparison to ad-hoc settings. As such, our analytic modeling is useful for early-stage studies of possible VSN deployments under collision-free MAC protocols prior to costly and time-consuming experiments in the field.

1 Introduction

The integration of low-power wireless networking technologies such as IEEE 802.15.4-enabled transceivers [1] with inexpensive camera hardware [2] has enabled the development of the so-called *visual sensor networks* (VSNs). VSNs

B. Krishnamachari, A.L. Murphy, and N. Trigoni (Eds.): EWSN 2014, LNCS 8354, pp. 150–165, 2014.

can be thought of as networks of wireless devices capable of sensing multimedia content [3], such as still images and video, audio, depth maps, etc. Via the recent provisioning of an all-IPv6 network layer under 6LoWPAN and the emergence of collision-free low-power medium access control (MAC) protocols, such as the time slotted channel hopping (TSCH) of IEEE 802.15.4e-2012 [4], VSNs are expected to play a major role in the evolution of the Internet-of-Things (IoT) paradigm [5].

1.1   Review of Visual Sensor Networks

An increasing number of VSN solutions were proposed recently with a focus on new transmission protocols allowing for high-bandwidth collision-free communications [6,4] and in-network visual processing techniques [7]. Most of the proposed VSN solutions can be abstracted as two tightly-coupled subsystems: a multimedia processor board and a low-power radio subsystem [2], interconnected via a push model. A cluster of such identical nodes can be organized into a VSN comprising a star topology that can operate in collision-free steady-state mode as illustrated in the example of Figure 1, with the consumption rate of each node being s bits for each interval of T seconds that the VSN remains active, or $\frac{s}{T}$ bits-per-second (bps). Within each node, the multimedia subsystem is responsible for acquiring images, processing them and pushing the processed data to the radio subsystem. For example, in the most typical application scenario for VSNs, the multimedia subsystem would acquire each image, compress it into a JPEG bitstream (e.g., using an MJPEG codec) and push the JPEG bitstream to the radio subsystem [2]. The latter transmits the processed data stream to the low-power border router (LPBR) [5], and eventually to a remote destination, which, under the IoT paradigm, could be any IPv6 Internet address.

Multimedia Processing Subsystem: The frame rate under which each VSN camera is operating, i.e. each node's temporal coverage, is controlling the frequency of the push operations. At the same time, the multimedia processing task itself (e.g., JPEG compression) controls the volume of bits pushed to the radio subsystem within each frame's duration.

Communications Subsystem: The number of sensors in the (single-hop) star topology, i.e. the VSN's spatial coverage (Figure 1), controls the bandwidth available to each sensor (i.e. its average transmission rate) under a collision-free MAC protocol [6,8,4]. Thus, there is a fundamental tradeoff between the spatial and temporal coverage in a network: high frame rate leads to high bandwidth requirement per transmitter, which in turn decreases the number of sensors that can be accommodated with the same LPBR. Conversely, dense spatial coverage via the use of a large number of visual sensors decreases the available bandwidth per sensor and this in turn reduces the achievable frame rate per sensor in order to maintain tight coupling.

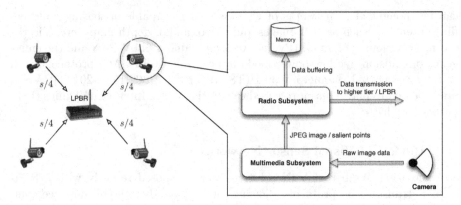

Fig. 1. Single-hop star topology in a visual sensor network, where every visual sensor (video camera) has its own spatial coverage, with s indicating the bits consumed by each node within each active interval of T seconds. Each camera node comprises two subsystems, which are illustrated in the figure expansion. If required, each node can buffer parts of its data stream for later transmission.

Overall System Perspective – Energy Consumption: Like traditional wireless sensor networks, VSN nodes are battery operated. Hence, energy consumption plays a crucial role in the design of a VSN, especially for those applications where a VSN is required to operate for days or even weeks without external power supply. In the last few years, several works have addressed the problem of lifetime maximization in VSNs: depending on the research area, solutions are available for energy-aware protocols and cross-layer optimization [4], application tradeoffs [5] and deployment strategies [2]. While existing work addresses transmission, scheduling and protocol design aiming for energy efficiency, it does not consider the impact of the spatio-temporal coverage in the energy consumption of VSNs. This is precisely the focus of this paper.

1.2   Contribution

In this paper, we derive analytic results concerning energy-aware VSN deployments under the push model of Figure 1. Specifically, we are interested in the link of the aforementioned spatio-temporal tradeoff with the incurred energy consumption under well known probability density functions modeling the pushed data volume of image and video applications, such as intra/inter-frame video coding and visual features extraction and transmission. We focus on the widely used case of single-hop VSNs comprising identical sensors connected to the LPBR via a star topology and we derive an analytic model that captures the expected energy consumption in function of: *(i)* the number of visual sensors deployed, *(ii)* the frame rate used by each camera sensor and *(iii)* the statistical characterization of the bitstream data volume produced by each sensor after on-board image analysis or compression. The extrema of the derived energy consumption function are then analytically derived in order to provide closed-form expressions for the minimum energy consumption of each case under consideration. The derived analytic results are experimentally validated with a VSN performing visual feature extraction and transmission to the LPBR.

2   Utilized System Model and Its Expected Energy Consumption

In the first four subsections we introduce the components of the utilized system model and the corresponding nomenclature. The key notations are summarized in Table 1, along with the practical settings used in the experiments of the paper.

2.1   Communication and System Infrastructure

Consider a wireless visual sensor network comprising a star topology. The network consists of n independent and identical camera nodes that process visual data and transmit multimedia streams to the LPBR. The MAC layer of the network is operating under a collision-free time-division (or time-frequency division) multiple access protocol [6,8,4], so that simultaneous transmissions (self-inflicted collisions) are avoided. Let $\frac{s}{T}$ bps be the average consumption rate of the LPBR over the VSN active interval of T seconds.

Within each node, the multimedia and radio subsystems work in parallel: while the multimedia system acquires and processes data corresponding to the current video frame, the radio subsystem transmits the multimedia stream stemming from the processing of the previous video frame(s). Examples of VSN applications that fit the communications model illustrated in Figure 1 are: multi-camera JPEG compression and transmission of video bitstreams [7], multi-sensor visual features extraction [9] and transmission, multi-camera compression and transmission for object recognition, etc.

2.2   Active Time Interval and Delay Tolerance

Given that applications based on visual sensor networks are subject to severe bandwidth requirements, it may not be possible to transmit the entirety of each multimedia stream within the transmission opportunities corresponding to the duration of one video frame. In such a case, buffering to on-board memory is required. This means that the application must tolerate certain delay until all multimedia streams are received by the LPBR. This delay is controlled by the chosen value of T and can be tuned to fit the constraints imposed by each deployment scenario.

After T seconds, each sensor stops gathering new data, completes the transmission of any data that may exist in its buffer and goes into suspension mode until the occurrence of the next active time interval. For example, setting $T = 5$ s indicates that the sensors are actively gathering and processing visual data for five seconds, complete any remaining data transmissions after that, and then suspend their activity until being reactivated. The VSN activation can either be event-driven (e.g., when activity or motion is detected) or periodic, with a certain duty cycle [2,4].

2.3   Spatio-temporal Coverage and Statistical Characterization of Data Transmission Volume per VSN Node

We consider that the VSN is established under the following two application constraints:

- *spatial coverage bounds*; the number of deployed nodes, n, is upper- and lower-bounded, i.e., $N_{\min} \leq n \leq N_{\max}$
- *temporal coverage lower bound*; the total frame acquisitions, k, within a predefined time interval, T, is lower-bounded, i.e., $k \geq K_{\min}$

The bounds of the spatio-temporal coverage stem from application specifics, such as: the cost of installing and maintaining visual sensors, the minimum and maximum spatial coverage required for the area to be monitored, and the minimum frame rate that allows for visual data gathering and analysis with sufficient temporal resolution for the application.

Since the multimedia subsystem of each visual sensor produces varying amounts of data depending on the monitored events and the specifics of the visual analysis and processing under consideration, the data stream volume produced by each camera in such multimedia applications is a non-deterministic quantity. We thus model the data volume produced when each camera processes k frames via a random variable (RV) $\mathcal{X}_k$, with marginal probability density function (PDF) $P(\chi_k)$, $\mathcal{X}_k \backsim P(\chi_k)$.

2.4   Energy Consumption Penalties

Following the push model illustrated in Figure 1, each node performs the following operations during the active time interval T:

1. *Acquisition:* A low-power camera sensor acquires k frames, each incurring a Joule (J) of energy expenditure. Hence, the energy consumed during T s is ka J.

2. *Processing and transmission:* Each captured video frame is processed with a CPU-intensive algorithm, realized by the multimedia subsystem. Each frame processing produces, on average, r bits (b) for transmission. These bits are pushed to the radio subsystem, which in turn transmits them to the base station. Let g J be the average energy required for processing and producing one bit of information and j the average energy required to transmit it to the LPBR. The average energy consumed for processing and transmission within the active interval is hence $(g + j) \int_0^\infty \chi_k P(\chi_k) d\chi = (g + j) \mathbb{E}[\mathcal{X}_k]$ J, with $\mathbb{E}[\mathcal{X}_k]$ bits comprising the statistical expectation of the data volume corresponding to k frames.

3. *Buffering and Idling:* As shown in Figure 1, the sensor network consists of n sensor nodes that communicate with the LPBR, which has pre-defined consumption rate of $\frac{s}{T}$ bps. Under balanced coupling, each sensor node can transmit $\frac{s}{n}$ bits during the analysis time interval of T s. We thus identify two cases: if the amount of data generated by the processing phase is greater

Table 1. Visual sensor energy and bitrate parameters, including settings used in this paper

Parameter	Description	Unit	Value
Radio Subsystem (measured on TelosB with Contiki & NullMAC/NullRDC)			
n, N_{min}, N_{max}	Number of nodes, min/max setting	–	$N_{min} = 2$, $N_{max} = 16$
$\frac{s}{T}$	Data consumption rate	kbps	144
j	Transmission energy per bit	J/b	2.197×10^{-7}
b	Beaconing/idling energy per bit	J/b	1.902×10^{-7}
p	Buffering energy per bit	J/b	2.861×10^{-7}
Multimedia Subsystem ASIC [10][2]			
k, K_{min}	Frames captured within T s, min. setting	–	$K_{min} = 2T$
a	Acquisition energy per frame	J	4.000×10^{-3}
g	Processing energy per bit (visual features)	J/b	1.907×10^{-8}

than $\frac{s}{n}$, then the sensor node has to buffer the remaining data in a high-power, typically off-chip, memory. Letting p J be the energy cost of storing one bit of information, the energy spent for buffering during the active time interval is: $p \int_{\frac{s}{n}}^{\infty} (\chi_k - \frac{s}{n})P(\chi_k)d\chi_k$ J. Conversely, if the data generated is less than $\frac{s}{n}$, the sensor node enters an "idle" state, where b J is consumed for beaconing and other synchronization operations corresponding to the duration of the transmission of one bit. The energy spent during the idle mode of the analysis time interval is thus: $b \int_0^{\frac{s}{n}} (\frac{s}{n} - \chi_k)P(\chi_k)d\chi_k$ J.

2.5 Expected Energy Consumption

Summing all contributions 1~3 described in the previous subsection, the energy consumption of the coupled system, E_c, over the time interval T is:

$$E_c(n, k) = ka + (g + j)\mathbb{E}[\mathcal{X}_k] + p\int_{\frac{s}{n}}^{\infty} (\chi_k - \frac{s}{n})P(\chi_k)d\chi_k + b\int_0^{\frac{s}{n}} (\frac{s}{n} - \chi_k)P(\chi_k,)d\chi_k.$$

(1)

Adding and subtracting $p\int_0^{\frac{s}{n}} (\chi_k - \frac{s}{n})P(\chi_k)d\chi_k$ to (1) leads to:

$$E_c(n, k) = ka + (p + g + j)\mathbb{E}[\mathcal{X}_k] - \frac{ps}{n} + (b + p)\int_0^{\frac{s}{n}} (\frac{s}{n} - \chi_k)P(\chi_k)d\chi_k.$$ (2)

The last equation forms the basis for the analytic exploration of the minimum energy consumption under the knowledge of the marginal PDF characterizing the data production and transmission process.

3 Analytic Derivation of Minimum Energy Consumption

Our objective is to derive the spatio-temporal parameters minimizing $E_c(n, k)$ in (2) subject to the spatio-temporal constraints defined in Section 2, that is:

$$\{n^\star, k^\star\} = \arg\min_{\forall n, k} E_c(n, k), \tag{3}$$

with

$$N_{\min} \leq n \leq N_{\max} \text{ and } k \geq K_{\min} \tag{4}$$

and $\{n^\star, k^\star\}$ the values deriving the minimum energy consumption.

In the following, we consider two different marginal distributions for $P(\chi_k)$ and derive the choice for n and k that minimizes the energy consumption, while ensuring the conditions imposed by the application constraints are met. While our analysis is assuming that n and k are continuous variables, once the $\{n^\star, k^\star\}$ values are derived, they can be discretized to the sets $\{\lfloor n^\star \rfloor, \lfloor k^\star \rfloor\}$, $\{\lceil n^\star \rceil, \lceil k^\star \rceil\}$ $\{\lceil n^\star \rceil, \lfloor k^\star \rfloor\}$ $\{\lfloor n^\star \rfloor, \lceil k^\star \rceil\}$ [if all four satisfy the constraints of (4)] in order to check which discrete pair of values derives the minimum energy consumption in (2). This is because: (i) the energy functions under consideration are continuous and differentiable; and (ii) we shall show that, for the data size PDFs under consideration, a *unique* minimum is found for (2) that is parametric to the setting of the temporal constraint ($K_{\min}$). As such, the analysis on the continuous variable space can be directly mapped onto the discrete variable set under the aforementioned discretization.

3.1 Illustrative Case: Uniform Distribution

When one has limited or no knowledge about the cumulative data transmitted by each VSN node during T, one can assume that $P(\chi_k)$ is uniform over the interval $[0, 2kr]$. That is,

$$P(\chi_k) = \begin{cases} \frac{1}{2kr} & 0 \leq \chi_k \leq 2kr \\ 0 & \text{otherwise} \end{cases} \tag{5}$$

with $\mathbb{E}_U[\mathcal{X}_k] = kr$ corresponding to the mean value of the data transmitted by a node that produces k frames of r bits each on average. Using (5) in (2) leads to:

$$E_{c,U}(n, k) = k\left[a + r(p + j + g)\right] - \frac{ps}{n} + \frac{s^2(b+p)}{4n^2 kr}. \tag{6}$$

To obtain the solution to (3) under the energy consumption given by (6), one can search for critical points of $E_{c,U}$. Imposing that the derivatives of $E_{c,U}$ with respect to n and k are both equal to zero leads to:

$$\begin{cases} \frac{\partial E_{c,U}}{\partial n} = \frac{ps}{n^2} - \frac{s^2(b+p)}{2n^3 kr} = 0 \\ \frac{\partial E_{c,U}}{\partial k} = a + r(p + j + g) - \frac{s^2(b+p)}{4n^2 k^2 r} = 0 \end{cases} \tag{7}$$

It can be shown that the solution of (7) requires $a < 0$ (the detailed derivation is omitted due to space limitations). However, this is not physically feasible since a is the energy cost to acquire one frame. Hence, under the physical constraints of the problem, *there is no single (global) solution* $\{n^\star, k^\star\} \in \mathbb{R} \times \mathbb{R}$ *to* (3) *in its unconstrained form, i.e. when one ignores the constraints of* (4). However, we may look at one or the other direction individually (i.e., along n or k) in order to find a local or global minimum for that particular direction and then choose for the other direction the value that minimizes (3) under the spatio-temporal constraints of (4). Subsequently, we can identify if the derived minima are unique under the imposed constraints and whether the entire region of support of the energy function has been covered by the derived solutions. These are investigated in the following.

n-direction. We examine the function $E_{c,U}$ along the plane $k = \bar{k}$, $\bar{k} \geq K_{min}$, and analyze $E_{c,U}(n, \bar{k})$ which is now a function of n only. It is straightforward to show by first-derivative analysis that the only candidate extremum or inflection point of $E_{c,U}(n, \bar{k})$ is $n_{0,U} = \frac{\beta_U}{\bar{k}}$, with

$$\beta_U = \frac{s(b+p)}{2pr} \tag{8}$$

defined as a "system-specific" parameter (which depends on average bits transmitted and the energy penalty rates). This candidate extremum or inflection point is valid under the assumption that: $N_{min} \leq n_{0,U} \leq N_{max}$, i.e. that the candidate point falls within the predefined spatial constraints of (4). Furthermore, we find that $\left. \frac{d^2 E_{c,U}(n, \bar{k})}{dn^2} \right|_{n=n_{0,U}} > 0$, which demonstrates that $n_{0,U}$ is a local minimum. Given that local extrema must alternate within the region of support of a continuous and differentiable function, the boundary points ($n = N_{min}$ and $n = N_{max}$) cannot be local minima. Thus, $n_{0,U}$ is the global minimum of $E_{c,U}(n, \bar{k})$ within $N_{min} \leq n \leq N_{max}$.

Having derived the global minimum of $E_{c,U}(n, \bar{k})$ along an arbitrary plane $k = \bar{k}$, $\bar{k} \geq K_{min}$, we can now attempt to find the value of k, $k \geq K_{min}$, that minimizes the energy function. Evaluating $E_{c,U}(n, k)$ on $n = n_{0,U}$ we obtain:

$$E_{c,U}(n_{0,U}, k) = k \left[a + r \left[(p+j) - \frac{p^2}{b+p} + g \right] \right]. \tag{9}$$

Evidently, the value of k minimizing (9) is the minimum allowable, i.e. $k = K_{min}$. Thus, the solution minimizing (3) in the n-direction is $\mathcal{S}_{n_{0,U}} = \left(\frac{\beta_U}{K_{min}}, K_{min} \right)$. This solution holds under the constraint:

$$N_{min} \leq \frac{\beta_U}{K_{min}} \leq N_{max}. \tag{10}$$

k-direction. Similarly, we cut $E_{c,U}(n, k)$ along the plane $n = \bar{n}$, $N_{min} \leq \bar{n} \leq N_{max}$, and minimize $E_{c,U}(\bar{n}, k)$ which is now function of k only. Following the steps presented earlier, we can show by first and second derivative analysis that the global minimum of $E_{c,U}(\bar{n}, k)$ occurs at $k_{0,U} = \frac{\gamma_U}{\bar{n}}$ with the "system-specific" parameter γ_U defined as:

$$\gamma_U = \frac{s}{2}\sqrt{\frac{b+p}{r\left[a + r(p+j+g)\right]}}. \tag{11}$$

The global minimum of $k_{0,U}$ given above holds under the assumption that $k_{0,U} \geq K_{\min}$ due the predefined temporal constraint of (4). Having derived the global minimum of $E_{c,U}(\bar{n}, k)$ along an arbitrary plane $n = \bar{n}$, $N_{\min} \leq \bar{n} \leq N_{\max}$, we can now attempt to find the value of n, $N_{\min} \leq n \leq N_{\max}$, that minimizes the energy function. Evaluating $E_{c,U}(n, k)$ on $k = k_{0,U}$ we obtain:

$$E_{c,U}(n, k_{0,U}) = \frac{1}{n}\left[a + r(p+j+g)\gamma_U - ps + \frac{s^2(b+p)}{4r\gamma_U}\right] \tag{12}$$

Evidently, the value of n minimizing (12) is the maximum allowable, i.e. $n = N_{\max}$. Hence, the solution when attempting to minimize (12) in the k-direction under the constraints of (4) is $S_{k_{0,U}} = \left(N_{\max}, \frac{\gamma_U}{N_{\max}}\right)$, under the constraint:

$$K_{\min} \leq \frac{\gamma_U}{N_{\max}}. \tag{13}$$

Uniqueness of Solution and Solution When (10) **and** (13) **Do Not Hold:** Starting from (10), with a few straightforward manipulations we reach $\frac{\beta_U}{N_{\max}} \leq K_{\min} \leq \frac{\beta_U}{N_{\min}}$, with β_U defined in (8). The second constraint for $K_{\min}$ is provided by (13). It can be shown that $\beta_U > \gamma_U$ (derivation omitted due to page limitation), which demonstrates that *the constraints of the two established solutions are non-overlapping*. Thus, the solutions $S_{n_{0,U}}$ and $S_{k_{0,U}}$ are unique within their respective bounds for $K_{\min}$.

To establish the optimal solutions when *neither* of these two constraints is satisfied, we have to analyze what happens when $\frac{\gamma_U}{N_{\max}} < K_{\min} < \frac{\beta_U}{N_{\max}}$ or $K_{\min} > \frac{\beta_U}{N_{\min}}$, as neither $S_{n_{0,U}}$ nor $S_{k_{0,U}}$ are applicable in such cases. It is straightforward to show that $\frac{\partial E_{c,U}}{\partial n}$ and $\frac{\partial E_{c,U}}{\partial k}$ are never zero within these intervals. Hence, the solution we are looking for must lie on one of the two boundary points: $(N_{\min}, K_{\min})$ or $(N_{\max}, K_{\min})$.

Let's focus on the case of $K_{\min} \in \left(\frac{\gamma_U}{N_{\max}}, \frac{\beta_U}{N_{\max}}\right)$ and evaluate $E_{c,U}(n, k)$ on the boundary plane $n = N_{\max}$. Since $E_c(N_{\max}, k)$ is monotonically increasing for $k > \frac{\gamma_U}{N_{\max}}$ the optimal point is $k = K_{\min}$, which leads to the solution $S_{\max\min} = (N_{\max}, K_{\min})$. Similarly, let's look at the k direction by evaluating the energy function on the $k = K_{\min}$ plane. Now $n_{0,U} = \frac{\beta_U}{K_{\min}}$ is larger than $N_{\max}$ and is thus not admissible. Since $E_{c,U}(n, K_{\min})$ is decreasing for $n < n_{0,U}$, the optimal point is $n = N_{\max}$, which also leads to the solution $S_{\max\min} = (N_{\max}, K_{\min})$. Hence we conclude that when $K_{\min} \in \left(\frac{\gamma_U}{N_{\max}}, \frac{\beta_U}{N_{\max}}\right)$, the optimal solution is

$\mathcal{S}_{\max\min} = (N_{\max}, K_{\min})$. Finally, when $K_{\min} > \frac{\beta_U}{N_{\min}}$, following a similar analysis we reach that the optimal solution is $\mathcal{S}_{\min\min} = (N_{\min}, K_{\min})$.

Summarizing, when the data transmitted by each VSN node follows the Uniform distribution of (5), the set of solutions giving the minimum energy consumption in (3) under the spatio-temporal constraints of (4) is:

$$\{n^{\star}, k^{\star}\}_U = \begin{cases} \left(N_{\max}, \frac{\gamma_U}{N_{\max}}\right) & \text{if } K_{\min} \leq \frac{\gamma_U}{N_{\max}} \\ (N_{\max}, K_{\min}) & \text{if } \frac{\gamma_U}{N_{\max}} < K_{\min} < \frac{\beta_U}{N_{\max}} \\ \left(\frac{\beta_U}{K_{\min}}, K_{\min}\right) & \text{if } \frac{\beta_U}{N_{\max}} \leq K_{\min} \leq \frac{\beta_U}{N_{\min}} \\ (N_{\min}, K_{\min}) & \text{if } K_{\min} > \frac{\beta_U}{N_{\min}} \end{cases} \tag{14}$$

with β_U and γ_U defined by (8) and (11).

3.2   Pareto Distribution

We present a second example with the Pareto distribution. This distribution has been used, amongst others, to model the marginal data size distribution of TCP sessions that contain substantial number of small files and a few very large ones [11]. It will also be shown by the experimental results of this paper that it presents a good fit to multimedia traffic generated by visual features extraction algorithms and hence it warrants detailed study under the proposed VSN framework.

Consider $P(\chi_k)$ as the Pareto distribution with scale v and shape $\alpha > 1$:

$$P(\chi_k) = \begin{cases} \alpha\frac{v^{\alpha}}{\chi_k^{\alpha+1}}, & \chi_k \geq v \\ 0, & \text{otherwise} \end{cases} . \tag{15}$$

Setting $v = \frac{\alpha-1}{\alpha}kr$ leads to $\mathbb{E}_P[\mathcal{X}_k] = kr$, i.e., we match the expected transmission data volume to that of the Uniform distribution.

Under (15), the energy expression of (2) becomes:

$$E_{c,P} = k\left[a + r(p + j + g)\right] + \frac{bs}{n} + (b + p)\left(\frac{v^{\alpha}n^{\alpha-1}}{s^{\alpha-1}(\alpha - 1)} - \frac{\alpha v}{\alpha - 1}\right). \tag{16}$$

Following the same analysis as for the Uniform PDF, we conclude that, when the data transmitted by each VSN node follows the Pareto distribution of (15), the set of solutions giving the minimum energy consumption in (3) under the spatio-temporal constraints of (4) is:

$$\{n^{\star}, k^{\star}\}_P = \begin{cases} \left(N_{\max}, \frac{\gamma_P}{N_{\max}}\right) & \text{if } K_{\min} \leq \frac{\gamma_P}{N_{\max}} \\ (N_{\max}, K_{\min}) & \text{if } \frac{\gamma_P}{N_{\max}} < K_{\min} < \frac{\beta_P}{N_{\max}} \\ \left(\frac{\beta_P}{K_{\min}}, K_{\min}\right) & \text{if } \frac{\beta_P}{N_{\max}} \leq K_{\min} \leq \frac{\beta_P}{N_{\min}} \\ (N_{\min}, K_{\min}) & \text{if } K_{\min} > \frac{\beta_P}{N_{\min}}, \end{cases} \tag{17}$$

with

$$\beta_P = \frac{s\alpha}{r\,(\alpha - 1)} \left(\frac{b}{b+p}\right)^{\frac{1}{\alpha}},$$ (18)

and

$$\gamma_P = \frac{s\alpha}{r(\alpha - 1)} \left(\frac{r(b-j-g)-a}{r\,(b+p)}\right)^{\frac{1}{\alpha-1}}.$$ (19)

The details of the derivation of (17) follow the same steps as the ones detailed for the Uniform distribution and are omitted for brevity of description.

3.3   Discussion

The results of this section can be used in practical applications to assess the impact of the spatio-temporal constraints and the data production and transmission process (as characterized by its marginal PDF) on the energy consumption of VSNs, under a variety of energy consumption rates for the radio and multimedia subsystems. For example, under particular technology specifications (i.e. given j, b, p, a and g parameters) and preset number of nodes and frames to capture within the activation time interval, one can determine the required energy in order to achieve the designated visual data gathering task. Similarly, under the proposed framework, one can determine the data production and transmission (marginal) PDFs that meet preset energy supply, spatio-temporal constraints and technology parameters (i.e. energy consumption per bit for each task). As a result, our proposed energy consumption model and the associated analytic results can be used in many ways for early exploration of system, network, and data production parameters in VSNs that match the design specifications of classes of application domains. Such application examples are given in Section 5.

4   Evaluation of the Analytic Results

For the radio subsystem of Figure 1, we used TelosB sensor nodes equipped with a 802.15.4-compliant CC2420 radio transceiver. Each TelosB runs the low-power Contiki 2.6 operating system and implements the open-source TFDMA protocol proposed recently [6] for time-synchronized multichannel communications with the LPBR. Given that the TFDMA protocol ensures collision-free packet transmissions by each node via application-layer adaptation of the transmission slots based on a desynchronization mechanism [6], we enabled the low-power NullMAC and NullRDC options of the Contiki OS. This led to data consumption rate at the application layer of $\frac{s}{T} = 144$ kbps. Evidently the usage of the TFDMA protocol is only for illustration purposes and any other protocol ensuring collision-free communications by centralized or distributed slot allocation, such as the IEEE 802.15.4e-2006 GTS [8] or the IEEE 802.15.4e-2012 TSCH [4] can be used.

All energy measurements were performed using a Tektronix MDO4104-6 oscilloscope to capture the real-time current consumption at a high-tolerance 1 Ohm resistor placed in series with each TelosB node running the described operations. Under these operational settings, the average transmission cost per bit, j J/b, as well as the cost for beaconing, b J/b, and buffering, p J/b, were established experimentally; their values are shown at the top half of Table 1.

Although capable of simple processing tasks, the TelosB is not a multimedia platform. However, it can be attached via its integrated FTDI USB chip to a more powerful platform such as the BeagleBone [12], or integrated with a low power DSP processor, as done in the CITRIC project [2]. Here, we assume that the multimedia sybsystem is based on an application-specific integrated circuit (ASIC), such as the one proposed recently for energy-efficient visual feature extraction [10] in images. Obviously, the processing cost per bit is application and hardware dependent; in the following, we use g (in J/b) derived from Park *et al* [10] and reported at the bottom half of Table 1. Finally, concerning image acquisition, we considered the energy cost of acquiring a frame (a J) derived from the specifications of the OV7670 camera sensor, which is widely used in low-power visual sensor platforms [2] and is also reported in Table 1.

Under the settings described previously and shown in Table 1, our first goal is to validate the basic analytic expressions of Section 3, namely (6) and (16), with respect to the energy consumption measured when performing Monte-Carlo–based experiments combined with actual energy measurement. To this end, we simulated the multimedia data production process on each VSN node by: *(i)* artificially creating several sets of data size values according to the marginal PDFs of Section 3 via rejection sampling and *(ii)* setting the mean data size per video frame to $r = 5.2$ kbit. The sets containing data sizes are copied onto the read-only memory of each sensor node during deployment. At run time,

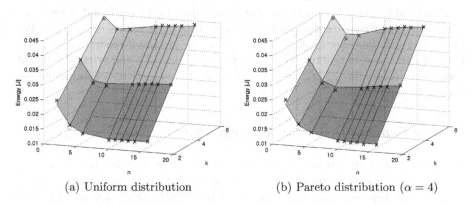

(a) Uniform distribution   (b) Pareto distribution ($\alpha = 4$)

Fig. 2. The grayscale surfaces show the energy consumption of a single camera sensor node in function of the number of frames per second and the total number of nodes. The blue crosses correspond to the value of the consumed energy as measured from the sensor network test-bed. All energy values and frames (k) are normalized to a one-second interval.

Table 2. Differences between theoretical and experimental results and the optimal value for the number of nodes and the frames-rates for the considered data transmission (marginal) PDFs under the settings of Figure 2

PDF	Mean Error (%)	Max Error (%)	R^2	Theoretical optimum
Uniform	1.08	4.81	0.9987	$\{n^\star, k^\star\}_{\mathrm{U}} = \{12, 2\}$
Pareto ($\alpha = 4$)	1.64	6.05	0.9973	$\{n^\star, k^\star\}_{\mathrm{P}} = \{14, 2\}$

each node fetches a new frame size from the preloaded set, produces artificial data according to it (akin to receiving the information from the multimedia subsystem) and transmits the information to the LPBR following the process described in the system model of Section 2. Depending on the frame size, the node can enter in idling/beaconing state or it can buffer the data exceeding the allocated TFDMA slots.

We report here energy measurements obtained under varying values of n and k. The chosen active time interval was set to be $T = 154$ s and, beyond measuring the accuracy of the model versus experiments, we also compared the theoretically-optimal values for k and n according to Section 3 with the ones producing the minimum energy consumption in the experiments. For the reported experiments of Figure 2 and Table 2, the spatio-temporal constraints were: $N_{\min} = 2$, $N_{\max} = 16$ and $K_{\min} = 2T$ frames, i.e. two frames per second. All our reported measurements and the values for k are normalized to a one-second interval for easier interpretation of the results.

As one can see from Figure 2 and Table 2, the theoretical results match the experimental results for all the tested distributions, with the maximum percentile error between them limited to 6.12% and all the coefficients of determination between the experimental and the model points being above 0.995. In addition, the theoretically-obtained optimal values for $\{n^\star, k^\star\}$ from (14) and (17), are always in agreement with the experimentally-derived values that were found to offer the minimum energy consumption under the chosen spatio-temporal constraints. We have observed the same level of accuracy for the proposed model under a variety of data sizes (r), active time interval durations (T) and spatio-temporal constraints $(N_{\min}, N_{\max}$ and $K_{\min})$, but omit these repetitive experiments for brevity of exposition.

5   Application in Visual Features Extraction

In order to assess the proposed model against application deployments, we consider the extraction and transmission of local visual features for image analysis. This scenario represents a wide range of practical VSN-related deployments proposed recently [2,7]. In a nutshell, salient keypoints of an image are identified by means of a *detector* algorithm, and the patch of pixels around each keypoint is encoded in a feature vector by a specialized *descriptor* algorithm. Here, we focus on corner-like local features, such as the ones detected by the FAST corner detector [9], which is optimized for fast and efficient detection on low-power devices.

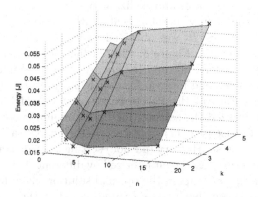

Fig. 3. The energy function for the considered application scenario. The grayscale surfaces represent the fitted energy function obtained with the Pareto PDF, while the blue crosses represent the experimental measurements. All energy values and frames (k) are normalized to a one-second interval.

Table 3. Energy consumption under varying spatio-temporal constraints with ad-hoc settings and with settings derived from the proposed Pareto model ($K_{\min}$, k and the energy values are normalized to a one-second interval)

	Spatio-temporal	Visual features extraction		
	Constraints	Ad-hoc deployment	Proposed approach	Gain
Case 1	$K_{\min} = 5$ $N_{\min} = 3$ $N_{\max} = 6$	$k_{\text{adhoc}} = 5$ $n_{\text{adhoc}} = 3$ $E_c = 0.031$ J	$k^\star = 5$ $n^\star = 6$ $E_c = 0.028$ J	10.30%
Case 2	$K_{\min} = 2$ $N_{\min} = 2$ $N_{\max} = 10$	$k_{\text{adhoc}} = 2$ $n_{\text{adhoc}} = 2$ $E_c = 0.022$ J	$k^\star = 2$ $n^\star = 10$ $E_c = 0.012$ J	48.65%

For what concerns the descriptor, several algorithms are available in the literature: here we assume to use the BRIEF descriptor, which produces a 64 bytes binary feature vector starting from intensity comparisons between pixels of the patch to be described, thus being particularly tailored for resource constrained devices. As input data, we considered the video sequences from the PETS2007 dataset[1], which are taken from an airport surveillance video system. The original resolution of all sequences is 768 x 576 pixels and the original frame rate is 25 frames-per-second. Similarly as before, the process is repeated for different video sequences and different frame rates (i.e. different values of k normalized to frames-per-second).

We repeated the experimental measurements described in Section 4 for this application scenario and under the same spatio-temporal constraints ($N_{\min} = 2$, $N_{\max} = 16$, $K_{\min} = 2T$, i.e. two frames per second), this time loading on the sensor network the traces of data sizes computed after the processing of the

---

[1] http://pets2007.net

video sequences in the two cases and utilizing the energy parameters of Table 1. Then, we fitted[2] the energy measurements with the ones produced by the Pareto distribution. The best fit was obtained under parameters $\alpha = 4$, $v = kr$ and $r = 11.7$ kbit, as shown in Figure 3, with coefficient of determination value $R^2 \cong 0.96$. Similarly as before, all reported energy values and number of frames are normalized to a one-second interval for easier interpretation of the results.

Given the high accuracy of the Pareto-based energy model against the application results, we utilized the settings for the minimum energy consumption derived for the Pareto case [see (17)] to ascertain the energy saving that can be potentially achieved against arbitrary (ad-hoc) settings. As an example, in Table 3, we consider two different cases, characterized by different spatio-temporal constraints. For each case, we compare the optimal solution given by (17) with an ad-hoc "least-cost" solution that assumes values equal to the minimum spatio-temporal constraints (under the intuitive assumption that less nodes and less frames-per-second lead to smaller energy consumption). Evidently, the proposed approach allows for significant energy savings, which can be more than 45% in comparison to the ad-hoc settings.

6   Conclusions

We proposed an analytic model for the energy consumption of wireless VSN arranged in a star-shaped topology under preset spatio-temporal constraints. We derived analytic conditions for the optimal spatio-temporal settings within the VSN for different PDFs characterizing the multimedia data volume to be transmitted by each node. Monte-Carlo experiments performed via an energy-measurement testbed revealed that the proposed model's accuracy is within 7% of the obtained energy consumption. Applying the model to the application scenario of visual features extraction demonstrated that substantial energy savings can be obtained via the proposed approach against ad-hoc settings for the spatio-temporal parameters of the VSN. As such, the proposed model can be used for early-stage studies of VSNs to determine the best operational parameters prior to cumbersome and costly real-world deployment and testing. Future research directions include the extension of the proposed framework to multi-tier cluster-tree topologies as well as other multimedia traffic distributions.

Acknowledgments. AR, MC and MT acknowledge the financial support of the Future and Emerging Technologies (FET) programme within the Seventh Framework Programme for Research of the European Commission, under FET-Open grant number: 296676. YA was supported by EPSRC, project EP/K033166/1.

---

[2] Fitting is performed by matching the average data size r of each distribution to the average data size of the set of visual features.

References

1. Lu, G., Krishnamachari, B., Raghavendra, C.: Performance evaluation of the IEEE 802.15.4 mac for low-rate low-power wireless networks. In: IEEE Internat. Conf. on Perform., Comp., and Comm., pp. 701–706. IEEE (2004)
2. Chen, P., et al.: CITRIC: A low-bandwidth wireless camera network platform. In: ACM/IEEE Int. Conf. on Distrib. Smart Cam., ICDSC, September, pp. 1–10
3. Charfi, Y., Canada, B.: Challenging issues in visual sensor networks. IEEE Wireless Comm. 16(2), 44–49 (2009)
4. Bachir, A., et al.: MAC essentials for wireless sensor networks. IEEE Comm. Surv. Tut. 12(2), 222–248 (2010)
5. Gubbi, J., Buyya, R., Marusic, S., Palaniswami, M.: Internet of Things (IoT): A vision, architectural elements, and future directions. Future Gen. Comp. Syst. J. 29(7), 1645–1660 (2013)
6. Buranapanichkit, D., Andreopoulos, Y.: Distributed time-frequency division multiple access protocol for wireless sensor networks. IEEE Wireless Comm. Letters 1(5), 440–443 (2012)
7. Kwon, Y., Shin, D.: The security monitoring system using IEEE 802.15.4 Protocol and CMOS Image Sensor. In: Proc. IEEE Internat. Conf. on New Trends in Inf. and Serv. Sci., NISS 2009, pp. 1197–1202. IEEE (2009)
8. Koubâa, A., Alves, M., Tovar, E.: GTS allocation analysis in IEEE 802.15.4 for real-time wireless sensor networks. In: IEEE Proc. Internat. Par. and Distrib. Process. Symp., IPDPS, p. 8. IEEE (2006)
9. Rosten, E., Porter, R., Drummond, T.: FASTER and better: A machine learning approach to corner detection. In: IEEE Trans. Patt. Anal. and Machine Intel., vol. 32, pp. 105–119 (2010), http://lanl.arXiv.org/pdf/0810.2434
10. Park, J.-S., Kim, H.-E., Kim, L.-S.: A 182mW 94.3 fps in full HD pattern-matching based image recognition accelerator for embedded vision system in 0.13 um CMOS technology. IEEE Trans. on Circ. and Syst. for Video Technol. 23(5), 832–845 (2013)
11. Park, K.: On the relationship between file sizes, transport protocols, and self-similar network traffic. In: Proc. IEEE Internat. Conf. on Network Protocols, ICNP, pp. 171–180 (1996)
12. Rachmadi, M., et al.: Adaptive traffic signal control system using camera sensor and embedded system. In: TENCON 2011 - 2011 IEEE Region 10 Conf., pp. 1261–1265. IEEE (2011)

K-Sense: Towards a Kinematic Approach for Measuring Human Energy Expenditure

Kazi I. Zaman, Anthony White, Sami R. Yli-Piipari, and Timothy W. Hnat

University of Memphis, Memphis, TN, USA
{kizaman,arwhite5,srylppri,twhnat}@memphis.edu

Abstract. Accurate energy expenditure monitoring will be an essential part of medical diagnosis in the future, enabling individually-tailored just-in-time interventions. However, there are currently no real-time monitors that are practical for continuous daily use. In this paper, we introduce the *K-Sense* energy expenditure monitor that uses inertial measurement units (IMUs) mounted to an individual's wrist and ankle with elastic bands to determine angular velocity and position. The system utilizes kinematics to determine the amount of energy required for each limb to achieve its current movement. Our empirical evaluation includes over 3,000,000 individual data samples across 12 individuals and the results indicate that the system can estimate total energy expenditure with a 92 percent accuracy on average.

Keywords: Body Sensor Network, Energy Expenditure, Kinematics.

1   Introduction

Obesity has reached epidemic proportions throughout the United States and was recently classified as a disease by the American Medical Association. It currently affects 35.9 percent of adults, 18.4 percent of adolescents, and 18 percent of children [20]. The estimated annual medical cost of obesity in the U.S. is $147 billion per year, with annual medical spending 42 percent higher for an obese individual compared to a normal weight individual [19]. The causes of obesity are as broad as the number of instances; however, most are contributed to individual lifestyles. Society has transitioned from manual labor style jobs such as factories or farms to office style environments where people sit at desks. Additionally, leisure activities have become more sedentary which include television or computer entertainment. All these factors contribute to the growing obesity epidemic.

Research has shown that a small amount of exercise is beneficial, but motivating individuals to change their behaviors is difficult [12]. However, there are currently no practical solutions for real-world precision energy expenditure measurement. Technologies such as metabolic carts [22] and calorimeter rooms [32] allow researchers to accurately measure energy expenditure; however, they are difficult and intrusive to wear or place a significant burden on the participant.

B. Krishnamachari, A.L. Murphy, and N. Trigoni (Eds.): EWSN 2014, LNCS 8354, pp. 166–181, 2014.

Most commercially available systems rely on waist or wrist mounted accelerometers which fail to capture the motion of body extremities. A common solution is the Actigraph system [1] which places an accelerometer on a elastic band worn under clothing around the waist. Other systems, such as the SenseWear arm-band [23], are bulky and worn on the upper arm. While it contains more sensors than most solutions, it not convenient to wear and has a limited ability to measure leisure activities. There is currently an influx of devices on the market that are designed to promote physical activity such as the FitBit [4], Nike's Fuel band [25], or Ubifit Garden [13]. They connect wirelessly to a smartphone or computer to provide feedback about the user's daily activities. These devices are primarily designed to help motivate individuals to exercise by assuming behaviors will change once they see how much or how little they are really moving during the day.

In this paper, we introduce the *K-Sense* energy expenditure monitor: a more accurate wearable monitoring system based on inertial measurement units (IMUs), consisting of 3-axis accelerometer, gyroscope, and magnetometer which are attached to the waist, wrist, and ankle of a person. These are combined with Bluetooth radios to transmit real-time motion data to a computer or smartphone. It measures motion and angular position, which are represented as quaternions, of each sensed point at approximately 50 hertz. The system uses the formula $\tau = I\alpha$, where τ is angular force, I is momentum and α is angular acceleration to estimate the amount of force required to achieve each successive position. K-Sense is a diagnostic technology designed for medical professionals in evaluating a person's behaviors or the effectiveness of an exercise treatment program. It will also enable a real-time feedback control mechanism for more effective obesity treatments. Our vision of the system involves integrating our techniques into a smartphone, wrist watch, and shoe, resulting in a solution without requiring any extraneous wearable devices.

K-Sense is a motion capture and analysis system; therefore, the main challenge is correctly measuring *energy expenditure*: the amount of energy a human body uses performing activities. The process of measuring limb and body motion is subject to many different sources of noise: the accuracy of each sensor, the basal metabolic rate which is the energy expenditure necessary to sustain the body's functions, individual characteristics of limb composition, and the variations of muscle and movement efficiency, among many others. Therefore, measuring limb motion on an arm and leg is not sufficient to capture this complete metabolic system. The insight behind K-Sense is that many times a person is performing similar actions with either their legs or their arms thus individual sensors are not necessary for each limb and that positional measurements provide more details about each activity. Additionally, there are many factors that contribute to energy expenditure which can not be measured based on motion. Instead, K-Sense considers the efficiency of limb motion and basal energy expenditure along with training data provided by a metabolic system.

In this paper, we present K-Sense's hardware design, signal processing algorithms, and kinematic system. We evaluate K-Sense with controlled experiments in a laboratory setting across six activities. Twelve test subjects followed a twenty-five minute action sequence consisting of standing, jumping, lying down, working on a computer, walking, and running. Each subject was connected to a laboratory metabolic system which captures the intake and expiration of oxygen and carbon dioxide. A total of over 300 minutes of data were generated for analysis and our results indicate that energy expenditure typically varies by 8.42 percent, or 6.65 kilocalories, on an average from ground truth. In comparison, the Actigraph system achieved a 14 percent energy expenditure error on the same set of experiments. K-Sense is computationally efficient: it is an online algorithm that could be easily implemented on an embedded platform. This indicates that the algorithm can be used on resource-limited platforms such as a smartphone.

2   Related Work

Systems designed to measure or estimate human energy expenditure can roughly be categorized into three groups: (1) direct, (2) indirect, and (3) non-calorimetric.

Direct calorimetry systems measure the heat loss from the body which is precisely the amount of energy expended. Systems such as an insulated chamber [31], indirect calorimetry room [32], or the Suit calorimeter [34] directly measure energy; however, the subject is placed within a very expensive and somewhat small environment where they must stay for the duration of the study. This significantly limits the types of activities they can perform. In contrast, our system is designed to be worn during everyday activities and is not constrained to particular rooms.

Indirect calorimetry systems typically measure the intake and expiration of gases which are converted into energy expenditure. Systems such as the Douglas bag [17] are difficult to operate and require the subjects to breath air from a sealed bag for a period of time. This is impractical for long duration studies. Other systems such as a metabolic cart [22] capture the air breathed through a gas sensor where it measures the concentrations of oxygen and carbon dioxide. These systems can be made small enough to be portable; however, their cost is prohibitive for large user studies and because they rely on the collection of gases, a mask must be worn over the nose and mouth making continuous wear difficult. Another common indirect measurement is doubly labeled water [15], where the hydrogen and oxygen molecules are tagged with a non-radioactive isotope. This allows researchers to measure energy expenditure over longer time durations without inconveniencing the participant except for occasional blood tests.

The class of systems most similar to K-Sense is based on physiological monitoring. Much research has been done based on using heart rate to estimate energy expenditure [9,30,35,28] In most cases, these solutions produce errors around 20 percent. Another solution that has the potential to be very accurate, electromyography [29], unfortunately requires each muscle group to be measured independently, thus making this impractical for daily use.

There has been a large influx of wearable sensor platforms on the commercial market recently which include the Nokia Activity Monitor [3], Sports Tracker [7],

Nike+ [6], Nike Fuelband [25], BodyBugg [8], Fitbit [4], Actigraph [1], Ubifit Garden [13], SenseWear Pro3 Armband and the SenseWear Mini [23]. Several of these system utilize GPS to track user movement along with accelerometers to aid in the estimation of energy consumption. Other systems such as the BodyBugg utilize machine learning to estimate energy expenditure but can be affected by types of movement not accounted for in the models. Because these systems are closed-source, it is challenging to evaluate their energy estimation algorithms. In one case, Darcy et al. evaluate the SenseWear devices and show an error rate of 8.2 percent with a deviation of 6.7 [23] but is in a relatively large form factor that be prohibitive for long-term wear.

Many other approaches are based on utilizing accelerometers to identify the activities and motions of individuals[11,30,10,35,27] All these techniques follow a similar approach where sensor data is collected and correlated with energy expenditure to produce an estimator. K-Sense utilizes a similar approach with its regression solution; however, by modeling the angular and translation motion of each limb, K-Sense is able to use kinematics to improve on this class of results without adding significant hardware to each individual.

3 System Design

The primary goal of the K-Sense hardware platform is to measure the position of a person's limb movements as they go about their daily lives. Secondary goals include energy consumption with a 16 hour minimum run-time and a small comfortable form-factor.

3.1 Hardware Design and Operation

K-Sense sensors utilize a Sparkfun Razor 9DoF inertial measurement unit (IMU), consisting of three axis accelerometers (ADXL345), gyroscopes (IDG3200), and magnetometers (HMC5883L), which are mounted on elastic bands that can be secured to a person's wrist, ankle, and waist, as shown in Figures 1 and 2. Each IMU was calibrated using the manufacturer's process. These three sensors are sampled by an on-board ATmega328 before being sent through a serial interface to our data collecting system. We modified the firmware to sample and output data as fast as possible, 50Hz per sensor-axis or 450Hz for each IMU board, and transmitted via a Bluetooth serial interface (RN-41) at 115200 bits per second. A computer connects to all three devices over separate Bluetooth channels to log the data. Each sensor platform is powered by a rechargeable 3.7 volt lithium-polymer battery which yields an approximate run-time of 16 hours. Our prototype would be further optimized and miniaturized before large scale deployment.

3.2 Signal Processing

K-Sense uses two main signal processing algorithms for each of its energy estimation algorithms. The first algorithm corrects each data stream's time stamps

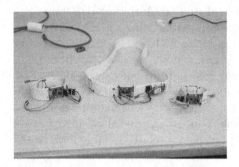

Fig. 1. The electronic suite is attached to elastic bands that are easily placed on the wrist, ankle, and waist of each participant

Fig. 2. The K-Sense evaluation environment where a person is walking on a treadmill in a metabolic lab

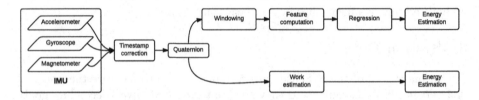

Fig. 3. K-Sense acquires data from an inertial measurement unit (IMU) and corrects the time stamps before converting to quaternions. Next, it utilizes two separate approaches for energy estimation: (1) a regression-based approach that utilizes windows and features and (2) a kinematic-based approach based on angular velocity.

and the second transforms the corrected raw data streams into quaternions. Next, there are two possible algorithm paths. The first utilizes regression over a set of features to approximate energy expenditure and the second utilizes a kinematic approach to estimate the amount of work done, and therefore, energy expenditure.

Time Stamp Correction. Data is collected by the IMU board, sent through a wireless Bluetooth link, and processed by our logging software where periodic errors in the time stamps occur. Figure 4 illustrates the manifestation of the time stamp synchronization errors as triangular shaped deviations where the logged time stamp is in the future. These events are periodic and consistent throughout the experiments . To correct these deviations, we utilize a robust linear regression technique [21] to fit a line and a predefined offset of 0.3 seconds to the data traces, effectively mapping the samples to a linear time sequence.

Quaternion. Each IMU produces data with three degrees of freedom for each sensor type or nine degrees of freedom for the whole board. This data is processed on our data logging computer which converts the raw sensor data

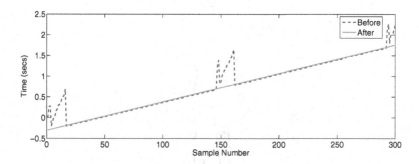

Fig. 4. The dashed line indicates the raw time stamp sequence with three instances of incorrect values. A corrected time sequence is identified with the solid line.

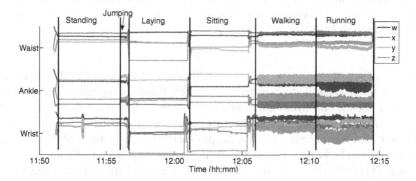

Fig. 5. Each participant performed six activities in a laboratory setting. Data is shown as a quaternion (w,x,y,z) plot for all three sensor platforms with each activity having distinct visual differences.

into quaternions [24]: a representation for the sum of a scalar and a three dimensional vector. Many IMU systems prefer to convert to Euler angles, yaw, pitch, and roll; however, this representation of three dimensional space suffers from a gimbal lock problem: the loss of one degree of rotational freedom [33]. Quaternions effectively add a fourth axis in an arbitrary orientation to always have an axis on which to rotate and are easily converted to Euler angles.

Energy Regression. K-Sense provides two mechanisms from which it estimates energy expenditure. The first is based on multi-dimensional linear regression. First, the raw data and quaternion values are represented as a 13 element vector: $V_i = q_a^i, q_b^i, q_c^i, q_d^i, a_x^i, a_y^i, a_z^i, g_x^i, g_y^i, g_z^i, m_x^i, m_y^i, m_z^i$ where element V_i at time i contains values q^i for the four quaternion components, a^i for all three accelerometer axis, g^i for all three gyroscope axis, and m^i for all three magnetometer axis. The goal of energy regression is to convert a sequence of the vectors V from up to three IMUs into a set of identifying features which can be used to correlate with energy expenditure.

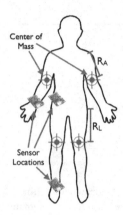

Fig. 6. Sensors are placed at the wrist, ankle, and waist on the right side of each participant's body. The distance between a joint and a limb's center of mass, R_A and R_L, is used in the kinematic model.

For each set of vectors $V_i, ..., V_{i+w}$, where w is the size of each window, K-Sense computes the following features over all columns independently: maximum, minimum, mean, amplitude and variance. These features are stored in a vector $F_i = F_1, F_2, ..., F_n$, where n is the total number of features generated. Thus, K-Sense's signal processing fuses multiple IMU platforms and different types of data into a single feature vector representing a fixed amount of time.

A model is constructed by computing all feature vectors and assigning a corresponding energy expenditure based on ground truth collected from a metabolic cart. Figure 5 is an example data trace which illustrates the basic activities used during our experiments along with corresponding quaternion representations for each of the waist, wrist, and ankle sensors. K-Sense utilizes a linear regression to map the multi-dimensional feature vectors to each assigned energy expenditure. We then utilize these regression parameters to estimate each window's energy and thus the total energy expenditure can be estimated by summing all windows.

Kinematic Energy. K-Sense's second mechanism is based on utilizing angular sensor data, provided by the IMU, to estimate amount of work necessary to accomplish that movement. For simplicity, we have placed sensors on the right side of the body on the wrist, ankle, and waist as shown in Figure 6. We are currently assuming each limb will be expending equal amounts of energy whether the arms are moving as a mirror image to each other, or the arms and legs are moving in a counteracting manner. Ultimately, total energy expenditure is a function of the angular movement of the arms and legs along with the basal metabolic rate for the core of the body, the amount of energy expended to maintain the body's core functions and is typically based on a person's height, weight, and age.

K-Sense estimates energy expenditure where rotational work, $W = \tau\theta$, is a function of τ, rotational force and θ, angular displacement. By combining momentum, I, and angular acceleration, α, work becomes $W = I\alpha\theta$. Angular acceleration, $\alpha = \alpha_c/r$, is a function of tangential acceleration, α_c and the radius, r, from the limb joint to the limb center of mass (Figure 6) resulting in work being defined as $W = I(\alpha_c/r)\theta$. Finally, by combining angular velocity, ω, with equations $\alpha_c = \omega^2 r$, and $I = mr^2$ we derive

$$W = mr^2\omega^2\theta \tag{1}$$

where work, W, is a function of mass, m, the radius squared, the angular velocity squared, and the angular displacement. This equation forms the basis of K-Sense's energy estimator.

3.3   Estimating Work

The amount of work done during each time interval needs to be estimated. Participants were required to provide their gender, age, height, and weight. The height and weight of each were used in conjunction with equations derived from Paolo et al. and Plagenhoef et al. [18,26] to compute the mass and lengths of individual body parts for each participant and the weight is used to compute basal energy requirements. Basal energy is the energy needed to carry out fundamental metabolic functions, such as breathing, ion transport, normal turnover of enzymes and other body components. The basal energy consumption of the human body is approximately 4 kilojoule per kilogram of body weight per hour [5].

The following equation is used to estimate the total amount of energy expended by each participant

$$E_{estimate} = 2xE_{Wrist} + 2yE_{Ankle} + zE_{Body} \tag{2}$$

where the estimated energy is two times the energy measured at the wrists plus two times the energy measured at the ankles and the energy of the body. Due to imperfect data and models, we have included a calibration factor, x, y, z, for each of the energy estimation components which will need to be tuned to minimize root mean square (RMS) error or total energy error. We utilized a *minimax* optimization process to derive the tuned values for x, y, and z, based on the RMS and end-to-end error for the data traces. Calibration data was taken from the metabolic measurement device used for ground truth data collection.

4   Experimental Setup

We built three K-Sense IMU bands and used them for a 12-person trial, where each person was subject to the same experimental protocol lasting approximately 25 minutes. Multiple versions of the K-Sense platform were initially tested before arriving at our current solution. The K-Sense platforms were attached to the right side of each subject's body. Each person performed a series of six different activities consisting of standing, jumping, laying, sitting, walking (3 mph), and running (6 mph). Jumping was performed for 30 seconds and all other activities

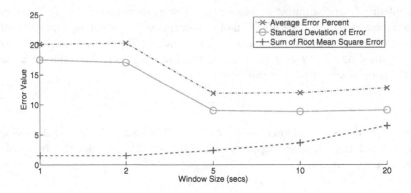

Fig. 7. The size of a window is determined by optimizing the average, standard deviation, and root mean square error

for four minutes. The study design and testing was done with the help of a kinematics lab (Figure 2). We have collected over five hours of data from the experiments. Due to the short duration of the jumping activity and the lack of data from the Actigraph system, we exclude it from our evaluation.

As a comparison to the current state of the art, each subject wore an Actigraph ActiLife version 6 [2] accelerometer during the experiment. This was placed around the waist according to the manufacturer's specifications. We calculated energy expenditure from Actigraph using Actigraph New 2-Regression Model defined by Crouter et. al. [14]. Additionally, ground truth was determined by a Parvo Medics TrueOne 2400 metabolic system which consists of a mouthpiece to collect expired gases and is hooked up to a sensor and computer via a six foot tube. This is one of the gold standards in metabolic measurement from which we are able to measure the accuracy of K-Sense and the Actigraph system.

5   Evaluation

The evaluation of the K-Sense platform is composed of two main components. First, we evaluate the effectiveness of the regression-based approach and second, an evaluation of the kinematics is provided. In each case, we illustrate the effects of different trade-offs on the total energy estimation error.

5.1   Regression Modeling

The linear regression model over feature vectors F_n (Section 3.2) is trained using a leave-one-out cross validation procedure. In other words, the parameters used for person n were derived from all the other participants' data and ground truth. This avoided the need for splitting the testing and training sets into two distinct groups. The window size was set to 5 seconds which provides an appropriate error minimization (Figure 7). K-Sense's regression model produces estimates of

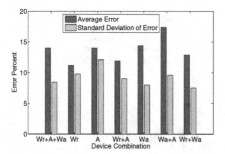 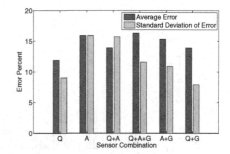

Fig. 8. Different device combinations, waist (Wa), wrist (Wr), and ankle (A) result in variations in energy prediction error. The wrist sensor alone provides the most accurate results at 11.2 percent; however, by utilizing the ankle sensor too, the error is slightly larger at 11.9 percent but reduces the standard deviation to 9.

Fig. 9. Different sensor combinations, quaternion (Q), accelerometer (A), and gyroscope (G), are evaluated for optimal performance. The quaternions provide the best performance trade off for both error and standard deviation. Magnetometers were not utilized due to interference from the laboratory equipment.

energy expenditure accurate to 88 percent of the ground truth measurements and has a standard deviation of 9 percent (Figure 10). In contrast, the current state-of-the-art system, Actigraph, estimates energy expenditure at 86 percent with standard deviation of 12 percent. Our system with its simple feature set provides approximately the same accuracy as Actigraph.

Component Evaluation. Figure 8 shows a comparison of how effective the sensors, ankle (A), wrist (Wr), and/or waist (Wa), are at estimating energy expenditure in different configurations. Most errors are between 11 and 14 percent with only the pair of waist and ankle sensors exceeding 15 percent. Additionally, the standard deviations fall into a slightly smaller range. The optimal error choice based on our data would be to utilize only the wrist sensor; however, the wrist with ankle sensor provides nearly the same error rate with a lower standard deviation. This results in a more consistent performance across all trials.

Figure 9 shows a comparison of the effects of different data sources on the regression error rates. We examine the effects of utilizing features from quaternions, accelerometers, and gyroscopes when combined with the wrist and ankle combinations from above. Magnetometer values are not directly used in the evaluation because the laboratory environment affects accuracy. The acceleration-based approach yields the worst performance in terms of accuracy and deviation. This is similar for any combination which contains the accelerometers. In this case, features solely based on the quaternions provide the best result at 88 percent accuracy with a 9 percent standard deviation.

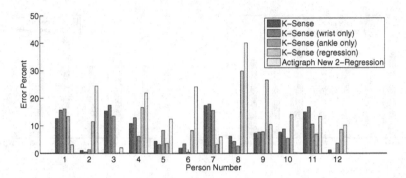

Fig. 10. Each of the four configurations of K-Sense is evaluated and compared with the Actigraph system. In most cases, K-Sense performs better that Actigraph; however, there are instances where Actigraph is better. In general, K-Sense is more consistent in its estimations.

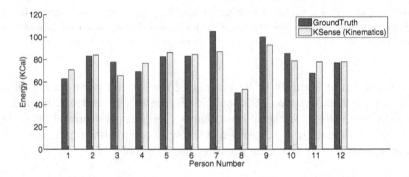

Fig. 11. The total amount of energy expended by each participant is shown along with K-Sense's estimation. In one instance, Person 7, K-Sense significantly underestimates energy and in most cases, the estimate is similar to ground truth.

5.2   Kinematic Evaluation

The second approach to estimating energy is based on K-Sense's kinematic modeling. Figure 10 shows that K-Sense is able to achieve an accuracy of 92 percent with a standard deviation of 5 percent by utilizing only the ankle and wrist sensors and applying a kinematic model to the data.

Figure 10 shows the error rate of several algorithms along with a comparison to Actigraph. There are cases such as Person 2 or 8 where both the Actigraph and regression approaches produce significant error rates. This is due to the particular motions performed by the test subjects which was unable to be accounted for by each algorithms. However, the K-Sense kinematic algorithm performed significantly better with error rates of 1 and 6 percent. In nearly all cases, the K-Sense kinematic solution produces comparable or better results then the current Actigraph system.

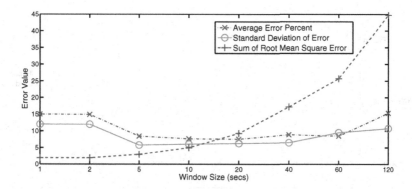

Fig. 12. The size of a window is determined by optimizing the average, standard deviation, and root mean square error. In the case of K-Sense's kinematic approach, this is 5 seconds.

Figure 11 shows the measured energy expenditure for each of twelve test subjects and their related K-Sense kinematic estimations. K-Sense overestimates the energy expenditure for eight people and underestimates the energy for four participants. In the worst case, K-Sense is off by 18 kilocalories and at best, it is within 1 kilocalorie. These results indicate that we are able to accurately and consistently estimate individual energy expenditure.

We compare the effects of window size, due to ground truth occurring at every breath instead of continuously, on the kinematic solution (Figure 12). We jointly minimize the average error over all trials, the standard deviation of these errors, and the average sum of root mean square (RMS) error per person. In this figure, average error and standard deviation are at a minimum in windows between five and twenty seconds. The smaller windows produce lower RMS error, thus we chose a window size of five seconds.

Figure 13 shows an example time series plot of one participant's data which includes quaternions, ground truth energy expenditure, and K-Sense's kinematic estimate. During sedentary activities, K-Sense's energy estimation is approximately 0.34 kilocalories in each five second window and increases as the activity level increases. When a person is walking, between 850 and 1050 seconds, this level increases to 0.64 kilocalories per window and further increases to 0.89 while running. These values are comparable to the ground truth measurements for each specific activity.

To understand the effects of K-Sense's kinematic solution, we show the cumulative energy over time for a single trial. Figure 14 illustrates that K-Sense estimates never exceed 9 kilocalories away from ground truth at approximately 800 seconds into the test. Our model is overestimating energy in this case; however, there are other examples where we consistently underestimate.

Table 1 shows the average end-to-end error percent and average sum of root mean square (RMS) error per person for each window. The best end-to-end error rate of 7.64 percent occurs when utilizing the ankle sensor; however, this

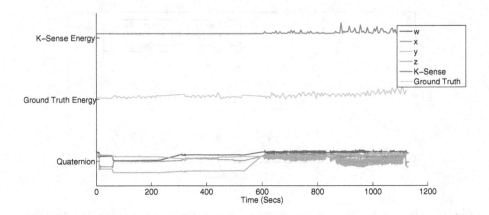

Fig. 13. The K-Sense estimation follows a similar pattern to ground truth which is correlated with the quaternion (w,x,y,z) representation

Table 1. Statistics for all experiments when averaged across all participants. K-Sense (ankle) provides the most accurate result but K-Sense provides a better average error and RMS error.

Method	Average error percent	Average sum of RMS error
K-Sense	8.42	0.24
K-Sense (wrist only)	9.07	0.26
K-Sense (ankle only)	7.64	0.26
K-Sense (regression)	11.9	0.20
Actigraph New 2-Regression	14	0.24

is less consistent through time then using both the ankle and wrist (K-Sense). We believe a good middle ground occurs for the first case with an average error of 8.42 percent and an RMS error of 0.24. Our regression-based approach was able to achieve a better RMS error; however, it was much worse in the average error metric. In both cases, K-Sense or K-Sense (regression) outperform the Actigraph solution which had an average error of 14 percent. By utilizing the K-Sense kinematic algorithm, we were able to reduce the measurement error by over 5 percent. The end-to-end root mean square errors percent for various devices including Actical (19%), DirectLife (14%), IDEEA (18%), ActiGraph (26%), and Fitbit (28%), which are larger than K-Sense's end-to-end root mean square error at 10.03 percent [16].

6   Conclusions and Future Work

In this paper, we present the K-Sense energy expenditure monitor that can estimate an individual's energy with a set of wearable bands. The system operates by measuring the angular velocity of limbs using a low-cost IMU sensor platform.

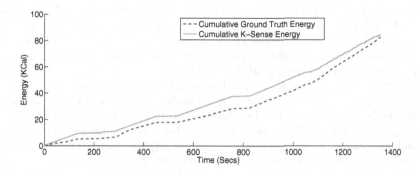

Fig. 14. Energy expenditure is cumulative over time and in this example, K-Sense's estimation tracks ground truth data while consistently overestimating energy. At the worst point, K-Sense is off by 9 kilocalories before converging to 1.6 kilocalories at the end of the trial.

We evaluate this system in a metabolic lab with twelve subjects, each performing the same controlled experiment, resulting in approximately five hours of data and 3,000,000 individual data samples. Our results exceed the Actigraph system by over 5 percent, reducing the total error from 14 percent to about 8 percent. Accurate energy expenditure monitoring will be the basis for many future intervention technologies such as an assessment of daily activity in a free living scenario or as a basis for just-in-time interventions for a variety of diseases including obesity and diabetes. In the future, we envision a kinematic solution that is integrated into common wearable platforms such as a smartphone, shoes, and watches. Additionally, we are continuing to work on identifying specific types of activities based on the kinematics and associated those movements with increases in work such as carrying an object, climbing stairs, or the efficiency of individual person's movement.

Acknowledgments. The authors would like to thank the anonymous reviewers for their comments and suggestions.

References

1. Actigraph, http://www.actigraphcorp.com/ (accessed September 4, 2013)
2. Actilife 6 official site, http://www.actigraphcorp.com/products/actilife-6/ (accessed September 4, 2013)
3. Activity monitor, http://research.nokia.com/page/529 (accessed September 4, 2013)
4. Fitbit official site, http://www.fitbit.com/ (accessed September 4, 2013)
5. Fones,energy consumption and body weight, http://www.bwl.admin.ch/themen/00509/00528/index.html?lang=en [Federal Department of Economic Affairs and Education and Research EAER] (accessed September 4, 2013)
6. Nike+, http://nikeplus.nike.com/nikeplus/ (accessed September 4, 2013)

7. Sports tracker, http://www.sports-tracker.com/ (accessed September 4, 2013)
8. Andre, D., Pelletier, R., Farringdon, J., Safi, S., Talbott, W., Stone, R., Vyas, N., Trimble, J., Wolf, D., Vishnubhatla, S., Boehmke, S., Teller, J.S.A.: The development of the sensewear armband, a revolutionary energy assessment device to assess physical activity and lifestyle. Bodymedia (2006)
9. Bradfield, R.B., Huntzicker, P.B., Fruehan, G.J.: Simultaneous comparison of respirometer and heart-rate telemetry techniques as measures of human energy expenditure. American Journal of Clinical Nutrition 22(6), 696–700 (1969)
10. Brage, S., Brage, N.: Branched equation modeling of simultaneous accelerometry and heart rate monitoring improves estimate of directly measured physical activity energy expenditure. Journal of Applied Phyliology 96, 343–351 (2004)
11. Choi, J.E., Lee, J., Hwang, H., Kim, J.P., Park, J.C., Shin, K.: Estimation of activity energy expenditure: Accelerometer approach. In: IEEE-EMBS Engineering in Medicine and Biology Society, pp. 3830–3833 (2005)
12. Church, T.S., Earnest, C.P., Skinner, J.S., Blair, S.N.: Effects of different doses of physical activity on cardiorespiratory fitness among sedentary, overweight or obese postmenopausal women with elevated blood pressure: A randomized controlled trial. JAMA 297(19), 2081–2091 (2007)
13. Consolvo, S., McDonald, D.W., Toscos, T., Chen, M.Y., Froehlich, J., Harrison, B., Klasnja, P., LaMarca, A., LeGrand, L., Libby, R., Smith, I., Landay, J.A.: Activity sensing in the wild: A field trial of ubifit garden. In: SIGCHI Conference on Human Factors in Computing Systems, pp. 1797–1806. ACM (2008)
14. Crouter, S.E., Clowers, K.G., Bassett, J.D.R.: A novel method for using accelerometer data to predict energy expenditure. Journal of Applied Physiology 100, 1324–1331 (2006)
15. Schoeller, D.A., Taylor, P.B.: Precision of the doubly labelled water method using the two-point calculation. Human Nutrition: Clinical Nutrition 41(3), 215–223 (1987)
16. Dannecker, K.L., Sazonova, N.A., Melanson, E.L., Sazonov, E.S., Browning, R.C.: A comparison of energy expenditure estimation of several physical activity monitors. Medicine and Science in Sports and Exercise (2013)
17. de Groot, G., Schreurs, A.W., Schenau, G.V.I.: A portable lightweight douglas bag instrument for use during various types of exercise. International Journal of Sports Medicine 4(2), 132–134 (1983)
18. de Leva, P.: Adjustments to zatsiorsky-seluyanov's segment inertia parameters. Journal of Biomechanics 29(9), 1223–1230 (1996)
19. Finkelstein, E.A., Trogdon, J.G., Cohen, J.W., Dietz, W.: Annual medical spending attributable to obesity: payer-and service-specific estimates. Health Affairs 28(5), w822–w831 (2009)
20. National Center for Health Statistics. Health, united states, 2012: With special feature on emergency care (2013)
21. Hollanda, P.W., Welsch, R.E.: Robust regression using iteratively reweighted least-squares. Communications in Statistics - Theory and Methods 6(9), 813–827 (1977)
22. Jensen, K., Jorgensen, S., Johansen, L.: A metabolic cart for measurement of oxygen uptake during human exercise using inspiratory flow rate. European Journal of Applied Physiology (2002)
23. Johannsen, D.L., Calabro, M.A., Stewart, J., Franke, W., Rood, J.C., Welk, G.J.: Accuracy of armband monitors for measuring daily energy expenditure in healthy adults. Medicine and Science in Sports and Exercise 42(11), 2134–2140 (2010)

24. Madgwick, S.: An efficient orientation filter for inertial and inertial/magnetic sensor arrays. Technical report Department of Mechanical Engineering University of Bristol (April 2010)
25. McDowd, K.B.: Life is a sport:how the nike+ fuelband gets it right and represents the evolution of design for wearables
26. Plagenhoef, S., Evans, F.G., Abdelnour, T.: Anatomical data for analyzing human motion. Research Quarterly for Exercise and Sport 54, 169–178 (1983)
27. Plasqui, G., Joosen, A.M., Kester, A.D., Goris, A.H., Westerterp, K.R.: Measuring free-living energy expenditure and physical activity with triaxial accelerometry. Obesity Research 13(8) (August 2005)
28. Rennie, K., Rowsell, T., Jebb, S.A., Holburn, D., Wareham, N.J.: A combined heart rate and movement sensor: proof of concept and preliminary testing study. European Journal of Clinical Nutrition 54, 409–414 (2000)
29. Seliger, V., Dolejs, L., Karas, V.: A dynamometric comparison of maximum eccentric, concentric, and isometric contractions using emg and energy expenditure measurements. European Journal of Applied Physiology and Occupational Physiology 1980 45(23), 235–244 (1980)
30. Shahabdeen, J.A., Baxi, A., Nachman, L.: Ambulatory energy expenditure estimation:a machine learning approach. In: Proceedings of the Twenty-Second Innovative Applications of Artificial Intelligence Conference (2010)
31. Snellen, J.: An improved estimation of mean body temperature using combined direct calorimetry and thermometry. European Journal of Applied Physiology 2000 82(3), 188–196 (2000)
32. Sun, M., Reed, G.W., Hill, J.O.: Modification of a whole room indirect calorimeter for measurement of rapid changes in energy expenditure. Journal of Applied Physiology 76(6) (June 1994)
33. Watt, A., Watt, M.: Advanced Animation and Rendering Techniques: Theory and Practice. Addison-Wesley (1992)
34. Webster, J., Welsh, G., Pacy, P., Garrow, J.: Description of a human direct calorimeter, with a note on the energy cost of clerical work. British Journal of Nutrition 1986 55(1), 1–6 (1986)
35. Wyss, T., Mäder, U.: Energy expenditure estimation during daily military routine with body-fixed sensors. Military Medicine 176(5), 494 (2011)

KinSpace: Passive Obstacle Detection via Kinect

Christopher Greenwood[1], Shahriar Nirjon[1], John Stankovic[1],
Hee Jung Yoon[2], Ho-Kyeong Ra[2], Sang Son[2], and Taejoon Park[2]

[1] University of Virginia, Computer Science Department
{cmg7t,smn8z,stankovic}@virginia.edu
[2] Daegu Gyeongbuk Institute of Science and Technology (DGIST),
Department of Information and Communication Engineering
{heejung8,hk,son,tjpark}@dgist.ac.kr

Abstract. Falls are a significant problem for the elderly living independently in the home. Many falls occur due to household objects left in open spaces. We present KinSpace, a passive obstacle detection system for the home. KinSpace employs the use of a Kinect sensor to learn the open space of an environment through observation of resident walking patterns. It then monitors the open space for obstacles that are potential tripping hazards and notifies the residents accordingly. KinSpace uses real-time depth data and human-in-the-loop feedback to adjust its understanding of the open space of an environment. We present a 5,000-frame deployment dataset spanning multiple homes and classes of objects. We present results showing the effectiveness of our underlying technical solutions in identifying open spaces and obstacles. The results for both lab testing and a deployment in an actual home show roughly 80% accuracy for both open space detection and obstacle detection even in the presence of many real-world issues. Consequently, this new technology shows great potential to reduce the risk of falls in the home due to environmental hazards.

Keywords: fall prevention, object detection, obstacles, safety, Kinect.

1 Introduction

Falls account for a large number of the injuries sustained in the home. Various studies estimate that from 33-52% of adults aged 65 or greater have at least one fall per year [2,13]. These falls are the leading cause of injury-related hospitalization for this population [13]. Behind motor vehicles, falls are the second largest contributor to the economic burden of injuries in the United States, and amount to almost $20 billion in estimated annual cost (about 1.5% of the national healthcare expenditure) [8].

It has also been shown that falls in the elderly population can largely be attributed to trips [3,20]. Researchers at Colorado State University estimate that about one third of falls in the elderly occur due to environmental hazards in the home, the most common of which is tripping over objects on the floor [20]. This gives clear motivation for the development of a system to assist in keeping living spaces free of obstacles in an effort to prevent falls.

B. Krishnamachari, A.L. Murphy, and N. Trigoni (Eds.): EWSN 2014, LNCS 8354, pp. 182–197, 2014.
© Springer International Publishing Switzerland 2014

Most existing solutions deal with the detection of falls as they occur, not the detection of environmental factors that cause falls. This, of course, does not actually prevent falls. Some research has been done in systems that detect obstacles to prevent falls, however existing solutions to this approach require that the user wear a camera system on the body. A system that is statically installed in the home and requires no repeated user input represents a significantly more scalable and user-friendly approach.

This paper makes the following contributions:

1. KinSpace, a passive, automatic, Kinect-based open space detection, obstacle detection, and alert system
2. A set of system features that address real-world complicating factors involved with in-home deployments of Kinect systems.
3. A lab evaluation of KinSpace that fully analyzes the accuracy of both open space and obstacle detection.
4. An deployment of KinSpace in two homes that demonstrates the handling of real-world issues, showing 80% overall obstacle detection accuracy.
5. A large deployment data set spanning several rooms and multiple classes of objects, with roughly 5,000 detection frames.

2   Related Work

Our work lies at the intersection of several existing bodies of research.

One area is object segmentation. These systems perform processing on depth data to gain additional information about the scene. Silberman [19] presents work on scene segmentation, in which individual objects are segmented from the background of a scene. Greuter et. al. [6] use depth information to control a robot for the Eurobot Challenge, in which the robot must navigate obstacles while moving objects about a predefined playing space. Similar projects leverage depth information from the Kinect or similar sensors in the field of object tracking for home healthcare [12].

When considering the application area of fall detection and prevention, existing work has primarily focused on detecting a fall after it has occurred. This has been done in various ways. Many systems have been developed to perform fall detection using wearable sensors [5,13,15,18]. Some systems employ the use of smart phones to reduce friction with the user [4,7]. Other systems, such as Life Alert, employ the user as a sensor and provide a simple notification system to alert others about a fall [10].

Work has been done in the area of fall prevention using a depth camera, mainly in the assistance of visually impaired users. Bernabei et. al. [1] present a real-time system in which the depth sensor is attached to the user and the system notifies the user through earphones of obstacles in his immediate path. Zöllner et. al. [23] propose a similar system that uses vibrotactile feedback to communicate obstacle notifications to the user.

Our work is also influenced by the research area of general home monitoring. Well Aware Systems [21] has developed a comprehensive monitoring system aimed at the elderly and disabled living independently. Wood and Stankovic [22] propose AlarmNet, which uses a similar wireless sensor network to learn resident patterns to further inform healthcare providers. We hypothesize that KinSpace could be added as one element of such deployments.

3 Obstacle Detection: The Problem and Issues

We define obstacle detection as the process of monitoring a room and detecting objects that are likely to cause a fall. An obstacle is likely to cause falls because of its size and position in the room relative to where individuals routinely walk. An obstacle detection system detects any such objects and notifies the proper person in the event of detection so that appropriate action can be taken to minimize risk of falls.

This problem is difficult for several reasons. First, it is difficult to identify the "open space" where misplaced objects would be considered falling hazards. Second, once the open space is defined, we have an equally complex problem of determining which elements in the scene are non-obstacles (floor, background, furniture, large movable objects such as a chair, etc.) and which are true obstacles. This understanding of which objects are truly obstacles can also potentially change over time.

Intervention Strategy: When an obstacle is detected by the system as a risk to the resident, an intervention should take place to minimize the risk of falling. This intervention could be a notification to the resident (visual, auditory, technological, etc.) or a notification to another individual such as a healthcare provider. There are several factors that affect the success of these different modalities of intervention, such as the physical/mental condition of the resident, the reaction time of non-residents, and the user's reaction to false alarms.

False Alarms: False alarms are a problem that must be handled in any safety system. Particularly in this type of system, if the system warns about numerous obstacles that happen to not be obstacles, the user will lose confidence in the system and any caregivers notified of obstacles may not take the proper precautions.

Real-World Environment: There are several real-world factors that make the problem of obstacle detection more complex in deployment than in lab testing. For in-home deployment, the open space may not be as rigidly defined as in lab environments. It may also change over time due to rearranging furniture, addition of permanent objects, changing travel patterns, natural settling of objects, or sensor drift. A robust obstacle detection system must be flexible in its definition of open space so as to evolve over time.

Another complicating factor about real-world deployment is that different people and different scenarios lead to different objects being considered actual obstacles. For instance, if a pair of shoes is left in the middle of a hallway with no residents currently in the room, we might all agree that this is an obstacle and potential falling hazard. But what if a resident comes into the room and sets a shopping bag down temporarily? Some might consider this an obstacle because the user may turn around and forget the bag is there. But a user that remembers the bag is there may not want to be notified each time that obstacle is detected.

Real-world environments also present the system with a much more varied set of objects and detection patterns. Even if a system is extremely reliable in its detection of large, rigid obstacles, there is inherent complexity introduced when the obstacle is smaller or non-rigid (a towel, an empty shopping bag, or even a spill). Obstructions and occlusions are complicating factors that any real-world system must address.

There is also noise that occurs in real-world sensor data that makes obstacle detection much more difficult. For instance, in deployment, the Kinect sensor may not detect the presence of humans in the scene depending on their distance from the sensor, their angle with respect to the sensor, and the angle at which they enter the scene. This may lead the system to consider parts of a user's person as potential obstacles. Noisy depth data and irregular objects may also cause the system to incorrectly segment a single object into multiple, further complicating the problem of determining a true obstacle from background.

4   KinSpace

KinSpace uses a statically-installed Microsoft Kinect sensor to perform open space and obstacle detection in a room so as to minimize the risk of falls. This section discusses the process by which KinSpace learns the open space in the scene and then detects obstacles in that environment.

4.1   System Overview

Each KinSpace system (one or more per room to account for sensor range) is made up of a Kinect sensor, a processing unit (laptop or embedded processing device), and a GUI feedback unit on a laptop. At installation time the system is placed in training mode through indication on the feedback unit. During training mode, the processing unit receives skeleton data from the sensor. It uses this skeleton data to record where users walk in the environment as well as information about the orientation of the floor relative to the sensor.

The user then places the system in detection mode. In detection mode, the processing unit receives depth stream data from the sensor and user input from the feedback unit. It detects obstacles in the scene and adjusts its understanding of the open space based on detection results and user input. It then passes detection results to the feedback unit for notification to the user.

4.2   Algorithm Description

Training - Data Collection: The sensor is installed at its desired location and enabled in training mode. KinSpace then monitors the room using the skeleton data stream from the Kinect sensor [11]. Whenever a skeleton is detected,

KinSpace checks the tracking state of each foot joint for each skeleton and records the position information for all foot joints that are marked as Tracked by the Kinect. The Kinect also provides an estimate of the floor plane equation (in a sensor-centric coordinate system), which KinSpace saves for normalization of these skeleton points.

Training - Data Processing: When the user places the system in detection mode, training data collection is complete, and post-processing occurs to produce the final training dataset. We use the latest floor plane equation to redefine the coordinate system for all depth points. The new coordinate system has its origin on the floor directly beneath the Kinect and a y-axis that is normal to the floor plane. KinSpace interprets the y-coordinate of a point as its height off the ground, and uses the Euclidean distance (considering only the x- and z-coordinates) between two points to represent the lateral distance (bird's eye distance) between those points. KinSpace calculates a transformation matrix (rotation and translation) that converts all Kinect coordinates into this new coordinate system. All foot points captured during data collection are transformed to generate a normalized training set of foot points. The system filters this set of projected points, removing any whose height is above a certain threshold. A large height value for a foot point indicates either that the user's feet were not on the ground in this frame or that a measurement error occurred. In either case, the foot point is probably not a good representation of the open space in a room. For example, if the user is lying on a bed, we do not want foot points to be captured and added to the open space. The transformation matrix for the scene and the resulting set of filtered projected foot points gives us the full training set to be used during detection.

Detection - Lateral Filter: In the detection phase, KinSpace captures and analyzes one frame per second. At each frame, all depth pixels are converted to the sensor-centric coordinate space by Kinect software, producing one 3D point per pixel. KinSpace then transforms these points into the floor-centered coordinate space. The system computes the lateral distance between each point and its nearest neighbor in the training set. That lateral distance is computed using a simple 2D Euclidean distance calculation, ignoring the y-coordinate. This results in a distance that does not take relative height of the objects into account. Any point with a lateral distance less than the *lateral distance threshold* is considered an obstacle pixel candidate.

Detection - Vertical Filter: After filtering by the *lateral distance threshold*, the set of obstacle pixel candidates will contain not only obstacle pixels, but also actual floor pixels in or near the open space. To account for this, the system filters the candidate set by the height of the pixel relative to the floor. Any pixel that has a height less than the *vertical distance threshold* is discarded. This gives us a candidate set of pixels that are within a specified distance of the open space and are above a specified height.

Detection - Cluster and Size Filter: This set of candidates is likely to contain some noise, or pixels that are not part of true obstacles. We make the assumption that actual obstacles are composed of mostly connected pixels, and that noise in the candidate set is mostly be made up of individual pixels or small patches of connected pixels. The system clusters candidate pixels into disjoint sets of pixels (segments) using binary connected component filtering [16]. To remove noise, KinSpace then filters the segment set to remove all segments whose pixel count is less than the *object size threshold*. All objects that remain are not just laterally close enough to the open space and high enough, but contain enough connected pixels to be considered a true obstacle.

Detection - Output: At every frame, the obstacle detection algorithm outputs this set of objects, each of which is made up of a set of pixels in the depth frame. This allows us to estimate the size of each object as well as its approximate location in the room.

4.3 Real-World Considerations

The algorithm described above performs very well in idealistic conditions. However, as discussed in Section 3, there are several real-world factors that make the problem of obstacle detection much more difficult in deployment, and KinSpace has several additional features implemented to address these factors.

The first real-world factor that must be addressed is false positives. KinSpace gives the user the ability to actively acknowledge an alert and provide feedback to the system. When an alert is raised, the user can either remove the true obstacle or push a button on the feedback unit that indicates to KinSpace that whatever is being detected at that time is not a true obstacle. KinSpace then adapts its detection process through what we call baseline filtering. When a false positive has been indicated by user feedback, KinSpace takes a snapshot of the pixels that were indicated as obstacle candidates during the frame in question. Then for future detection, candidate pixels in the baseline filter are discarded from the candidate pixel set. One possible use case for this would be if a resident places a new piece of furniture in the room. KinSpace would likely detect this obstacle and the user would be alerted to it. Once the user notifies KinSpace that the piece of furniture is meant to be there, all of the pixels detected as part of that chair are ruled out from future consideration, and the piece of furniture effectively becomes part of the background.

Sensor drift and natural settling of the environment lead to additional false positives. KinSpace provides more continuous false positive reduction through baseline evolution so as to minimize false positives caused by these phenomena. When KinSpace is first placed in detection mode it performs an initial baseline filtering to remove any false positives in the environment at startup time. This could occur if the user stepped particularly close to a background object, for instance. After this initial calculation, baseline evolution begins. At each detection frame, KinSpace has knowledge of its current baseline filter. It computes the obstacle candidate segments as described in Section 4.2. It then scans these candidate segments searching for segments that are (1) adjacent to existing baseline regions, and (2) small in segment size relative to the size of the adjacent baseline region. Pixel segments that satisfy these two conditions are considered not as obstacles but instead portions of the evolving baseline. These pixel segments are added to the existing baseline (and thus not detected as obstacle pixels for the current and all subsequent frames).

To account for objects being split into multiple discontiguous pixel segments, KinSpace uses isotropic dilation to fuse segments that are close to one another into a single detected obstacle. The more prevalent problem with signal noise is that users can be erroneously detected as obstacles themselves. To solve this problem, we implement a temporal consistency process. After obstacles are detected in the current frame, KinSpace checks each obstacle for temporal consistency with the previous N frames (N being defined by the *temporal consistency factor*). Temporal consistency is satisfied when a given obstacle in frame 1 and any obstacle in frame 0 have similar size (relative to the size of the object itself) and similar location (relative to the size of the frame). An obstacle is only considered a true obstacle if it maintains temporal consistency with all previous N frames (we use N=2 in our experiments). There is a tradeoff here in that when an object is initially placed in an open space, there is a slight delay as the object establishes temporal consistency with previous frames, during which time the obstacle is not detected. However, we found this to be a reasonable tradeoff since the intended use of KinSpace is detecting objects that have been misplaced, and are thus not in motion.

The final real-world factor we address is the position of detected obstacles relative to users in the scene. It is a trivial task to ensure that any pixels detected as obstacles do not lie on the users themselves. But we also do not want KinSpace to detect an obstacle when a user places an object down with the intention of picking it right back up. Because of this desired behavior, we implement the following protocol. When an obstacle is detected and there are valid skeletons detected in the scene, KinSpace delays an alert about this obstacle until one of two conditions are met: (a) the user moves a certain distance away from the detected obstacle, or (b) a certain period of time passes without the obstacle being moved. Both the user distance threshold and the time threshold are configurable parameters. This protocol aims to reduce frustration with the system by reducing false positives that occur when the user is fully aware of his or her placement of objects in the room.

5   Evaluation

We evaluate KinSpace using an extensive set of controlled lab experiments and several in-home deployments.

5.1   Lab Experimental Setup

Our lab experiments involve placing a Kinect in the lab and marking off a portion of the visible floor space as an open area. This allows us to test the effectiveness of the system at detecting objects within the open area while ignoring objects that are outside the open area. After designating the open area, we actively train the system by having an experimenter traverse the open area by foot.

We test the system under three different floor layouts (see Figure 1). These layouts simulate those we would expect to see in a real deployment. Layout A is the simplest of the three, defined by a rectangle in the center of the frame of view with no obstructions. This is similar to what one would see in a hallway that is generally kept with little furniture. Layout B also has no obstructions, but the open area is defined as an L shape instead of a simple rectangle. For layout C, we started with the same simple rectangle as in layout A, but placed a table on one side. Users are forced to walk around the table when navigating the open space, and thus we expect to see the open space omitting space under the table. The sensor has a view of both under the table and the floor on the opposite side of the table to test detection accuracy under both cases.

After the training phase, we place obstacles inside and outside the open area to test the detection accuracy of our system. We capture 3 individual frames with each configuration of objects in the scene. Our first experiment tests the accuracy of the system at adapting its detection to the three different layouts. We do this by placing a series of objects about four inches in height at distances between seven and fourteen feet from the sensor throughout the open space. We visually inspected the detection results to ensure that the detected objects were not disjoint from the actual objects in the scene. We then conduct an experiment to quantify the maximum usable distance of the system by training on layout A as well as space directly behind layout A. We vary the distance from the sensor and at each distance, place multiple objects both inside and outside the open area. Finally, we perform an analysis of the accuracy of the system as the size of the object changes. Because of the measurement resolution of the Kinect and the lateral and vertical distance thresholding done by the system, we know that at a certain point an object is too small to detect. By using variably sized items, we aim to quantify the effect of these parameters.

5.2   Lab Results

Open Space Calculation: Figure 1 depicts the open space calculated by KinSpace when trained under each layout. In these images the bright areas represent portions of the scene that that KinSpace determines to be open space. We see that in each layout, KinSpace is able to learn nearly 100% of the open space through active training. We note that each calculated open space region also includes some overlapping onto non-open space areas - we define this as the false positive open space. This is due to the lateral distance threshold, which we set as 0.2 meters for all detection experiments. Decreasing this threshold would lead to less false positives caused by the border around the open space, but also leaves the potential for gaps in the true open space. We discuss the effect of this parameter in more depth in Section 5.3.

It is clear from inspection that the system adapts its understanding of the open space based on the foot patterns of users during training. Additionally, we note that in Layout C, the system effectively excludes portions of the scene that

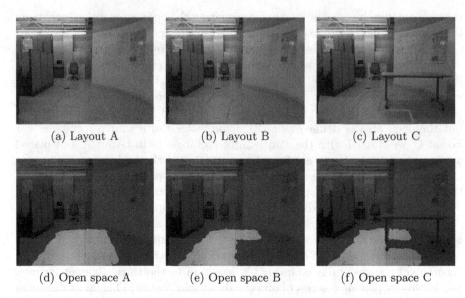

(a) Layout A   (b) Layout B   (c) Layout C

(d) Open space A   (e) Open space B   (f) Open space C

Fig. 1. Figures (a)-(c) show the three layouts defined for our lab experiments. Figures (d)-(f) depict the open space calculated by KinSpace when trained under each layout.

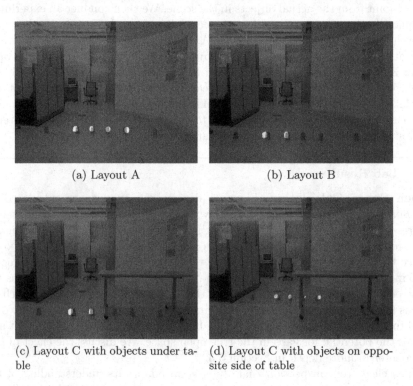

(a) Layout A   (b) Layout B

(c) Layout C with objects under table   (d) Layout C with objects on opposite side of table

Fig. 2. The layout used to train the system dictates which objects are detected as obstacles by KinSpace

are not true floor space even if they are close to the walking path of the user (the legs of the table).

Effect of Layout: In Figure 2a, we see that under Layout A, the system successfully detects the four objects that lie within the defined open space of the environment while ignoring objects placed outside this open space. In layout B (Figure 2b), KinSpace again is able to detect objects inside the open space and discard objects that lie in areas not covered by the new training region. Under Layout C, we see that the system is effective both at discarding objects that lie underneath the table (thus outside of the open space) as well as correctly detecting obstacles on the opposite side of the table.

Effect of Distance from Kinect: This analysis is performed on layout A. We trained the system using a large area and attempted to detect objects as they were moved further from the Kinect. From Figure 3a we observe consistent detection accuracy in the range of 7-13 feet from the sensor, after which point the accuracy decreases sharply. This can be attributed to the maximum depth sensing distance.

Effect of Size of Object: The large objects used are roughly 4-5 inches in height, while the small objects are roughly 2-3 inches in height. From Figure 3b we observe that as the size of the object decreases, the effective detection distance decreases as well. This makes sense - the smaller an object is, the less distance it has to be from the sensor before the number of pixels it occupies falls below the threshold. As the object gets smaller it will also fall below the vertical distance threshold, which was set to roughly 1.5 inches for our experiments. A possible improvement to the current system would be to vary the object size threshold based on how far away the object is or use additional Kinect systems in the room.

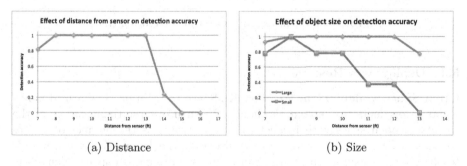

(a) Distance   (b) Size

Fig. 3. Controlled lab experimentation that evaluates the effect of distance from the sensor and object size on detection accuracy

5.3 Deployment Experimental Setup

In the second phase of our evaluation, we deploy the system into two home environments. The first goal of these deployments is to evaluate how well the system can estimate the open space of a room by using passive training only. We install KinSpace in the room and allow it to train while residents of the home go about their normal activities. The system uses the activities of the residents to determine which portions of the room should be deemed open space.

We then test the system's calculation of the open space in the scene. A trial participant uses a color image of the scene to hand label the perceived open space, which provides us with ground truth. We compare the open space determined by KinSpace to this ground truth to determine how well KinSpace calculates the open space. An analysis is also done on this data to test the effects of the lateral distance threshold parameter. We do so by varying the parameter and testing the accuracy of KinSpace's open space determination with respect to ground truth.

The second goal of our deployments is to test the system's detection of obstacles in a real-world environment. We do so using a scripted set of actions performed by a test user over the course of several minutes (see Figure 4). The script is performed five times for various classes and sizes of objects. We test small objects that are likely to cause tripping, such as water bottles and shoes, as well as large objects that a resident may run into, such as chairs and light fixtures. We hand label each trial with the true number of obstacles in the scene at each frame and then compare the output of KinSpace to this ground truth.

1. Walk in, drop object 1, walk out
2. Walk in, pick up object 1, drop object 2, walk out
3. Walk in, drop object 1, walk out
4. Walk in, pick up object 2, drop object 3, walk out
5. Walk in, drop object 3, walk out
6. Walk in, pick up all objects, walk out

Fig. 4. Deployment experiment script used for all trials

5.4 Deployment Results

Open Space Calculation: We allow KinSpace to train on the natural movements of residents throughout the home. We then observe the accuracy of the calculated open space with respect to ground truth, as the number of frames considered by KinSpace increases. We also vary the *lateral distance threshold* to observe the effects of this parameter on the resulting open space calculation. One would expect that as the lateral distance threshold increases, passive training allows the system to learn more of the ground truth open space, but also increases the false positive rate.

The left graph in Figure 5 shows the portion of the true open space that is captured in the system's determination of open space as the number of frames considered increases. The right graph depicts the false positive rate as the system considers more frames. Note that the number of considered frames includes only

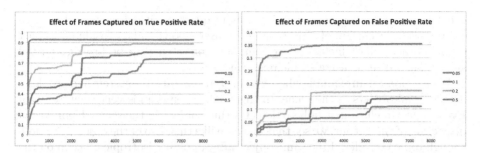

Fig. 5. Accuracy of passive open space detection, showing true positive and false positives rates as the number of training frames increases

those in which a valid skeleton was detected. We observe several distinct points in the training process where there is a sharp spike in the portion of the open space that is recognized by the system - these spikes represent times when a resident moved into a portion of the open space for the first time. These spikes in the system's knowledge of the open space come with a smaller increase in false positives. As the resident moves about that space, additional knowledge of the open space slows.

After observing these results, we decided to use a lateral distance threshold of 0.2 meters for all experiments, as it offered the best tradeoff between true positive and false positive rates.

Obstacle Detection: We first present two examples of a scripted trial. Over each trial, KinSpace monitors the environment and indicates the number of obstacles it detects in the scene. We present this output over time, along with the hand-labeled ground truth.

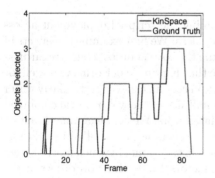
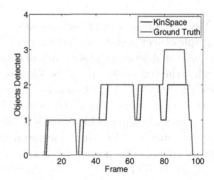

Fig. 6. Examples of scripted trial output. (a) Note very high detection accuracy except for transitions when user is actually manipulating objects; (b) An object is missed after Event 5, likely due to isotropic dilation.

In the first example (see Figure 6), for sections where the system is in a stable state and the user is not in the process of dropping or picking up an object, the system proves to be extremely reliable. The main source of detection error occurs when a user is near the obstacles in question, which causes objects to be in motion, occlusion of objects, and the user's body to be considered as part of an obstacle. Such factors cause temporal consistency to be broken and the system fails to recognize a stable obstacle.

We also present an example where even in a stable state, the system had problems detecting all objects in the scene. In this trial, the system is very accurate until Event 5, at which time it fails to detect a third object in the scene. Upon visual inspection of the output, we see that in a case like this, two of the objects are close enough to be considered the same object after applying isotropic dilation on the object segments. Though this is a potential source of inaccuracy of the system, since the main goal of the system is to detect the presence of obstacles at all, the confusion between one obstacle and several obstacles is not a critical flaw.

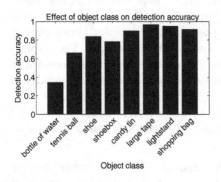 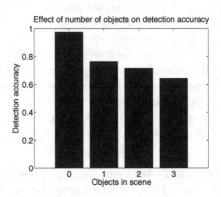

Fig. 7. (a) KinSpace detected most objects with high accuracy, but had trouble in particular detecting bottles of water; (b) Over all object classes, there was a consistent degradation of detection accuracy as number of objects increased

We next present aggregate results of running the scripted deployment across multiple object classes, for 5 trials per object class. We first examine the effects of the class of object on the accuracy of detecting the correct object count, regardless of what the true object count is. We observe that KinSpace performs very well for a wide variety of object classes, but struggles on certain classes, particularly water bottles. This is likely due to the relatively small size of the water bottle combined with its translucence, which causes Kinect data errors. We next examine the effect of the number of objects in the scene on detection accuracy across all object classes. We saw consistently poorer detection accuracy in the frames in which more objects were present. This is likely due to a number of factors. First, with more objects in the same amount of area, it is more likely that occlusion (an external factor) or isotropic dilation (an internal factor) causes KinSpace to fuse two objects and consider them one, causing an erroneous detected object count. Second, the majority of frames in which a human was manipulating the scene were those in which the ground truth object count was greater than one. If we were to disregard these frames completely and focus on stable state we would likely see an increase in detection accuracy with multiple objects.

Figure 8 shows a confusion matrix between the ground truth obstacle count and the obstacle count detected by KinSpace for all object classes and trials (over 5000 frames of deployment data). We observe over 79% detection performance overall and note that when an error does occur, KinSpace is more likely to detect fewer objects than actually exist in the scene. This gives us confidence that if KinSpace alerts the user to one or more object in the scene, these are actually obstacles and not false positives.

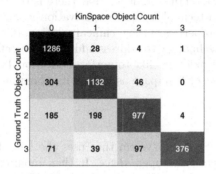

Fig. 8. Confusion matrix incorporating 5000 frames of deployment data. Error cells in the bottom left portion indicate false negatives (18.8%), while error cells in the top right indicate false positives (1.7%).

6 Discussion

KinSpace shows promising results both in lab and in deployment. However, there are several limitations of the system, as well as additional considerations that would have to be addressed in a production system.

One limitation is the size and profile of an object that can be detected by KinSpace. Because KinSpace applies a threshold to both an object's height and the number of contiguous pixels, objects that are small enough will not be detected. We adjusted the parameters of the system to minimize the effect and note the effect of this limitation in our results section. Furthermore, we note that if an object is small enough to be filtered out by the thresholding process of KinSpace, it is likely that its depth profile will be lost in the measurement accuracy of the Kinect sensor itself. This indicates that although object size is a limitation of KinSpace, it is a limitation that is (to some extent) imposed by the Kinect itself and applies to any similar system.

Another limitation of the system is the inherent inaccuracies that occur when a user is in the process of manipulating objects in the scene. As an object is being picked up or set down, there is often a 1-2 frame range on either end of the event during which time detection is inaccurate. Though this is a source of error, this is not a major limitation with respect to the primary motivation of KinSpace - to notify users about the presence of obstacles that may cause falls. Though the number of obstacles is helpful, the key information we want to capture is whether or not an object is there at all. As such, the confusion between two and three obstacles, for instance, is a minor issue. Also, KinSpace is primarily useful when a user forgets that an object has been placed in an open space. In fact, a production system would likely not notify the user of an obstacle for a certain period of time, during which time we can assume the user intends for that object to be there. Because of this, we felt it best for the system to default to not detecting obstacles when in doubt. This reduces the number of false positives and ensures that when KinSpace detects an object in the scene, it has a relatively high level of confidence that there is truly an obstacle there.

This work develops a technology whose motivation is fall prevention. We develop and analyze the properties of the technical solution. In the future, we would like to extend current technology to address additional object classes such as flat objects and spills. We would also like to perform additional analysis to evaluate the user feedback aspect of KinSpace as well as its potential to prevent falls.

7   Conclusion

We have presented KinSpace, a system that uses the Kinect sensor to observe an environment and learn the open space. It then monitors that open space for the presence of obstacles and notifies the resident if an obstacle is left in the open space. KinSpace employs a feedback loop with the user and with its own output to allow it to evolve its understanding of the objects in the scene. We have tested KinSpace extensively in lab to prove the potential of using the Kinect sensor for obstacle detection in open spaces. We have also presented two in-home deployments and produced a large data set that spans multiple rooms and numerous object classes (5,000 total frames of testing data). Through this deployment experimentation we have shown an obstacle detection accuracy of 80%. We have shown a very low false positive rate, proving the reliability of KinSpace as a tool for notifying residents about falling hazards. KinSpace is shown to be an easily-deployable, low cost system that helps keep open spaces clear in the home, potentially preventing falls and injuries for residents.

Acknowledgements. This work was supported in part by NSF CNS-1319302, and by the DGIST R&D Program of the Ministry of Science, ICT, and Future Planning of Korea (CPS Global Center).

References

1. Bernabei, D., Ganovelli, F., Benedetto, M.D., Dellepiane, M., Scopigno, R.: A low-cost time-critical obstacle avoidance system for the visually impaired. In: International Conference on Indoor Positioning and Indoor Navigation (2011)
2. Blake, A.J., et al.: Falls by elderly people at home: Prevalence and associated factors. Age and Ageing 17(6), 365–372 (1988)
3. Chen, H., Ashton-Miller, J.A., Alexander, N.B., Schultz, A.B.: Age effects on strategies used to avoid obstacles. Gait & Posture 2, 139–146 (1994)
4. Dai, J., Bai, X., Yang, Z., Shen, Z., Xuan, D.: Mobile phone-based pervasive fall detection. Personal Ubiquitous Comput. 14(7), 633–643 (2010)

5. Diaz, A., Prado, M., Roa, L.M., Reina-Tosina, J., Sanchez, G.: Preliminary evaluation of a full-time falling monitor for the elderly. In: 26th Annual International Conference of the IEEE Engineering in Medicine and Biology Society, IEMBS 2004, vol. 1, pp. 2180–2183 (2004)
6. Greuter, M., Rosenfelder, M., Blaich, M., Bittel, O.: Obstacle and game element detection with the 3D-sensor kinect. In: Obdržálek, D., Gottscheber, A. (eds.) EUROBOT 2011. CCIS, vol. 161, pp. 130–143. Springer, Heidelberg (2011)
7. Hansen, T.R., Eklund, J.M., Sprinkle, J., Bajcsy, R., Sastry, S.: Using smart sensors and a camera phone to detect and verify the fall of elderly persons. In: European Medicine, Biology and Engineering Conference (2005)
8. Heinrich, S., Rapp, K., Rissmann, U., Becker, C., Konig, H.: Cost of falls in old age: A systematic review. Osteoporosis International 21(6), 891–902 (2010)
9. Khan, A., Moideen, F., Lopez, J., Khoo, W.L., Zhu, Z.: KinDectect: Kinect detecting objects. In: Miesenberger, K., Karshmer, A., Penaz, P., Zagler, W. (eds.) ICCHP 2012, Part II. LNCS, vol. 7383, pp. 588–595. Springer, Heidelberg (2012)
10. Life alert, `http://www.lifealert.com/`
11. Microsoft kinect coordinate spaces, `http://msdn.microsoft.com/en-us/library/hh973078.aspx`
12. Nirjon, S., Stankovic, J.: Kinsight: Localizing and Tracking Household Objects using Depth-Camera Sensors. In: Proc. of Distributed Computing in Sensor Systems, Hangzhou, China (2012)
13. Noury, N., et al.: A smart sensor based on rules and its evaluation in daily routines. In: Proceedings of the 25th Annual International Conference of the IEEE Engineering in Medicine and Biology Society, vol. 4, pp. 3286–3289 (2003)
14. Noury, N., et al.: Monitoring behavior in home using a smart fall sensor and position sensors. In: 1st Annual International Conference on Microtechnologies in Medicine and Biology, pp. 607–610 (2000)
15. Li, Q., Stankovic, J.A., Hanson, M.A., Barth, A.T., Lach, J., Zhou, G.: Accurate, fast fall detection using gyroscopes and accelerometer-derived posture information. In: Sixth International Workshop on Wearable and Implantable Body Sensor Networks, BSN 2009, pp. 138–143 (2009)
16. Rosenfeld, A.: Connectivity in digital pictures. J. ACM, 17(1), 146-160 (1970)
17. Rubenstein, L.Z., Josephson, K.R.: The epidemiology of falls and syncope. Clinics in Geriatric Medicine 18(2), 141–158 (2012)
18. Shan, S., Yuan, T.: A wearable pre-impact fall detector using feature selection and support vector machine. In: 2010 IEEE 10th International Conference on Signal Processing (ICSP), pp. 1686–1689 (2010)
19. Silberman, N., Fergus, R.: Indoor scene segmentation using a structured light sensor. In: 2011 IEEE International Conference on Computer Vision Workshops (ICCV Workshops), pp. 601–608 (2011)
20. Tremblay Jr., K.R., Barber, C.E.: Preventing falls in the elderly (2005), `http://www.ext.colostate.edu/pubs/consumer/10242.html` (2013)
21. Well aware systems, `http://wellawaresystems.com`
22. Wood, A., Stankovic, J.A., Virone, G., Selavo, L., He, Z., Cao, Q., et al.: Context-aware wireless sensor networks for assisted living and residential monitoring. IEEE Network 22(4), 26–33 (2008)
23. Zöllner, M., Huber, S., Jetter, H.-C., Reiterer, H.: NAVI – A proof-of-concept of a mobile navigational aid for visually impaired based on the microsoft kinect. In: Campos, P., Graham, N., Jorge, J., Nunes, N., Palanque, P., Winckler, M. (eds.) INTERACT 2011, Part IV. LNCS, vol. 6949, pp. 584–587. Springer, Heidelberg (2011)

Author Index

Andreopoulos, Yiannis 150

Beutel, Jan 66
Buchli, Bernhard 66
Buranapanichkit, Dujdow 150

Cattani, Marco 100
Cesana, Matteo 150
Christmann, Dennis 84

dos Santos Ribeiro Júnior, Nildo 34

Engel, Markus 84

Gnawali, Omprakash 34
Gotzhein, Reinhard 84
Greenwood, Christopher 182
Gregorczyk, Michal 1
Gunningberg, Per 116

Handziski, Vlado 50
Hermans, Frederik 116
Hnat, Timothy W. 166
Hollick, Matthias 133

Ignjatovic, Aleksandar 17
Iwanicki, Konrad 1

Jha, Sanjay 17
Jurdak, Raja 17

Kanhere, Salil S. 17
Kusy, Branislav 17

Langendoen, Koen 100
Li, Kai 17
Löscher, Andreas 50

McNamara, Liam 116

Nirjon, Shahriar 182

Park, Taejoon 182
Pazurkiewicz, Tomasz 1

Ra, Ho-Kyeong 182
Redondi, Alessandro 150
Riecker, Michael 133
Rohner, Christian 116

Son, Sang 182
Stankovic, John 182
Sutton, Felix 66

Tagliasacchi, Marco 150
Thiele, Lothar 66
Tsiftes, Nicolas 50

Vieira, Luiz F.M. 34
Vieira, Marcos A.M. 34
Voigt, Thiemo 50

Wennerström, Hjalmar 116
White, Anthony 166
Woehrle, Matthias 100

Yli-Piipari, Sami R. 166
Yoon, Hee Jung 182
Yuan, Dingwen 133

Zaman, Kazi I. 166
Zuniga, Marco 100